D0800686

19.95/

9th Vermont Military Register

Chromolithograph rosters such as this one for Company C of the 9th Vermont commemorated a regiment's brutal battles as well as the lofty idealism of the men who left home to fight for the Union in the Civil War.

LETTERS *TO* VERMONT

FROM HER CIVIL WAR SOLDIER CORRESPONDENTS TO THE HOME PRESS

VOLUME I

Edited and compiled by
Donald H. Wickman

IMAGES FROM THE PAST

Cover:
John Q. Dickinson, 7th Vermont Regiment, corresponded with the Rutland Herald *while he was a soldier in the Civil War; his letters appear in Volume II.*

All rights reserved under International and Pan-American Copyright Conventions. No part of this book may be reproduced in any form or by any electronic, photographic, or mechanical means, including information storage and retrieval systems, without the permission in writing from the publisher.

1 2 3 4 5 6 7 8 9 10 XXX 05 04 03 02 01 00 99 98

Library of Congress Cataloging-in-Publication Data

Letters to Vermont from her Civil War soldier correspondents to
  the home press/edited and compiled by Donald H. Wickman

  p.   cm.

  Includes bibliographical references and index

  ISBN 1-884592-10-4 (v. 1: hard cover). — ISBN 1-884592-11-2 (v.1: paper).

  1. United States Army. Vermont Brigade, 1st (1861 - 1865) 2. United States.
  Army. Vermont Brigade, 2nd (1862 - 1863) 3. Vermont — History — Civil
  War, 1861 - 1865 — Personal narratives. 4. United States — History — Civil
  War, 1861 - 1865 — Personal narratives. 5. Soldiers — Vermont
  Correspondence. 6. Vermont — History — Civil War, 1861 - 1865 —
  Regimental histories. 7. United States — History — Civil War, 1861 - 1865 —
  Regimental histories.
                                                                    98-12293
                                                                        CIP

I. Wickman, Donald H. (Donald Harvey), 1953-
E533.4.L47   1998
973.7'443 — dc21

Copyright © 1998 by Donald H. Wickman

Published by Images from the Past, Inc., P.O. Box 137, Bennington, VT 05201
Tordis Ilg Isselhardt, Publisher

Printed in the United States of America

Project Editor: Stuart Murray
Design and Production: Ron Toelke Associates, Chatham, NY
Printer: Thomson-Shore, Inc. Dexter, MI
Text: ITC Century; Display: Poster Bodoni
Paper: 55lb. Glatfelter Supple Opaque Recycled Natural
Cover: 12pt. C1S

To Betsy, who
supported this
lengthy project,
and
"A.A.C.," whose letters
sparked the idea

Editor's Note

In transcribing these letters, occasional incorrect spellings, especially with regard to place names, were corrected. Where words in the printed newspaper letters were blurred or incomprehensible, a [?] has been placed to indicate this. Otherwise, the letters are exactly as printed by the *Rutland Herald*, including the use of capitalization and italics (or lack of them), except where achieving consistency within each letter required an alteration. These letters (which include both the date of publication and the date they were written) are extremely close to what the public would have read in the *Herald* during the Civil War years, 1861-65. The difference is that readers now know who the writers were.

Preface

This is the first of two volumes of collected, annotated letters from several young Vermont soldiers who wrote to the *Rutland Herald* about their day-to-day experiences during the Civil War, 1861-65.

In their letters, these men — who were known to the home press only by initials or pseudonyms — related what they believed was important and interesting to friends and family at home. *Letters to Vermont* is their story, and it is not intended to be a definitive history of Vermont in the Civil War.

This collection — which includes virtually every letter these men wrote to the *Herald* — began as an offshoot of another Civil War research project back in 1990. After first finding the correspondence in old newspapers, I was led to more thorough research that convinced me they should be published in a book.

Over the years, my correspondence went to Washington, D.C., Somerville, Mass., Denver, and Chicago, following the routes of these soldier-correspondents. In Vermont it led me to graveyards, where I saw the final resting place of men whom I felt I had come to know. It is my hope that the reader will feel the same.

Don Wickman
Rutland, Vermont
January 1998

Vermont in the 1860s
*The home towns of the writers are as follows: Bridport — A.A.C.; Danby — J.C.W.;
Goshen — L.T.D.; North Clarendon — E.R.R.; Rockingham — Sigma; Rutland — M.J.M.*

❦ CONTENTS ❧

Introduction ☞ **Page 1**

Chapter 1 ☞ **Page 12**
First to go, with the 1st Vermont
"M.J.M." • Martin J. McManus
1st Vermont Regiment

Chapter 2 ☞ **Page 26**
Reporter to Soldier
"Sigma" • Albert R. Sabin
9th Vermont Regiment

Chapter 3 ☞ **Page 58**
In the Peninsular Campaign of 1862
"L.T.D." • Lewis T. Dutton
5th Vermont Regiment

Chapter 4 ☞ **Page 96**
A Transplanted Vermonter in the 21st Massachusetts
"E.R.R."/"America" • Edwin R. Reed
21st Massachusetts Regiment

Chapter 5 ☞ **Page 126**
With the 12th Vermont Regiment
"B" • Unknown
12th Vermont Regiment

Chapter 6 ☞ **Page 146**
Tales of the 2nd Vermont Brigade
"J.C.W." • John C. Williams
14th Vermont Regiment

Chapter 7 ☞ **Page 170**
From Battlefield to Campground with the Vermont Brigade
"A.A.C." • Albert A. Crane
6th Vermont Regiment

Afterword ☞ **Page 204**

General/Chapter Notes ☞ **Page 206**

Acknowledgments ☞ **Page 219**

Sources of Illustrations ☞ **Page 220**

Bibliography ☞ **Page 221**

Index ☞ **Page 223**

The Editor ☞ **Page 237**

Ye tried, and true, and loyal ones, what words of mine can tell

How in your country's inmost heart, your memories shall dwell?

The record of your glorious deeds shall live forever more,

Till heaven and Earth shall pass away and Time itself be o'er.

And oh! ye honored dead who lie in unmarked graves this day,

O'er which no friend may ever weep, nor wife nor mother pray —

Yet earth shall hold in glad embrace the sacred solemn trust,

And God and His angels watch over each soldier's dust.

excerpted from

The Vermont Volunteer

Julia C.R. Dorr

Rutland, Vermont

January 11, 1864

LETTERS TO VERMONT

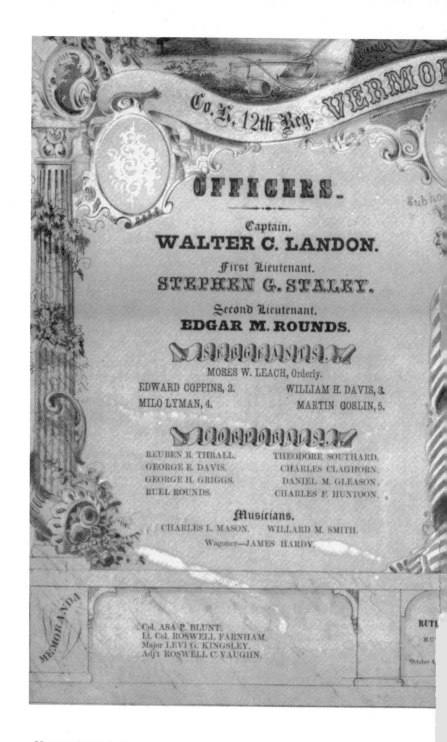

Mustered into Federal service

*Rosters such as this one for the 12th Regiment's Company K, known
as the "Rutland Light Guard" Vermont Volunteer Militia, honored the
officers and men going off to war in the South.*

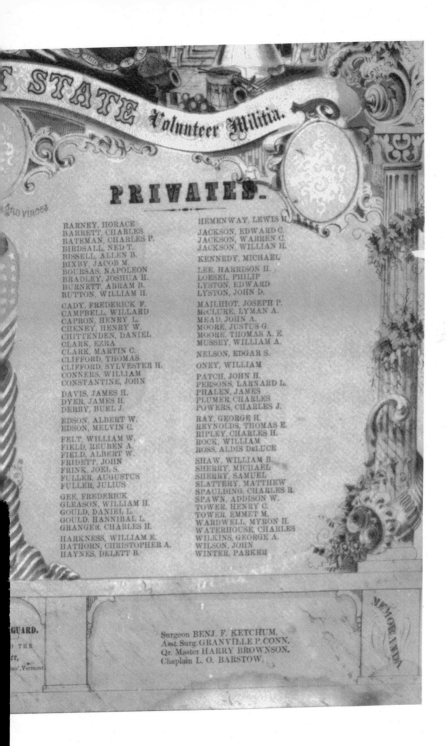

STATE Volunteer Militia.

PRIVATES.

BARNEY, HORACE
BARRETT, CHARLES
BATEMAN, CHARLES P.
BIRDSALL, NED T.
BISSELL, ALLEN B.
BIXBY, JACOB M.
BOURSAS, NAPOLEON
BRADLEY, JOSHUA H.
BURNETT, ABRAM B.
BUTTON, WILLIAM H.

CADY, FREDERICK F.
CAMPBELL, WILLARD
CAPRON, HENRY L.
CHENEY, HENRY W.
CHITTENDEN, DANIEL
CLARK, EZRA
CLARK, MARTIN C.
CLIFFORD, THOMAS
CLIFFORD, SYLVESTER H.
CONNERS, WILLIAM
CONSTANTINE, JOHN

DAVIS, JAMES H.
DYER, JAMES H.
DERBY, BUEL J.

EDSON, ALBERT W.
EDSON, MELVIN C.

FELT, WILLIAM W.
FIELD, REUBEN A.
FIELD, ALBERT W.
FRIDETT, JOHN
FRINK, JOEL S.
FULLER, AUGUSTUS
FULLER, JULIUS

GEE, FREDERICK
GLEASON, WILLIAM H.
GOULD, DANIEL L.
GOULD, HANNIBAL L.
GRANGER, CHARLES H.

HARKNESS, WILLIAM E.
HATHORN, CHRISTOPHER A.
HAYNES, DELETT B.

HEMENWAY, LEWIS H.

JACKSON, EDWARD C.
JACKSON, WARREN C.
JACKSON, WILLIAN H.

KENNEDY, MICHAEL

LEE, HARRISON H.
LOESEL, PHILIP
LYSTON, EDWARD
LYSTON, JOHN D.

MAILHIOT, JOSEPH P.
McCLURE, LYMAN A.
MEAD, JOHN A.
MOORE, JUSTUS G.
MOORE, THOMAS A. E.
MUSSEY, WILLIAM A.

NELSON, EDGAR S.

ONEY, WILLIAM

PATCH, JOHN H.
PERSONS, LARNARD L.
PHALEN, JAMES
PLUMER, CHARLES
POWERS, CHARLES J.

RAY, GEORGE H.
REYNOLDS, THOMAS E.
RIPLEY, CHARLES H.
ROCK, WILLIAM
ROSS, ALDIS DeLUCE

SHAW, WILLIAM B.
SHERRY, MICHAEL
SHERRY, SAMUEL
SLATTERY, MATTHEW
SPAULDING, CHARLES R.
SPAWN, ADDISON W.
TOWER, HENRY C.
TOWER, EMMET M.
WARDWELL, MYRON H.
WATERHOUSE, CHARLES
WILKINS, GEORGE A.
WILSON, JOHN
WINTER, PARKER

Surgeon BENJ. F. KETCHUM.
Asst. Surg. GRANVILLE P. CONN.
Qr. Master HARRY BROWNSON.
Chaplain L. O. BARSTOW.

The Rutland Herald

Six days a week — not on Sundays — the Rutland Herald *carried war news and uncensored letters to the editor from Vermont soldiers and sailors, whose families and friends eagerly awaited news of their boys fighting for the Union in the Civil War.*

Rutland Daily Herald.

VOL. 2 — NO. 209. RUTLAND, VT., MONDAY MORNING, JANUARY 5, 1863. PRICE, THREE CENTS.

THE LATEST NEWS.

BY TELEGRAPH.

THE ATTACK ON VICKSBURG.

Terrible Fighting!

REBEL INTRENCHMENTS CARRIED BY STORM!

The Conflict not ended.

REBEL ACCOUNTS.

From Murfreesboro.

Terrific Fighting all last Week.

TREMENDOUS CARNAGE!

THE REBELS FINALLY DRIVEN ON SATURDAY.

BRAGG REPORTED KILLED

Great Loss of Federal Officers.

PARTICULARS OF THE CONFLICT

The Monitor Foundered

Loss of Officers and Men.

IMPORTANT FROM ARKANSAS.

Introduction

Within two weeks of the firing upon Fort Sumter in Charleston Harbor on April 12, 1861, the *Rutland Weekly Herald* began printing a daily paper, except for Sundays, in addition to the regular weekly edition. The daily paper became popular, for it kept readers up–to–date with war news and told how the Vermont boys were managing in the conflict.

Small, local papers like the *Rutland Herald* did not possess the resources to send correspondents to report the war. The editors were dependent on the daily reports of journalists of the major city papers such as the *New York Herald* and its competitor, the *New York Times*, among others. An additional source of war information soon came directly from Vermont: soldiers in the field were a wealth of talent willing to share, through letters, their military experiences.

By late May 1861, the *Rutland Herald* commenced printing soldiers' letters addressed to the editor, but meant for the public. These letters brought camp life and battlefield incidents alive as the participants told their stories. Many newspapers in both Union and Confederate states instituted the same policy. It was the press at its best, describing the war and satisfying its customers.

Another factor contributed to the situation: except for the short Spanish-American War in 1898, the Civil War was the last major conflict in which the national government did not censor press reports or correspondence home. Freely printed in newspapers were reports written from regimental, brigade, division, corps, and army levels, lists of casualties, and uncut letters from soldiers. These last provided an indispensable wealth of news. They described camp life, where soldiers were stationed, food, weather, sad and humorous events, and descriptions from the participants of battle — details the public clamored for throughout the four years of war. Many of these details were not recorded elsewhere until numerous regimental histories appeared in print during the 1880s.

This lack of wartime censorship posed problems that were recognized but never remedied. Although a paper like the *Rutland Herald* took several days to reach soldiers at the front, when the war news would be old, this was not the case with large city dailies that had access to railroads. New York papers reached the soldiers in camp on the same day they were printed. Soldiers could read fresh war news that described the movement of troops and other strategically important information. This would not have been a problem if the newspapers remained in camp, but newspapers were great bartering tools when trading with Confederates for their much-esteemed fresh tobacco. Eventually, newspapers ended up in the hands of ranking officers in the Army of Northern Virginia, who could accurately follow the movements and gauge the morale of the opposing Army of the Potomac.

At least one Union general realized this problem. When Joseph Hooker was appointed as commander of the Army of the Potomac he demanded reporters accompanying the army provide a byline to their stories so he could trace any intelligence leaks. Also, as he commenced his secret flanking movement towards Chancellorsville in May 1863, Hooker ordered the mails halted for a day so news of the army's move would not reach print in the papers. This decision helped disguise the maneuver, for Lee at first was unable to anticipate Hooker's plans. Though the generals knew the lack of censorship was a detriment to their operations, it was never corrected during the war.

Over the course of the conflict, numerous soldiers sent letters to the editor of the *Rutland Herald* for publication. Some soldiers-turned-correspondents communicated sparingly, providing glimpses of camp life in one or two letters, and were never heard from again. Others corresponded on such a regular basis that it was easy to follow the affairs of Vermont regiments in the field.

The soldiers guarded their identities when signing this correspondence. Many created acronyms formed from their initials; others concocted pseudonyms. The frequent reader of the *Herald* read letters from "A.C.B," "J.A.L.," "America," or "Sigma." Protecting his identity safeguarded the correspondent from any possible discipline if he had commented unfavorably about officers or military policies.

This fate befell Lieutenant Henry M. Hall, Company E, 2nd United States Sharpshooters. Hall, of Danby, Vermont, wrote to the *Rutland Herald* in January 1862, describing the poor sanitary conditions in camp and hospital, and noting the need for certain articles of clothing not adequately provided by the military. He also criticized the recently issued weapons. He signed his full name, rank, and regiment. In his next letter, the lieutenant was extraordinarily brief, because he had been placed under arrest for two days after word of his complaints reached his regimental commander. Hall wrote, "I would like to give you a little history of how things are here, but as I have some objection of having my freedom of loco-motion curtailed, I think it best to hold my thoughts in reserve for the present."

Defending Washington
The 5th Vermont parades at Camp Griffin, in northern Virginia, where the Vermont regiments spent the winter of 1861-62.

So, the unwritten rule was to let the folks at home know the news of camp and conflict, but to avoid any direct obvious identification.

Newspapers not only provided information to the people at home, but were more than appreciated by the soldiers in the field. The men craved Vermont news, and also read about the exploits of their fellow soldiers. Captain Aldace Walker of Wallingford, an officer in the 1st Vermont Artillery Regiment, wrote to his father that a letter from his regiment published in an 1863 *Rutland Herald* could be attributed directly to his company clerk. Homesickness, often referred to as "melancholy," became most apparent at mail call, and the state papers were unrolled for everyone to read.

George Cantine, 7th Vermont Regiment, urged Vermonters to send the local paper, and he described the excitement the arrival of a newspaper made.

"Your paper is now and then seen, even at so remote a place as Ship Island, and coming as it does from old Rutland, its columns teem with peculiar interest to her absent soldiers. And here let me suggest to those who have friends in the Seventh, to send now and then a *Herald* — it will cost you nothing. Could you but see the crowd of soldiers a Rutland paper attracts, you would unhesitantly mail one every week."

James Barrett, 1st Vermont Cavalry, echoed Cantine's sentiments when he wrote about the newspaper, "Your visits to us are not very frequent, but when you do make your appearance you are welcomed with joy. We liked you when at home, but now to sit down perhaps upon the battlefield and peruse the pages of the *Rutland Herald* right from home, is indeed a pleasure." So the press filled a second niche in responding to the needs of the distant soldier.

Most Vermont troops fought in Virginia during the war, but other units discovered themselves in much more unfamiliar territory: the bayous of Louisiana, a paroled prisoner-of-war camp in Chicago, and along the Atlantic Ocean or Gulf of Mexico coasts. Letter-writers narrate the journeys of these far-traveling, adventure-seeking

Vermont youths, many of whom had never before left the state. At first, these soldiers carried with them the impression that war was all glory and sufferings were minimal. That attitude expired over the first several months as comrades died of disease or in battle.

Not only did the folks at home read about the actions of a regiment and the distresses felt by the men, but they also learned about regions and their inhabitants that were foreign to many of them. The richness of this soldier correspondence lies in its eloquence. These letters were not written for family or friends, but for the general public.

It is not difficult to become attached to several of these writers, for they describe a scene so clearly. One has reason to mourn when research details their deaths in battle or from the ravages of disease. Others were discharged for disabilities or illness from exposure. They returned home alive, but suffered for the remainder of their lives as a result of their service in the Union Army.

Newspapers remain one the greatest untapped Civil War resources. One reason they are so underutilized is the great effort required to scrutinize various papers and all their pages. Also, papers were not always the most punctual information sources for various reasons. Some accounts of an incident might take months to surface in Rutland, for they were picked up and printed in one paper after another before they finally reached Vermont. Though belated, the descriptions still made good reading. A letter written by Colonel Edward Cross of the 5th New Hampshire Regiment describing the Federal assault at Fredericksburg in December 1862 was not published until after the colonel had died at Gettysburg the following summer. The letter had been printed first in a Kentucky paper and eventually found its way into Vermont newsprint.

Most of the time mail service was rather swift; a letter might appear in the press within a week of being composed. Others took longer as their delivery depended on water travel from Louisiana. Often, letters were delayed because the rigors of a campaign took precedence, with free time at a minimum. Still, there were dedicated soldiers who regularly put pen and pencil to paper and wrote

Winter in Virginia
*The Vermont Brigade's 1862-63 winter quarters outside Fredericksburg, Virginia,
are pictured in this painting by James Hope, a captain in the 2nd Regiment;
Hope used his own sketches of the camp for an oil painting finished in 1864,
one of several Civil War campaign scenes he painted.*

home to the local newspaper. It was not out of self-gratification, as explained by a writer known only as "B," who stated in his initial letter, "you will pardon me if I make myself the humble medium of communication for the present time with those who have always taken such a kind interest in the fortunes and welfare" of the soldiers. People at home craved information on their soldiers, and since some men were not letter-writers, family members had to be dependent on newspapers for word of them or their regiments.

This book and Volume II are a collection of letters from thirteen of the most dedicated writers to the *Rutland Herald* from 1861 to 1865. They represent a cross-section of Vermont: college graduate, student, mechanic, writer, teacher, painter, harness maker. They were as young as sixteen when they departed for war and were members of twelve units, representing the infantry, artillery, and cavalry. All but one correspondent served in Vermont units, the exception being a transplanted Vermonter in the 21st Massachusetts.

Grouping the letters by author establishes a bond with each as the reader learns of their upbringing, their military careers, and their postwar lives. Chapters are arranged in chronological order according to the primary event each writer is describing. Some of the writers provide narrow pictures, for death, disease, or discharge may have limited their time of service. These soldiers are easy to place in the course of events. The men who survived pose a more substantial problem, for they corresponded over a number of years. They have been placed where they most belong in the scope of the Civil War and the role of Vermont.

Letters have not been altered except to correct obvious spelling errors and to provide punctuation where necessary.

Except for the correspondent known as "B," all the writers have been identified. This was accomplished by first identifying their regiments and companies, checking the appropriate rosters for matches of the initials or, in the case of "Sigma," tracing his career from hints found in articles he had written in earlier editions of the *Rutland Herald.* "B" remains an enigma.

The narrative tells about the soldiers' careers and describes when and where the letter was written. If large gaps exist between letters — as during the captivity of "J.B." or because the soldier failed to write regularly — a transitional narrative offers a glimpse of the war and the life of the regiment.

The prewar and postwar lives of the soldiers were researched in pension and service records, newspaper accounts, obituaries, regimental histories, and town histories. These biographies show the lives of the men when times were less dangerous and not as adventuresome. For most of these soldiers-turned-writers, the Civil War was the most exciting and memorable time of their lives.

UNITED STAT[ES]

CIVIL WAR 1861-65

☐ Union States   ☐ Secession

× Battlefields

Longitude West 90 of Greenwich

Map text labels include:

CANADA

Lake Huron, L. Ontario, Lake Erie

Toronto, Rochester, Buffalo, Syracuse, Albany

NEW YORK

VERMONT, Montpelier, NEW HAMPSHIRE, Concord, MAINE, Augusta

MASSACHUSETTS, Boston, Cape Cod

Hartford, CONNECTICUT

MICHIGAN, Lansing, Detroit, Toledo, Cleveland

OHIO, Columbus, Cincinnati

PENNSYLVANIA, Harrisburg, Carlisle, Oak Hill, Gettysburg, Chambersburg

Wheeling, Ohio R.

NEW YORK, NEW JERSEY, Trenton, PHILADELPHIA, Long Island

W. VIRGINIA, Charleston, Beverley, Cheat Summ., Philippi

VIRGINIA, Richmond, Lynchburg, Petersburg, Staunton, Gordonsville, Chancellorsville, Appomattox, Malvern Hills, Harrison

Pt. Pleasant, Cynthiana, Lexington, Paintsville, Prestonburg, Pikeville, Danville, Beckley, Barbourville

KENTUCKY, Somerset, C. Wild Cat, Rogersville

TENNESSEE, Knoxville, Chattanooga, Chickamauga, Bloyntsville

N. CAROLINA, Raleigh, Williamston, Washington, Goldsboro, Kinston, New Berne, Beaufort, Fayetteville, Wilmington, Ft. Fisher

Roanoke I., Pamlico Sd., C. Clarke, C. Hatteras, C. Lookout

S. CAROLINA, Columbia, Charleston, Ft. Moultrie, Ft. Sumter, Ft. Beauregard, Pt. Royal

GEORGIA, Atlanta, Augusta, Milledgeville, Macon, Millen, Savannah, Ft. Walker, Ft. Pulaski, Ft. McAllister, Altamaha, Andersonville

St. Simons, Brunswick, St. Marys, Ft. Clinch, Fernandina, Jacksonville, Olustee, St. Augustine

FLORIDA, Apalachicola

ATLANTIC OCEAN

BAHAMA ISLANDS

English Miles
0   50   100   200   300

John Bartholomew & Son, Ltd. Edinburgh.

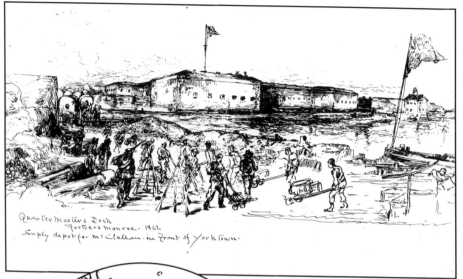

Quarter Masters Dock
Fortress Monroe - 1862
Supply depot for McClellan in Front of Yorktown.

**Fortress Monroe's
quartermaster's dock**
*Supplies for the garrison and for
troops on campaign inland were
transported by ship to the fortress,
where they were off-loaded
and transferred onto carts
and wagons to be taken to
warehouses and supply depots.*

**Ten miles around
Fortress Monroe**
*In May 1861, a few weeks after
hostilities began, the 1st Vermont
was sent to garrison strategic
Fortress Monroe, which
commanded the narrows where
Virginia's James and York rivers
empty into Chesapeake Bay.*

**Fortress Monroe
in peacetime**
*Pictured just before
the Civil War,
Fortress Monroe
included a hospital,
in the foreground,
which saw
considerable use for
wounded soldiers
as the fighting
intensified.*

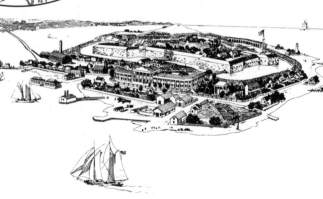

Chapter 1

First To Go with the First Vermont

"M.J.M."

Martin J. McManus, 1st Vermont Regiment

In April 1861, when the summons for military assistance came from Washington at the onset of the Civil War, Vermont was there. Within a month the 1st Vermont had been mustered into Federal duty and sent to the front. Its men represented the first of thousands of Vermonters who would serve during the course of the war. The unit did its share of duty, and at the end of its term many 1st Vermont members returned home to re-enlist in subsequent regiments raised in the state.

The 1st Vermont Regiment saw service as an infantry regiment enlisted for three months and was the first from Vermont to answer Lincoln's call to arms after the surrender of Fort Sumter. Governor Erastus Fairbanks authorized the raising of the regiment from the various militia units in the state. The militia companies vied for the honor to serve, and the "Rutland Light Guards" was one of ten units selected. Their captain was William Y. W. Ripley, son of a marble manufacturer. Captain Ripley would make a name for himself before being wounded at Malvern Hill on July 1, 1862.

The Rutland Company prided itself on its eager volunteers. Among them was Martin J. McManus, a twenty-two-year-old Irish immigrant with a talent for music, who had been working as a clerk at E. Foster Cook's Bardwell House.

When the gray-uniformed regiment[1] was mustered in on the Rutland Fairgrounds on May 9, 1861, McManus was promoted. He found himself no longer attached to the Rutland Company, now officially Company K, but a member of the non-commissioned staff of the regiment as fife-major. Holding this rank throughout the regiment's three-month term, McManus must have shown additional talent, for he also earned an assignment as assistant regimental quartermaster.

Vermont native Colonel John W. Phelps, a West Point graduate and veteran of the Mexican War, commanded the 1st Vermont Regiment when it headed south on May 9, 1861, to Fortress Monroe, at the southern end of Virginia's Tidewater Peninsula. The regiment became part of the garrison guarding that strategic Federal post on the edge of the Confederate state of Virginia.

Times were busy for the men of the 1st Vermont. McManus proved to be one of the few soldiers in the regiment to communicate with the home state newspapers.

One of the first Vermonters to volunteer
Pictured in late 1861 wearing the uniform of a lieutenant colonel, First United States Sharpshooters, William Y. W. Ripley was among the first from Vermont to volunteer to defend the Union; more than a year later, in the summer of 1862, he was wounded at Malvern Hill, Virginia.

May 25, 1861

Letter from Fortress Monroe

The Sewall's Battery Engagement — One Sailor fatally wounded
Number of men at the Fortress — Senator Wade, with friends,
visits the Fort — Popularity of Col. Phelps
The Funeral of Private Underwood — The Weather, &c.

Fort Monroe

May 20.

This afternoon, about 3 o'clock, a brisk fire commenced at the mouth of James River, which lasted for three hours, between the steam-tug *Monticello*, together with two other crafts, and a secession battery on shore. The force now stationed at Fortress Monroe [?] a force much larger than many are now aware of. I have been informed by Captains and Lieutenants of the regulars now in the Fort, that there is at least 3500 in the Fort, including regulars. The general supposition is, that the force in the Fort is 2000.

In the action to-day, between the *Monticello* and the land battery, one of the sailors manning the guns was severely wounded and died at a late hour to-night. One of the Vt. Regiment, from the Bradford company, whose name is Benjamin Underwood,[2] a very handsome soldier, and much respected member of the regiment, died about 12 o'clock this night, which throws a shade of gloom over the Vt. Regiment.

The scene of action to-day was indeed a view which brought to the minds of those who saw it, a recollection of the old and heroic engagements of the Revolution as they have read it. As I saw the momentary flash and heard the roar of cannon, it called to my memory the engagements of ancient and modern times. Hundreds watched it from the shore, and every man wished to be ordered to the scene of action.

To-day Senator Wade,[3] and friends, visited our post, and met with the hospitality of Col. Phelps,[4] who, by the way, is beyond all question, the most popular and gentlemanly Col. in the Fortress; so say the regulars, as they know him from old experience in this and other places. Our regiment are highly pleased, and well they may be, at having an old and experienced officer at their head. Col. Phelps is proud of his regiment, and every man in the regiment is proud of Col. Phelps.

The funeral of our comrade, Underwood, took place about four o'clock May 20th, and the occasion was very impressive [?] as we followed his remains to the place of burial along the coast of Old Virginia, the boisterous waves dashed with majestic swell, and broke in mournful sound beneath the wheels of the ambulance which conveyed his remains to

Eastern approach to Richmond
Control of the Tidewater region of eastern Virginia, with several navigable rivers, was considered by the Union to be of crucial importance in threatening Richmond and blockading Confederate seaports.

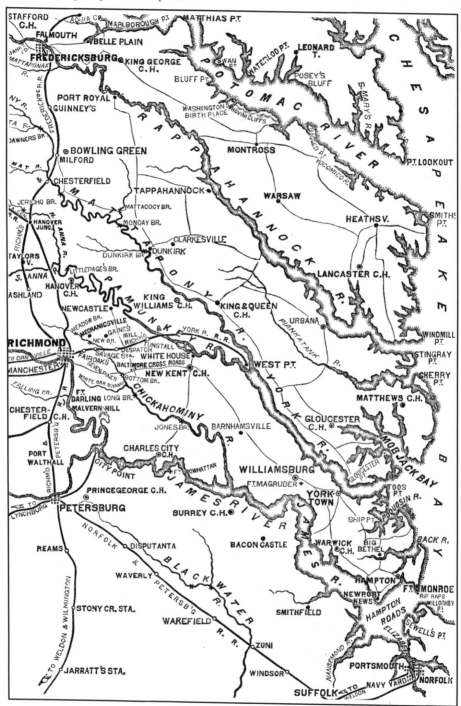

their last resting place. The usual salute was fired over the grave of the young hero, and the grave quickly filled by brother soldiers, whose eyes were moistened with the soft tear of sorrow, and all was over. Then again the martial airs of music filled with animating liveliness the grove in which he rests [?] and drowned, to a great extent, the feeling of gloom and sadness.

This afternoon the Rutland company and Woodstock company went into the woods on a scouting expedition, all ready for action, and equipped in the best possible manner. They returned under a heavy rain in the evening and were as they termed it, comfortably soaked through.

To-day the war vessels, *Minnesota* and *Cumberland,*[5] are preparing to move toward the places where land batteries are being erected, and will, undoubtedly, pay them their respects ere returning. The weather is quite cold, more so than in Vermont. For the last two or three days the men have worn their overcoats, and are chilly at that. We are receiving daily mails from Baltimore and other points. At present there is a grand opening for northern men in the way of speculating in flour and potatoes. The former is worth $16 per barrel, the latter $1.75 per bushel.

M.J.M.

The close proximity of Fortress Monroe to the Confederate lines led to some anxious moments for the Union garrison. The men were constantly on edge, awaiting the moment the enemy might advance on their works.

June 11, 1861
Letter from Camp Butler
Camp Butler, Newport News, Va.
June 6th, 1861.

Yesterday morning about 9 o'clock the steamer *Harriet Lane* fired upon a rebel battery directly opposite to this camp, to which the battery briskly responded, by firing 30 guns, only one of which took effect aboard the steamer, by the way of slightly wounding two of the gunners. The action lasted thirty minutes, and was looked upon with much interest by the whole Brigade at Camp Butler. The firing from the vessel was far more accurate than that of the battery, the former firing 20 shots, ten of which took effect upon the battery, doing considerable damage. There appeared to be heavy guns, and rifled cannon on the shore, judging from the report and the distance which they threw shot &c. The action being over, the steamer proceeded immediately to Fortress Monroe and returned in the evening at six, with a small schooner laden

The 1st Vermont in camp
The newly raised 1st Vermont encamped at Brattleboro, Vermont, beginning a three-month enlistment in response to President Lincoln's call for soldiers to defend Washington, D.C., against threatening Confederate forces.

with mutton, veal, and whiskey. There were three rebels on board who were also captured, one of whom is a Negro: they have not revealed anything in regard to matters on the other side. They are now on their way to the Fort in the *Harriet Lane*.

2 o'clock P.M.

There is great excitement in the Camp this moment [?] the picket guards have discharged their guns, which is an indication of trouble in the woods. Soldiers are rushing from the woods, while others are going under arms in that direction. Regiments are in line ready for the conflict. One of the Massachusetts Regiment, a member of the Boston Rifle Company, while forming into line was accidentally shot, by the discharge of a gun which fell to the ground in his own company. It is thought he cannot live till night. Another Massachusetts soldier was in the vicinity of the woods riding a mule which was shot under him about the same time, by a party of four horsemen, [?] he escaped and came into camp rather lively, having lost his hat in the skirmish. I saw him when he arrived and conversed with him; he was apparently but little frightened. He said when the rebels fired, they rode off at full speed, and were, he thought better horsemen than marksmen. Mr. Hatch the Assistant Quarter Master General of Vt., arrived here yesterday, and is inquiring into the necessary wants of the Regiment, which he is ready to furnish, by order of the Governor of the State.

I saw in the Bellows Falls Argus, an editorial of the most shameful kind, denouncing Quarter Master Morse[6] of the 1st Regiment, and charging him with that which the whole Regiment know to be a downright falsehood, as do all who know anything about the manner of doing business in the Quarter Master's department of a regiment, and especially as it is done here at present. He says the sum of three hundred and fifty dollars is placed in the hands of the Quarter Master each day for supplies for the privates. This is not so; it only shows the ignorance of the person who made the statement as well as the characteristic meanness of the source from which it comes to us in print.

All provisions furnished the Vermont Regiment are taken out of the Government stores in Fortress Monroe, or other Government places, and under the superintendence of the Government officers or agents, who deal it out in bulk to the Quarter Master of each regiment, for which the latter receipts, but pays nothing. Don't our friend of the Argus wish he could do likewise. Those who know Mr. Morse, know him to be an honest and straightforward business man, of good standing in society, and cannot avoid censuring the editor of the Argus, for his abusive and uncalled for attack upon the unstained reputation of Quarter Master E.A. Morse of the 1st Regiment of Vermont.

I assure you that I know of but one way for any Quarter Master now in Camp Butler to make anything by dishonesty, that is by stealing salt pork or sea biscuits, which will undoubtedly be left open for little editors who love mean and little things.

Mr. E.A. Morse has been appointed Quarter Master of the post, which is an evidence of his popularity and the confidence placed in him by his superior officers commanding the Brigade.

Respectfully yours,
M.J.M.

Two days after McManus composed this letter, five companies of the 1st Vermont, under Lieutenant-Colonel Peter Washburn, joined a short expedition against the fortified Confederate position at Big Bethel, in one of the first engagements of the Civil War. The men of the 1st Vermont were onlookers. No Vermonters were injured in the battle, considered a defeat for the Union forces. Apparently McManus did not accompany the detachment, for the fight would have certainly received mention in a letter to the paper.

July 20, 1861
From Newport News
Camp Butler, Newport News, Va.
July 14, 1861.

Having some leisure hours after the usual Sabbath ceremonies, I thought it would be appropriate to inform you in regard to what little has transpired within a few days thereabouts. On the morning of July 12th, a party of Germans,[7] thirty-five in number, went some seven miles into the country upon a scouting expedition, as parties frequently do, in order to ascertain the locality, if any there be in that vicinity, of the numerous detachments of rebel horsemen, who frequently make their appearance.

About three in the afternoon a few of the Germans returned with one of their men who was shot through the hand, and stated that they met and fought with a party of three hundred horsemen, and that they killed two of our officers, and took 14 privates prisoners. However, they are missing, up to noon to-day. This morning we received a telegraphic dispatch from the Fortress, that Gen. Butler[8] would visit the camp. The steamer arrived about 12 o'clock with the Gen'l and Staff, together with Mr. Russell[9] the correspondent of the London Times, also John B. Page and F. Chaffee[10] of Rutland, Vt. The two latter named gentlemen were

Big Bethel

The earliest real battle of the war took place in Virginia on June 10, 1861, at Big Bethel, just northwest of Fortress Monroe; although Federal troops — with the 1st Vermont nearby but not engaged — were repulsed with the loss of about a hundred men, the rebel force withdrew from their defenses later that night.

received with great enthusiasm and heartfelt welcome, which was made manifest by the long and warm shake of the hand from every member of the Rutland Light Guard, and I assure you, that for a time the place looked much like Rutland.

Respectfully yours,
M.J.M.

The 1st Vermont completed its three-month term of service on August 2, 1861. It returned home, and the men received their final pay, although many did not end their military service with the mustering out of the regiment. Of 753 officers and men, more than 600 volunteered to serve three-year enlistments in new Vermont regiments. McManus was among those who immediately rejoined.

The 5th Vermont issued a call for volunteers, and McManus received a second lieutenant's commission in the regiment on September 4, 1861, in Company G, primarily of Rutland men. He went south with the regiment, which assumed garrison duty at Camp Griffin outside Washington, D.C. In November, after appearing before a military board of evaluation, McManus was requested to submit his resignation. No explanation is given in his service record regarding the resignation, which became effective November 22, 1861. A soldier corresponding with another paper, not knowing the true circumstances behind McManus's departure, wrote of the resignation as being "a loss to the company and the regiment."[11]

There exists a sketchy record of what employment McManus held after his return from the Army of the Potomac. Newspaper accounts of January 1864 find him employed at the Brandon House. When the re-enlisted veterans of the 5th Vermont attended a banquet held in their honor at the Brandon House on February 3, 1864, McManus was called on to provide an inspirational speech. By the words he delivered that evening it was apparent he never lost his allegiance to the regiment. On September 27, 1867, Martin J. McManus died in Castleton, Vermont. The twenty-eight-year-old veteran was interred in Rutland's Old Catholic Cemetery under a simple stone stating his military service as an officer in the 5th Vermont Regiment.[12]

Letter from Camp Griffin
This flag design — printed in red, white, and blue — was on stationery used in December of 1861 by a Vermonter with the "Army of the Potomac, Camp Grifin [sic], Va."

Captain A. R. Sabin

Albert R. Sabin was an idealistic, newly wed young captain in the 9th Vermont when he departed with the regiment in the summer of 1862 to campaign in the Shenandoah Valley.

In support of the Union

Pro-Union women of Maryland offer refreshment and kindness to Federal troops passing through Baltimore, which had a population that was notorious in the North for its pro-Secession sentiments.

View from Union positions above Harper's Ferry, toward Maryland Heights across the Potomac

A strongpoint with a railroad bridge crossing the Potomac on the invasion route northward, Harper's Ferry was captured in September 1862 — along with the garrison and the 9th Vermont — after a heavy bombardment by Stonewall Jackson's artillery.

Chapter 2

Reporter to Soldier

"Sigma"

Albert R. Sabin, 9th Vermont Regiment

Soldiers came from all professions, and not all were captured by the "war fever" of 1861. One chose first to report on the raising of one Vermont infantry regiment before himself enlisting a year later. He therefore provided two perspectives of military life.

As a Middlebury College student in 1860, Albert R. Sabin was well-known for conducting a singing quartet of fellow students and for giving voice lessons in Rutland and Brandon. He went on to direct choruses, and word of upcoming performances began to appear in letters to the *Rutland Herald* under the name "Sigma."

When Sabin enlisted as an officer in the 9th Vermont Regiment, the correspondence from Sigma continued, and when he resigned, the correspondence ended. Sigma's easy contacts with the officers of both the 2nd and 9th Vermont Regiments indicates a man with some rank in society.

Sabin was from Rockingham, born September 30, 1838. He entered Middlebury College, and when the first shots were fired on Fort Sumter he was still a student. He did not join up immediately, but wrote about the troops for the *Rutland Herald* as a special correspondent. His first dispatches detail the assembling of the 2nd Vermont Regiment in Burlington. For almost two weeks the *Herald* published Sigma's news of the 2nd Vermont from Camp Underwood, the regiment's rendezvous in Burlington. It had been named after the state's lieutenant-governor, Levi Underwood.

From Camp Underwood

A Private Drummed Out. Private's Name Stricken from the Roll.
COMPANIES UNIFORMED. REGIMENTAL APPOINTMENTS.
A Captain Inspected Out.

Special Dispatch to the Herald

Camp Underwood, Burlington

June 12th.

Nothing of note transpired in camp to-day excepting that a private by the name of Wesley Spaulding, of the Fletcher Company, was drummed out, as the reporter understood, for not taking the oath. Gen. Baxter[1] struck from the roll the name of Alexis Mead, a private in the same company, on account of disobedience and mutinous conduct. The Bennington Companies, the Montpelier, and the Waterbury Company named respectively A, F, and D were uniformed this morning. The business of parcelling out the respective uniforms will be continued from day to day until completed. This is of course a work of some time, as each man has to find his fit in the variety of garments. The uniforms furnished thus far add very much to the appearance of the troops.

The following appointments were made this afternoon under special order: No. 9. — Wm. Guinon 1st Sergeant of Company F is appointed Sergeant Major of the 2nd Regiment; Wm. J. Cain is appointed Quarter Master Sergeant of the 2nd Regiment; Louriston D. Stone is appointed Commissary Sergeant of the 2nd Regiment upon the recommendation of Surgeon Ballou.[2] Eli L. Stearns a recent graduate of our Medical College, receives the appointment of Hospital Steward. The hospital is admirably arranged to meet the wants of the Regiment.

Through the courtesy of Capt. R. Smith[3] of the Tunbridge company, your reporter has been enabled to secure many advantages in the way of looking on. Capt. Smith maintains very strict order and discipline, but is nevertheless a very popular officer and a gentleman. The Captain of the Fletcher company being inspected out on account of his age, it is understood that Capt. Burnham[4] of Montpelier, is to take his place. The whole matter however rests in conjecture as yet. I shall be able to give further details tomorrow.

Sigma

June 14, 1861
Letter from Camp Underwood
(From our Own Correspondent)

"Inspecting out" — The 2nd Regiment receiving Uniforms and making disposition of various Officers for service.
New Appointments, &c., &c.

Camp Underwood, Burlington
June 13th, 1861.

The morning broke clear and beautiful over the camp of the 2nd Regiment, though it was somewhat chilly, unusually so, for this season, and considering the late very warm weather. Although to one unskilled in military requirements it might seem as though time was unnecessarily consumed in making this Regiment ready for marching, still the fact is the very contrary. The officers are at work incessantly, and hurrying to make all ready for their marching orders, and are looking care-worn and jaded, even this early in their campaign, from their devotion to the tedious rounds of duty. Despite all their energy, however, much remains to be done before the Regiment can be put into readiness. The inspections of the respective companies, officers, &c., &c., conducted as regularly as it is with a view to send out none but able bodied "fit" men, occupies a great deal of time, and occasionally results in the rejection of a man much to his disappointment and disgust. I was so late at the camp yesterday that I had not time to give you details in my last dispatch of the rejection of Sergeant Z.G. Chase of Company H for a physical infirmity. That he was a good officer and a favorite with his comrades was attested not alone in their loud murmurs of regret and disappointment, but in the public presentation to him of a very beautiful silver watch and chain by the company. The loss to the company occasioned a marked expression of esteem for him among his comrades by whom he was deservedly "petted." The rejection of Capt. Strite of the Fletcher Company on account of his age, (having over-lived the limits of the rule in such appointments) was the subject of many heart-felt regrets to his Company, and of grief and chagrin to himself. It does seem hard to exclude a good and favorite officer (and Capt. Strite at that) because Providence had been merciful to him and spared his life. It was evident, however, that he was a little too far advanced in years to make it entirely safe to subject him to the fatigues of a military life in active service.

His zeal and patriotism prompted him to accept the position given him by his company, and his rejection is a very severe blow to his ambition, though he will remain as true to his country as ever. I dwell thus at length on this subject, since it seems richly to merit it.

In the place of Capt. S. the Company at an election last evening chose Wm. T. Burnham of Montpelier, who had raised a Company for this regiment, which was not detailed, however, the Regiment being already filled by Companies having a prior claim. Capt. Burnham has seen considerable service as a militia Captain, and Major. He is the son of a warrior of 1812; a fine-looking, soldier-like man, who will no doubt head the Company very acceptably to themselves. The compliment was a greater one to him from the fact that it was altogether unexpected and unlooked for by him. He accepts the position however with zeal and the spirit of a war lover. I will hazard the prediction that he will make a favorite and excellent officer. He sympathizes deeply with the Captain whom he supersedes, for no fault in the one, nor unworthy motives in the other.

Capt. Walbridge[5] of the Bennington Company, is the officer of the day. The courtesy of the officers of this Regiment affords every facility to "members of the Press" to be as inquisitive as they please, and questions are cheerfully answered ad infinitum. Last night was the most quiet night the Regiment have had since they were encamped. Disturbances and noisy conduct have not been unfrequent of nights heretofore, but the quiet prevailing last night betokens a better state of discipline. Everything about the camp looks more promising as time gives a chance for the soldiers to learn and to appreciate their duty.

Sigma

June 15, 1861
Camp Underwood
(From our own Correspondent)

Tidings from the 2nd Regiment — Uniforms — Camp life
Our boys in good spirits — Discipline more thorough.

Camp Underwood, Burlington
June 14, 1861.

Another beautiful day, another reveille, another squad drill, monotonously vary the monotonous round of camp duties and camp life! Capt. V.S. Fullam,[6] of Company "J," (Ludlow) is officer of the day. Lieut. D.L. Sharpley[7] is officer of the guard for today.

I had the privilege of looking closely at the uniforms afforded to this regiment, and am convinced that the stricture heretofore asked by some of our papers are undeserved, misbestowed. That fact is, that our Quarter Master General Davis (a State officer not the regimental quarter master) has done his duty to the very letter as well as in the spirit of the law which governs him. He has provided most excellent uniforms, well

George J. Stannard

As commander of the 9th Vermont, Stannard was destined to be captured with his regiment at Harper's Ferry, and later to lead the Second Vermont Brigade in some of the most critical fighting of the Battle of Gettysburg.

made out of excellent cloth, and giving very general satisfaction. The Regimental Quarter Master and his Sergeant, are exerting themselves to the utmost, in aid of the disposition of the State, to do justice by the boys as far as wearing apparel is concerned. The uniform consists of grey cloth frock coat and pants; the pants have a blue stripe sewed into the seams; the coats are trimmed with blue, and gilt buttons (very thickly gilded too) are prominent. Straps are sewed upon the shoulder pieces of the coats to fasten knapsacks to, and taken altogether, with the grey loose overcoat, the uniform is comfortable and complete, and in strict accordance with "regulations."

The fare at the camp in the eating line is very wholesome and good. I supped last evening with Capt. Walbridge of Company A (of Bennington) and can avow that I never fared better as in good wholesome diet. "Our boys" — by which I mean our regiment — are in good health and fine spirits; while the great majority miss the luxuries and considerable provisions of a rich "homestead," yet they accept the duties of a soldier's life with a very cheerful acquiescence to the requirements of the camp, knowing that their country, their houses and everything dear to them demand this sacrifice. It is a sacrifice to their country, and every patriotic citizen feels and knows it, as he looks upon the camp life of these brave fellows.

The discipline grows every day more and more strict; demanding of every man in the regiment that he should be "on hand" at a moment's warning and ready for duty. If the letters of your correspondent should not look as well as the genteel chirography of the itinerant writing master, and if his ideas should not come together on paper as smoothly as the polished sentences of the quiet rhetorician, please bear in mind that he writes in the marques (or tent) of the Lieut. Colonel (Stannard)[8] who affords him a sitting place surrounded by the noise and confusion of a thousand men and the roll of drums innumerable. He will try to accustom himself to these normal annoyances and do better in the future.

Sigma

(From our Special Correspondent)
The Second Regiment

A "damper" on Camp life — Visitors from Montpelier
Presentation of a stand of Colors to the Capital Guard
Distributions of uniforms still going on.

Camp Underwood, Burlington

June 15th, 1861.

It makes a distinct difference as to the comfort of the soldier whether or not the weather behaves itself respectably! Bah! such a cold, wet, drizzly morning, as the reveille called out "the boys" to drill under, very effectually takes the romance all out of life under canvas! I must confess, however, that there is much less murmuring and silent determination evinced by their looks and actions, to make the best of even the worst things falling to their lot, which surprises every one who witnesses the good conduct of our good fellows in the field. The guard house is pretty much an obsolete institution; it is an unfrequented concern. The few cases which have occurred requiring its use, have been the result of a thoughtless playfulness altogether free from any malice or mutinous motives. The reflection that the majority of this thousand yeoman are young, healthy, nimble fellows, full of life and animal spirits, will account at once for an occasional outburst of frolicsome little peccadilloes, rather outside the stern and unyielding laws of the soldier's life, but not (for all that) deserving of anything more than a trifling rebuke.

We had to-day a visit from a large concourse of the citizens of Montpelier, and two of its Fire Companies, No's. 3 and 5. They arrived in the 11 o'clock train — were received and escorted by the Burlington Fire Companies in full uniform. The Ethan Allen, under Capt. E. W. Peck, and The Boxers, under Capt. J.J. Duncklee, and the Capital Guards, [Co. F, Capt. F.V. Randall[9]] of Montpelier. After marching to the Camp, and a short visit among their acquaintances, they were escorted to the Lake House, (in regular line of march) where they dined, faring most sumptuously too, as your Reporter happens to know from his own tried experience in the matter (and he claims the right of passing an opinion on all matters connected with the trencher!). Altho' Curtis, (the host of the house,) had had but a very short notice, the dinner was one of his own peculiar successes, and that in the opinion of your Reporter is enough to say of any reflection.

At 5 o'clock yesterday (Friday afternoon) the Montpelier Company F, Capt. Randall, were publicly presented (the Regiment being on parade) with a beautifully wrought Flag, the gift of the patriotic ladies of

Montpelier, a very large number of whom were present to see that it was well conducted, and to "add countenance" and give encouragement to our men by their many fair faces and sunny smiles. When woman with lovely patriotism bestows the flag, what man can desert it?

The presentation was made by Rev. W.H. Lord, on behalf of the afore-said ladies. He made a most eloquent and effective address to the recipients of this handsome compliment, which altho' kindly furnished, the Reporter finds to be too long for the limits of a letter. Capt. Randall responded on behalf of the "Guard," in a very patriotic and thrilling speech.

I will hazard the prediction that that company will never desert that flag. Very excellent promotions have been made from that company, and is very evident that it is a favorite corps of the men in the Regiment. The men are all large-sized, stalwart and high-spirited men, who will not be found "wanting" when "weighed," their average weight being a very uncommon one. The whole ceremony of the presentation passed off to the great credit of the parties concerned.

The regiment is mostly uniformed; the arms are expected today. The shoes furnished are most excellent ones for the service they are designed for. They are a very thoroughly made, sewed shoe; broad on the bottom, reaching well up the ankle and will prove not only durable, but easy to walk in. Some fault is found with their size, being too large, but the fault is a good one. They are large for their respective sizes according to numbers, but are well made, easy-fitting shoe. From the close scrutiny I can make, I can only say that the duties of Quarter Master General Davis have been most faithfully and honestly attended to.

Capt. Lonergan, of the Winooski Co. (Green Mountain Guard) is officer of the day, and Lieut. J.B. Chase, of the Fletcher Company H, is officer of the guard. The Rutland County boys are in fine spirits, and excepting two or three cases among the Pittsford men, who expect to be sent home for ill health, are all well in body as well as mind. The entire regiment, under the watchful eyes of its commanding officers, gives evidence that experience is doing much to make them an effective, handsome body of men. The Vermont 1st, which went away in such eclat, will have to work hard to keep up with the boys of the 2nd, in point of discipline, looks, and pretty much every thing which goes to make up a complete soldier. Some smears have been thrown out by the Montpelier Patriot, regarding Col. Whiting.[10] The people in this section of country, think that Col. W. is unquestionably as good an officer as Hon. E.M. Brown[11] would have made. Col. W. has had a thorough military education, and has seen service, neither of these facts can be predicated of Mr. Brown, we believe.

I have just time to add before closing, that the Juvenile company from Rutland, uniformed in red shirts and black pants, and armed with lances, have just been most handsomely received, and escorted by Bennington Company A, Capt. Walbridge, who seems to be much pleased to notice the little fellows. The "boys" ("boys" they are in this instance most literally) are bearing their honors becomingly and are indeed a handsome little corps of nice little men. We learn, to our regret, that they return home as soon as to-night. We hope our Burlington Juveniles will forsake their tops and kite-flying, and copying after these gallant little fellows will enter the ranks of a goodly company, for they have enough of them to make a full company "and to spare."

In my next, I shall be able to give you a full roll of the Regiment, as the Field and Regimental, and company appointments have all been made.

As I write amid all the "hurly-burly" of the Camp, I beg indulgence for the periods and punctuation of this scrawl.

Sigma

June 19, 1861

From Camp Underwood

Gossip from Camp — Companies filled — Arrival of Regimental Band — Receipt of Knapsacks, Belts and Cartridge Boxes Sunday in Camp — Pleasant little Presents from Citizens, &c., &c.

(From our Special Correspondent)

Camp Underwood, Burlington

June 18th, 1861.

The unavoidable absence of your correspondent for a short time interrupted his communication that should have been made yesterday. On Saturday the ranks of the Fletcher Company (a little deficient from "inspections out," "drumming out," &c., &c.,) were filled by the arrival of eighteen men from the company already raised at Montpelier by Capt. Burnham, as I have heretofore mentioned. They more than make good the deficiency occasioned by the default of their predecessors. This, I believe, makes the Regiment's complement of men according to "regulations."

The Regimental Band, from Bennington, came into camp Saturday evening. They were "received" by the Bennington Company in due and handsome form and are a most excellent Band of twenty-four "pieces."[12] Its members are well trained, and show evidences of thorough practice. Its selection is a very judicious one, although made to the disappointment of one most excellent corps of musicians.

Yesterday this Regiment received its knapsacks, belts, and cartridge boxes, all which appear to be made thoroughly and fully up to the requirements of the omnipotent "regulations." The arms are expected to-day. Should they arrive, we outsiders can see no reason why the Regiment should not take up its line of march for the duties of the campaign by day after to-morrow; but there may, nevertheless, be very operative reasons known to the authorities for keeping them here. No one knows anything about it, (I suppose) as yet, when they will march.

I have not yet been able to procure the "roll" of the Regiment, but hope to be able to give it complete in my next.

Sunday morning was very unpleasant, a thick misty rain was drenching everything. The afternoon, however, was favorable, and at 5 o'clock religious services of an impressive and appropriate kind were held in the camp. The exercise comprised the usual prayers, the singing of a beautiful hymn, and a thoughtful, instructive discourse by the Rev. Dr. Witherspoon of the 1st Methodist Church here, on the subject, "The Christian Soldier." We were deprived the pleasure of listening to this gentleman's production, but from what we have heard from him, and more especially from the comments made upon this sermon by those fortunate enough to be present, I am ready to vouch for its ability and its abiding interest for his soldier audience.

A pleasant variety in the larder of the camp was thoughtfully and kindly made Sunday at dinner, by the ladies of Burlington, in the way of a donation of innumerable delicious pies, mountains of dough-nuts, with a due accompaniment of cakes, cheese, &c., &c., to render an agreeable relish to their supper of the same day. It will be long ere the men of the Second Regiment lose their fond remembrances of the ladies of this place, enhanced as they are by so many little tokens that the ladies hold them and the cause they are working for in very high esteem. Such kindness may have a much deeper impression upon the recipients of them, in the trying times they are to encounter, than even the generous donors can ask for; greater than they imagine at the time. Men thus cared for are fortified by a sweet remembrance of the past as much as they are stimulated by their visions of glory in the future. Too much zeal cannot be shown in providing for the soldier.

Sigma

P.S. — Since writing the foregoing gossip, I learn that what the past day or so was a mere surmise, proves to be a fact, that the Winooski Company K, Capt. Lonergan, has been disbanded on account of insubordination. There are various rumors in camp respecting the matter. It is said that they are disbanded without any chance to reform themselves. Another rumor says that if a few good men can be found to join a few good men belonging now to the company, its organization may still be maintained. It is said again that they are disbanded, and dismissed, and that their place is to be supplied at once by a company from Vergennes, or, as some say, from St. Johnsbury. I will endeavor to give further details to-morrow.[13]

S.

From Camp Underwood

More activity in Camp — Arrival of Arms and Equipments
Dissatisfaction of the men with their Arms
Marching orders, &c., &c.

(From our Special Correspondent)

Camp Underwood, Burlington

June 20th, 1861.

But little has transpired in camp out of the usual monotonous course of camp drill and other duties, for the past two days, until (and except- ing) the arrival and distribution of the lacking equipments (canteens, bayonets sheaths, cap boxes) and the arms. Since then more activity and bustle has necessarily prevailed in the speedy distribution of these among the men, alterations in size and form being occasionally neces- sary, and some articles being rejected occasionally on trial. Very much dissatisfaction prevails among the men because of their being provided with the smooth-bore musket of 1852, instead of the rifled musket, which it was so confidently expected they would have. The men have been taught to suppose they would certainly have the latest improved musket, and consequently to undervalue any other. Many of them think that they are not armed at all as compared with the arms heretofore given out, and think it hazardous not to say criminally wrong to send them out into battle with (what they deem) so inefficient an arm. The arms are, of course, well made, coming from Springfield; they show well and add everything to the appearance of the men, and for aught I know are a good and effective weapon. At any rate they may enjoy the reflec- tion that they are probably much better than nine-tenths of the arms in the hands of the rebels. The men are being incessantly drilled in the "manual" — the use of the arm — and appear to take hold with zeal and enthusiasm. They evidently learn quickly and appreciate a difference between a drill with arms and a drill without any. It adds a relish to the exercises which takes away the weight of the arm.

The Regiment were notified last night to be in readiness to march on Friday (to-morrow) but I have it from high authority in the matter that such a thing is hardly probable. I do not believe, and it is not generally believed, that they can "get away" before Monday next. I understand that Gov. Fairbanks[14] does not expect them to march before Saturday at the earliest, and, in view of the preparations made in New York City for the "reception" of the Regiment, it is much to be hoped that they will not leave on that day. If they do so, they will be obliged either to remain somewhere over Sunday, to everybody's inconvenience and discomfort, or else to treat our friends in New York with great discourtesy, and almost contempt. Either alternative is to be avoided if possible; the latter more especially, and at all events.

In speaking of the arms furnished by the Government, I would not cast blame on our "Uncle Sam," for perhaps he could do no better than he has; yet if he has good arms, this Regiment, under the circumstances of its enrollment, and the peculiar position in the army which it must take, deserves the very best arm[15] in the gift of the Government. The fact that they are better than the great majority of arms handled by the enemy is hardly a complete satisfaction in case they should happen by the advance fortunes of war to fall in with a body of men who happened to have (by the same ill luck) the best of arms. The range of these guns is limited; their aim, especially on a windy day, very uncertain; they are more liable than the improved arm to get strained and become "untrue"; but above and beyond all these objections they begat an unconscious want of confidence in the men holding them, which is the very worst thing for the holy cause which brings them into use.

More delightful weather for camp life could not be. The temperature is very even and not intolerably warm. The men are in fine health and good spirits, and as each day adds to their equipments (which is now completed) they look more and more soldierly and warlike. Too much praise cannot be awarded the officers of this Regiment in their untiring efforts to make it creditable and praiseworthy; to provide for the health and comfort of the men, and to make it the "crack" Regiment of Vermont. If any one supposes that an officer has nothing to do but wear becoming buttons and stripes, let him sojourn a while with Col. Whiting or Stannard, or Adjutant Ladd, and soon will his folly depart from him! The truth is that it is a laborious responsible life, that of a commander of other men and their welfare.

The officer of the day is Capt. Wm. T. Burnham, Fletcher Co., and the officer of the guard, Lieut. N. Stone.[16] Capt. Burnham is rapidly growing is favor with his men. It will be remembered by your readers that he superseded Capt. Strite in command of that Company.

It has been utterly impossible for me as yet to procure a correct, accurate muster roll. That already published in some of the State dailies, is incorrect in many particulars. I have promised the roll so long I will make no further promises, but hope to give it to you very soon.

Sigma

From Camp Underwood

(From our Special Correspondent)

Throngs at the Camp — The time fixed for the departure of the 2nd Regiment — Presentation of the Regimental Colors.

Camp Underwood, Burlington

June 21, 1861.

The delightful weather and the "hurrying season" among the farmers having passed, brings crowds of strangers to the camp; some actuated by a curiosity to see what camp life is; some to see their friends among the troops now soon to be separated from them perhaps forever, and some because their neighbors have, perhaps, set them the example of visiting the camp (an example which they had better not follow so far as their own reputations for decency is concerned). It is astonishing what a throng of boobies and boors, will crowd in among respectable people on occasions like these. One such specimen is now looking over my M S., and were I certain that he could read good penmanship, I should allude to him in terms not very flattering to his vanity. Never mind him now — he has just left; so I leave that subject for a future discussion.

The time is at last definitely decided upon for the departure of this regiment. They leave here on Monday next en route for the theatre of their action in this momentous struggle of right against wrong. It is very affecting to witness the leave takings between visitors to the camp, and their devoted soldier friends, who are now about to separate from their kindred and kind, many perhaps forever. One may at almost any moment, during the hours when visitors are allowed in camp, witness scenes which afford food for reflection upon the tender ties which bind man to his fellows; I have sometimes turned away with a moistened eye and a saddened heart, from these touching little encounters.

The fault found with the arms furnished by the government, I am very much afraid, will have a bad influence against any effort to raise any more regiments in Vermont. It will operate as a great drawback upon the enlistment of men in the future, unless they can be officially assured that they will be furnished with the best, latest improved, arms.

Perhaps, however, the department will change the arms of this regiment; whether it does or not, we may feel well assured that it does the best it can to provide well for the men.

Yesterday at 5 o'clock P.M., the imposing ceremony of presenting the regimental colors by the Governor[17] to Col. Whiting, took place. The Governor, in a feeling and emphatic speech alluding among other things to the expectations he and the freemen of Vermont held respecting this regiment, put the colors into Col. W's hands, who replied in appropriate and stirring terms; satisfying the immense throng who witnessed the ceremony, that he will stand by his colors come what may.

The troops were paid off yesterday by Quarter Master Pitkin,[18] the regimental, and not the State officer of the same official name. It is superfluous to say that this proceeding, on his part, was productive of great satisfaction to these creditors of Uncle Sam. Capt. Richard Smith, of the Tunbridge company, is officer of the day, and Lieut. Jno. Howe,[19] officer of the guard. Major Joyce commanded at the dress parade last evening. Owing to the receipt of arms, and the excellence of the music, added to the growing experience of the men, the parade of last evening was the most creditable one we have had as yet.

Sigma

Second Brigade headquarters flag
This flag flew over the headquarters of the Second Brigade, 2nd Division,
18th Army Corps; the 9th Vermont belonged to this brigade from September to December 1864,
when it was transferred to the 24th Army Corps.

Letters to Vermont

From Camp Underwood

(From our Special Correspondent)

The Second Regiment taking leave of its encampment
Throngs of people visiting the Camp for "farewells"
Active preparations for departure — Efficiency of the officers
Enthusiasm and goodwill of the citizens openly exhibited and
generously betokened — Court martials — Distribution of Bibles
and Prayer Books — Stringent rules adopted at the last, regarding
visitors, and those soldiers who desired to visit outsiders
Final breaking up of Camp, &c., &c., &c.

Camp Underwood, Burlington

June 22, 1861.

Since it has become a settled conviction on the part of the civilians
that this stalwart regiment of valorous Vermonters are to leave on
Monday next; and since the "orders" leave no alternative to the "parties
in interest" themselves, every necessary preparation has been made,
(and I judge very skillfully made too,) for their final departure — knapsacks are packed; blankets folded; rations being laid in, and every need-
ful step taken to secure the comfort and insure the reputation of the
regiment. If the second regiment is not a regiment of soldiers, then
Vermont ought not to make another effort to send out her sons to war.

Of course, this being the last (week) day of its sojourn, throngs
crowd to camp for the final interviews; some to see, (and nothing
more) but many, a one, to bid a farewell to near ones and dear ones
whom they fear never to meet again — (the fear is not unfounded!).
It has saddened me, "many a time and oft," reflecting that of this stalwart thousand, so many may never see their native land, the ever-
green, ever-glorious hills of old Vermont again! Many little "comforts"
are bestowed by thoughtful and parents; many a token exchanged in
tears between parents and children; between brothers and sisters,
and (nearer and dearer than all either relations) between husband and
wife, or, (better still — holier still) between the lad and lassie
betrothed to each other!

The officers of the regiment and the captains of the several companies
are unceasingly at work to do "all things well." It is a long, tedious task to
get a regiment of men into proper shape according to the "military
ideas." If I am to judge of this regiment by the numberless "attentions"
which it receives, and the bouquets of flowers in the hands of many of its
officers, I shall be obliged to decide that this regiment is a favorite one.

It was found necessary in order (among other things) to inspire the regiment with correct ideas of discipline, to hold a court martial to-day upon the individual cases of about seven privates, who had been absent from camp (without any permission) during the previous day. The court consisted of Capt. F.V. Randall, Montpelier Company, as President; Lieut. Wm. Henry,[20] Waterbury Company, and Lieut. Jno. S. Tyler,[21] Brattleboro Company. A fine was imposed upon the offenders, upon trial, of $5, severally, and imprisoned in the guard house until 6 o'clock Sunday evening. At the dress parade on Saturday evening, the several sentences were read.

This afternoon a very interesting spectacle took place, with very little ceremony, but the better appreciated. Testaments having been previously distributed to the regiment, the Rev. D.H. Buel, on behalf of his denomination (the Episcopalian) announced the distribution of the common Prayer Book in a very thrilling, eloquent and patriotic address. Although having listened to this Rev. gentleman many times in the pulpit, and altho' fully aware of the excellence of his discourse, I never heard him acquit himself as well as upon this occasion. The influence upon the men of such an address cannot be but a good and a lasting one.

Burlington, June 23d.

To-day, (Sunday) no one was allowed the liberty of the camp; no one, (except a soldier) so potent with the powers which rule the tented field, as to be able to visit it upon this its last Sabbath among us! When friends from the outer world would see their soldier friends, the Col. upon due representation, would allow the individual sought to be seen, to go inside the gate (or what would be the "line" in the absence of a high fence) but upon no account could your correspondent find an opportunity to cross the line into camp. He was as powerless as innumerable others who "tried and couldn't," and a rude boy laughed at the disappointment which the aforesaid official (your humble servant) manifested at the decree of the Colonel, who could not be brought to believe that people "connected with the Press" should enjoy immunities uncommon to less favored individuals. So "we" (of the press) were obliged to guess at what went on within.

It was no doubt feared that the men, having been paid off, and finding themselves so near their leave taking of friends and home, would desert if allowed the same liberties which they had before that enjoyed. This was guessed at among us outsiders, especially as some members of a company which had given no little trouble by its insubordination, (the name I forbear to give) did actually desert, and three or four could not be recaptured in time to march with the regiment for the south. A bad time was chosen to pay them. This pleasant ceremony had better been postponed until their arrival in New York, or at their head quarters. Not even to the dress parade nor the religious services of Sunday evening, were the public admitted. This stringency may have been necessary, but the many who had traveled miles, from all parts of the State to take leave of friends in the regiment (whom they have small hopes of ever seeing again) "don't see it so."

June 24.

This morning reveals the fact that no little work was done yesterday. The complete readiness of the men was very remarkable; the more so since so little time was allowed for packing. At half past seven the tents were all down ("struck" I believe it is termed) and packed, and the regiment with colors flying, and its splendid music playing, marched through the principal streets of the village to the Rutland & Burlington Railroad depot, where a long train of cars awaited them. It took no little time to "file in." The cars were filled after a while, and at last moved slowly out of the depot, cheered by such a throng as Burlington seldom gathers together.

Of the "closing scenes" of their sojourn, winding up with the immense crowd assembled at the depot to bid good bye, and the many thrilling partings there, I can say but little. I can only confess to a weakness of the tear-fountains of my eyes as they watched the scene. After all, the nature of the errand on which these brave fellows are sped; the cruel necessity they are compelled to yield to in arranging themselves against common countrymen — traitors though they may be — adds a pang to this parting, which words cannot portray fully. I find myself inadequate to this painful task. A fortnight of the encamped life of a thousand men, with the hurley-burley noise, confusion, throngs and general activity consequent, will leave us very lonesome now that we are without all this. God speed, and in His mercy bless the brave "boys" who go out upon this great errand! May He in His mercy restore them to us — a hope with small foundation.

Sigma

After the 2nd Vermont departed on June 24, Sabin continued to write short dispatches for the paper. He remained at Middlebury College until the authorization to raise the 9th Vermont was announced in May 1862. Though the Union Army had a half a million men in the field, a number thought to be sufficient to end the war, Confederate threats plus falsely inflated enemy numbers prompted the War Department to call up more troops. This time Sabin put away the college books and gained an appointment as the recruiting officer for the Middlebury company. By June 24 the company was organized, and Albert R. Sabin was its captain. Soon, the regiment reported to Brattleboro and was equipped. The official mustering-in ceremony occurred on July 9, 1862.

On July 11, six days before the regiment headed south, Sabin exchanged marriage vows with Mary Barber of Middlebury. When the 9th Vermont departed Brattleboro, it proceeded directly to Washington, then found itself at the end of July in Winchester, Virginia, at the lower end of the Shenandoah Valley[22] guarding against the rebel army of Gen. Thomas "Stonewall" Jackson. This was to be their base for the next five weeks. As did many other correspondents, Sabin attempted to dispel various rumors that had reached the state.

August 13, 1862
Letter from Winchester
Camp Sigel, Winchester, Va.
August 6, 1862.

You, or any other man, had you been in my place two days since, would have been inclined to smile with unusual longitude, bow and salute with unaccustomed urbanity — step with greater alacrity — and give signs of extreme satisfaction in general — and more, too. For until that time for nearly two weeks not a word or letter from old Vermont cheered our anxious hearts. During this time what events might not have happened! Young fellows who had left their hearts behind and expected a ten page letter six times a week, seemed to feel it badly. The sun scorched them. They could not eat, nor drink — much. I felt sorry for them. Also for those whose honeymoon had been abridged. The rest of us did better; had less headaches, heartburn, dizziness, cough, catarrh indigestion and blue — I almost said it. But our mail came at last, and your smiling and intelligent face among the rest. I then learned the cheering news from the embryo 10th, and then looked for the 11th. Hurrah for Vermont, the "Banner State." Today we hear of the call for 300,000 more. Better and better. I declare, somebody is getting converted in Washington. Those immaculate kid gloves are thrown aside — off comes the coat and up the sleeves — and the fist really is clenched! Will anybody be hit? Patience good friends, work is ahead. Activity, severity, and victory by consequence. Only send men. Nothing has given me so much courage as the announcement that drafting is to be substituted for volunteering if men will not respond. That is orthodox. It is time to coax and tease. But I don't fear for Vermont. She won't allow such infamy and disgrace to come upon her. The fame of the backbone State will forever remain untarnished.

I suppose it would be highly improper for me tell you how many troops are here, or how many guns we are placing in our fort. But give us a little more time and we won't be "skedaddled" out of Winchester by any small force. Secesh[23] is the rule here; a real Union man is worth as much as a white blackbird for a curiosity. There are a few, I am told, but they are mostly mystical. By the way, the account you got up of our reception in Baltimore is the biggest lie on record. I have seen men who could tell large stories — I have heard things in the way of more fabrication which I though evinced genius, but the Baltimore correspondent of the N.Y. Times towered above them all — like Saul in Israel or Satan among his staff and aide-de-camps. He is above genius himself. Let all common or uncommon liars stand abashed, send in their hats, and acknowledge their master. The Union men of Baltimore fed us — and nobler men than they cannot be found. One faint cheer from some two dozen spectators did greet us, but it sounded like the first abortive attempt of an ambitious but very juvenile rooster to crow. Sulky, sour, revengeful countenances peered from windows and graced the corners of the streets. The friends of those who fired upon the Mass. 6th are still in that city, and they would repeat it if they dared. I would not say a word if I could see the utility in such lies. We have had too many. Truth is better, if only by way of variety. De Quincey treats of "Murder as a fine art." If ever lying comes to be classed among the fine arts, let me place upon record my solemn conviction that the man who could say that the officers of our regiment "were literally loaded with bouquets in Baltimore," should have the first Professorship. Let the Father of Liars resign the sceptre to his gifted son.

Our boys are enjoying themselves well. The country is delightful and fruit plenty. I see your company officers every day, and they are worthy of their country. Captain Ripley[24] is following in the footsteps of his brother, as he should, to be a popular and efficient commander. My friend, Lieut. Kelley[25] seems to be as popular and successful here as in teaching, and what more need be said? He has been acting as adjutant during a temporary illness of Adjutant Stearns.[26] Lieut. Ballard[27] can wield the spade as dexterously and effectively as the pen or sword. Count on him anywhere. The boys like our field officers immensely. They don't go in for show, but work and discipline. Our pickets are fired upon nearly every night by bushwhackers — the name given to the meanest of thieves and most devilish of murderers. The people expect Jackson up again soon. We shall be happy to receive him, if he can find it convenient to give us a call. You like brief letters, but I cannot help it. I couldn't stop now only my sheet is full, to that you are greatly indebted. Let us give thanks.

   Sigma

The seat of war

Fighting raged in the region from Washington, D.C., westward to Harper's Ferry, where the Shenandoah River meets the Potomac, the armies maneuvering and clashing in a seesaw struggle to control the river crossings, rail heads and towns between Fredericksburg and Winchester.

Though secure in Winchester, the 9th Vermont still suffered the effects of Confederate raiders attacking the rail line connecting the town with Harper's Ferry. Few things were worse than losing the mail. Morale suffered when the troops read of men at home refusing to enlist and fight in the war. Sabin blasts those individuals who were healthy and left others to do the fighting, such as that in the recently concluded Peninsular Campaign, where Union casualties were heavy.

September 3, 1862
Army Correspondence
Letter from Winchester
Camp Sigel, Winchester, Va.
Aug. 29.

It is with gratitude and pride that we read in our veracious journals, the record of our gallant deeds, learn how bravely we bore ourselves in the deadly strife, and how our thinned ranks bore unmistakable testimony of our valor. For if our friends and neighbors have confidence enough to say all this for us now, what eulogies shall we not receive where there is some foundation of truth upon which to base them. We have been in the battle of Culpeper it seems — yet every day hundreds of letters have been mailed from us at Winchester. Capt. Jarvis[28] has made such statements has he? Mr. Herald, won't you ask the papers on the east side of the mountain to tell the truth. It would have saved some anxiety, I presume. We ought to be ashamed to acknowledge that we have been cut off from Harper's Ferry by a squad of rebel cavalry, but it is so.

Last Saturday, the mail train was captured, several soldiers on board taken prisoners, the mail and express matter carried away, and our men compelled to carry fuel and burn the cars. And this about ten miles from us! Understand distinctly, however, it was no fault of ours. The railroad is under Gen. Wool's[29] control. Now, there is a guard on the train as there should be.

Ten of the R.I. cavalry[30] were taken prisoners last week, while outside our perimeter. They were boys from Dartmouth College. Per contra — the R.I. cavalry took ten of Ashby's cavalry at Newtown, seven miles west, this week. One rebel Captain was shot by a Union man near us day before yesterday, and yesterday one was captured after a long pursuit. Small bodies of cavalry hover about us on all sides, but disappear when our troops approach. We are experiencing some sickness. Nearly one half of the line officers are unfit for duty, but none of them dangerously ill. The climate and dietetic changes can but have an influence.

It is possible that we have Vermonters so mean, so cowardly, so utterly destitute of honor, manliness, and decency, as to slink off to Canada, lest they be compelled to serve their country! I blush for shame every night as I lie with uncovered head upon the soft earth — or perchance a block of stone — and gaze up to the quiet stars, beaming so calmly upon me and saying "Peace, be still, War is for the hour; Peace forever. The hand which supports us in our trackless orbits will protect and shield the faithful soldier." I thank God every day of my life that I came out when I did to serve our common country. I think our ancestors, the brave Green Mountain Boys of Vermont, must look down with wonder upon their degenerate sons, going about in crowds with certificates of disability in their pockets. No one, more than I is aware of the folly of sending invalids to the army. We are reminded of the painful consequences every day. But would any one imagine that a town could be found in Addison County with only five able bodied men? Yet I am told such is the fact. What a record of everlasting infamy some are leaving for posterity in this time that tries men's souls and bodies. I must leave this point — it is distasteful and sickening. But I will glory in the men who are now coming into the field. They are saving our State from disgrace. Posterity will call them heroes. But I cannot help wishing sometimes, that there would be a draft. I would pray day and night for the lot to fall on some men, or rather human beings I know of.

If I do not stop I shall get excited and take hand and hit somebody, and that would be naughty.

Yours moderately,
Sigma

After the Union loss at the Second Bull Run in August, rumors spread that Lee was about to enter the Shenandoah Valley and threaten the Federal forces there. The War Department issued orders for the forces at Winchester to march directly to Harper's Ferry. On September 3, the 9th Vermont abandoned Winchester, leaving behind forty men in the hospital. After the troops arrived in Harper's Ferry they waited while Lee's army marched into Maryland. The Union force that included the 9th Vermont hoped to be assisted by the Army of the Potomac.

Relief never arrived, and Jackson's army encircled the town. Surrounded by an enemy on commanding heights, the Union force in Harper's Ferry had no chance. On September 15, Colonel Dixon Miles surrendered the entire garrison without much of a fight, a decision that angered many Union soldiers. The general opinion was that Dixon, a native Marylander, had sold out, revealing his real sympathies for the Confederacy. Dixon could not answer those charges for, in the final moments of the siege, he had been mortally wounded by a cannonball.

The 9th Vermont and other Union regiments were paroled, and they headed north by train to special camps to await exchange for paroled enemy prisoners. Until then, they would not be permitted to take up arms again. The men learned their new camp would be in Chicago, many miles from Vermont.

September 27, 1862
Army Correspondence
From the 9th Regiment — Surrender of Harper's Ferry
The Regiment to go to Chicago.
Annapolis, Md.
Sept. 22, '62.

We are out in the world again, and I feel gratified — altho' we did not get out in a desirable manner. We left Winchester under an order from the War Department, on very short notice, leaving our sick in the hospital, and destroying large quantities of commissary stores which we could not bring away. We left about 11 o'clock in the night of Sept. 3d, and reached Harper's Ferry about 6 the next day afternoon, having marched 32 miles, and being quite fatigued.

Two days after reaching Harper's Ferry communication was cut off, and for 12 days we heard nothing from the north. On Saturday the 13th inst., the enemy appeared on Maryland Heights,[31] and after a sharp engagement our troops left the Heights and three batteries, magnificent ones, were spiked and dismounted. Here was the blunder, or worse, of Col. Miles; for when we had lost the Heights, we had really lost everything, and it was only a question of time. The Heights, so termed, is a mountain like that east of Lake Dunmore, rising precipitously and commanding everything. This point should have been held, if every man were required to defend it, and we then could have received our reinforcements in season. On the same day large numbers of the enemy's infantry were discovered on the west and north and [enemy] batteries on Loudon Heights,[32] across the Potomac from Maryland Heights. We sent them a few shell, but could do no more, as our force was little more than 10,000, the force above us nearly or quite ten to our one. To sally out to attack them was to weaken ourselves and be cut to pieces. To remain where we were, was the only way left, and this left the enemy at liberty to plant batteries all around us.

On Sunday afternoon they opened with two batteries of 10-pound Parrot guns from Loudon Heights, sending shell and shot into our camps. We went over the hill to escape the fire, cavalry and infantry together, our batteries replying. No sooner were we nicely out of fire there, than a battery opened on us from the opposite direction, and we sought a ravine for protection. About 5 o'clock tidings were brought that an infantry force was approaching from the south, and the 9th Vermont, 3d Maryland[33] and 32d Ohio went out to meet them. The 9th were drawn up in the woods, our right supported by the 3d Maryland. Firing commenced there first, and our right was drawn out in one terrific volley, which the rebels acknowledged killed and wounded fifteen or twenty, although scarce a man was in sight. They then forced the Maryland 3d, and we were compelled to retire towards our battery to prevent being flanked and to protect the battery. Here we lay during the night, and near morning took position about twenty rods south of Rigby's battery[34] to support it. About sunrise the rebels opened upon us with seven batteries, and Capt. Rigby[35] replied in splendid style, dismounting two guns in one place, killing some gunners in another, and doing good business all around. After two hours' fire, his ammunition was exhausted and he hoisted the white flag and left the fort. During this time the 9th Vermont lay on the ground expecting an attack of infantry, and with the fire of five batteries passing over our heads, and shell and shot plunging around us on every side. It seems singular that no one was killed and but two wounded. At first the danger seemed imminent, but soon it became obvious that there were many places for balls to hit without touching us. Besides, we were every moment expecting the enemy's infantry to charge upon us. Col. Stannard[36] was surprised and chagrined to see a white flag, and the feeling was shared by all his boys. Surrounded on all sides by a force from 100,000 to 150,000,[37] it was folly to waste life when defeat was sure and speedy. The victorious party was magnanimous; no insulting language was used; the officers were allowed their side arms, and private property was left unmolested except some that was plundered before a guard was placed over it. Two teams to a regiment were allowed us to bring away baggage, and altogether we were surprised at the gentlemanly treatment we received. One reason was doubtless that they were themselves severely pressed by McClellan, and commenced moving away baggage as soon as we surrendered. To come so near holding our position and lose it, losing a splendid victory, and most vexing to our pride; but sorrow for the great loss to our country was the thought uppermost in every patriotic heart.

Col. Miles was hit by a canister shot, and I learn died soon after. But he sold us — intentionally or otherwise — and a feeling of hatred exists towards him which his death cannot remove.

The day after we arrived at Harper's Ferry, Col. Stannard was invited to look over the defenses and make suggestions. He advised to plant batteries on the top of Maryland Heights, to take possession of and fortify Loudon Heights, and to cut down all the woods within five miles, so that no enemy could approach under cover. Nothing was done but to cut a few trees. Had our brave and competent Colonel been in command, the country would have been saved a great loss, and the 9th Vermont a great misfortune. Had we held out longer, we should have had a terrible slaughter. Three brigades were drawn up ready to charge upon our battery, and our regiment would have met two of them.

We left Harper's Ferry on Tuesday noon, went to Frederick, Ellicott's Mills, and thence to this place, in all about one hundred miles. The last day we came twenty-five miles, and were exhausted, hungry and thirsty when we reached here.

Now we are told we are to go to Camp Douglas, Chicago. So far since we were paroled, we fare much worse than when in service, and find it seems to be so generally. There are men here who have been here since the Bull Run battle. Prisoners experience all the privations and none of the indulgences of active service. We were sold and shall be glad when we can be exchanged and put into the field again. But in the meantime railroads and contractors must fatten from us — who may be considered in respect to government, as "encumbrances," as some one styled children.

Lieut. Ballard was left sick in the hospital at Harper's Ferry, and Lieut. L.E. Sherman[38] and three other officers at Winchester.[39] Such are the fortunes of war. To take them all philosophically requireth verily great attainments.

Sigma

On September 28, the 9th Vermont and Albert Sabin arrived at the parole camp in Chicago. They were first quartered at Camp Tyler, then Camp Douglas. The men waited there to be exchanged, while the officers, who had greater freedom than the enlisted men, could travel throughout the city. Sabin composed a letter to the Rutland Herald to dispel rumors concerning the actions of the officers of the 9th Vermont. This time, he elected not to use his pseudonym, but his real name.

Parole camp in Chicago
After their capture at Harper's Ferry, the men of the 9th Vermont
were released by the enemy — paroled — on their promise not to be
employed again as troops until officially exchanged for Confederate prisoners;
the parolees were quartered in Camp Douglas, near Chicago.

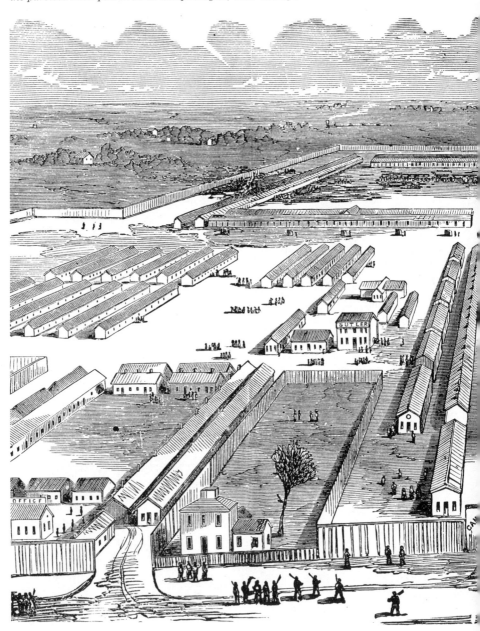

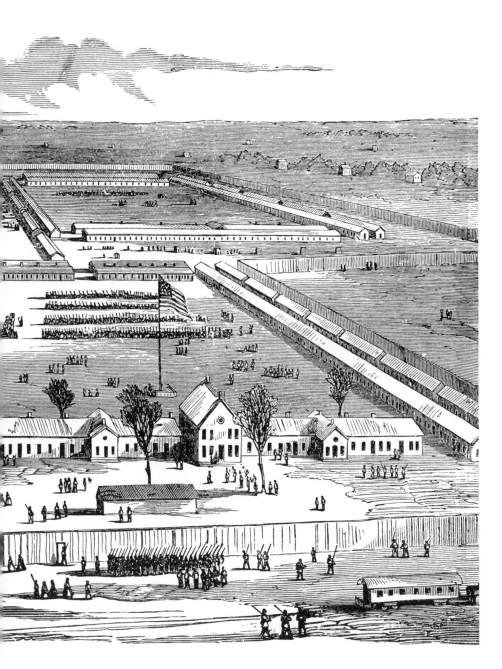

From the 9th Vermont Regiment
Vindication from recent newspaper attacks
Camp Tyler,[40] Chicago, Ill.
October 25, 1862.

The Burlington Times of October 18th contains the following paragraph:

"SHAMEFUL CONDUCT. We are assured upon excellent authority that some of the officers in the 9th Vt. Regiment were so wanting in self respect and patriotic feeling that after the capture of Harper's Ferry they sold their equipments, swords, field glasses, overcoats, &c., to the rebel officers. We should not credit the statement which is so disgraceful to the recreant poltroons, were it not attested by one of the best officers in the service of the State and country."

This is by no means the first attack made upon the ill-fated 9th by this sheet. Almost every issue that has come to us for the last fortnight has contained some report of insubordination or riotous acts perpetrated by the soldiers of the 9th, such as refusing to do guard duty; defying the authority of the officers; burning barracks, &c., all of which are totally false or grossly misrepresented. And now, as if not satisfied with making the rank and file out as knaves and rowdies, it makes this most libelous and flagitious attack upon the officers of the regiment that ever defiled the white surface of an innocent medium. We are accused of being guilty of "shameful conduct," of having lost our "self-respect and patriotism." In short and in fine we are no longer men but recreant poltroons,[41] because, for sooth, as is alleged, some of the officers sold their equipments, field glasses, swords, revolvers, overcoats, &c. to the rebel officers; all of which is attested by "one of the best officers in the state."

Now, Mr. Editor, I must deliberately and above my own signature affirm that the accusation is false not only in its verbal diction but in its intent. I know not who the very excellent officer referred to is, nor do I care, but it is perfectly apparent as I will show you by a candid statement of facts, that the author of the libel is actuated by malicious motives with which the Times seems to be in lively sympathy. Admitting for the moment the accusation to be true that at the surrender of Harper's Ferry, the officers of the 9th did dispose of certain side arms and field glasses, and that rebel officers paid us money for them; does it necessarily follow that we were miscreant to our trust in so doing? that we sacrifice sentiment? that we made ourselves poltroons? Who has constituted the Times our judge? Or if he be self constituted will he please state to the people of Vermont candidly the condition and circumstances in which we were placed, and the motives that might have actuated us, and then he may pass his judgment, but not before. He has no right to do it before. Has he done this? Or has he not rather heard with a biased mind the statement of some prejudiced officer, jumped at his conclusions, and meanly arraigned us before the public with a lie.

What means has either the Times or its superlatively excellent officer of knowing the circumstances which may or may not have influenced our actions at this time?

In the first place every officer in the regiment looked upon the white flag that acknowledged the rebels our victors as the inevitable sentence of each one of us, to a winter's berth in a Richmond prison. We had not the slightest hope of retaining our personal effects, save the clothes upon our bodies. We had received no pay and few of us had any money. Now, admitting that some Captain or Lieutenant did receive $18.00 or $20.00 for his revolver from a rebel officer, supposing that it would be taken from him anyway, is it anybody's business but his own? Was it so very shameful to replenish an empty pocket, with which to go into Dixie, with six months imprisonment in prospect? Is the Times so exceedingly pure and good that it sees evil in such a transaction. Or, if some officer, had some article of clothing which he was unable to carry with him for want of transportation, is it indicative of a total loss of self respect that he received $5.00 for it instead of leaving it common property for the lousy legion of rebel privates around us?

But we have denied the accusation and branded it with the lie. I am happy to inform the friends of the 9th at home that its officers are fully equipped with the swords and revolvers with which they left Brattleboro, that they are all well protected with good warm overcoats; and that if we are, perchance, minus a field glass, we are yet able to see very clearly the malicious, cowardly and contemptible motive which prompted the sneaking assault of the Times.

Some of the officers threw their weapons into the Shenandoah, who afterwards recovered them, and in one or two cases they were left there. Many of them swore the rebel officers should never lead their ragged crew with their swords. Col. Andross[42] had ordered his horses to be shot rather than they become the property of rebels. Such were the manifestations of the feelings of the officers, both field and line on the lamentable occasion, and these are facts which every officer in the regiment will attest.

We feel deeply our misfortune and we feel that we are the greatest sufferers. For weeks we labored on forts and fortifications but were obliged to witness their destruction in one short night.

A fortnight after, we were sold by a "traitor."[43] We have worked, we have been cattle carred here and cattle carred there; we have pillowed our heads upon mother earth, and found a hard cracker and piece of raw salt pork a greater luxury than ever the daintiest dish of chicken back home, but we have taken all these things for granted. We have not complained nor do we wish to, but we do complain, and we think with reason, when such nefarious libels are put before the public mind in our own State and among our own friends as is contained in the offensive article of the Times. It is intended to mislead the public and destroy their confidence in us, who feel that we are grossly injured and insulted.

It is thought to be so very fine to hold a commission in the army? Do any envy us our bountiful pay? Let me assure any such that if they will clear us of the sacred obligation of duty and honor that holds us, our mantles shall fall upon the croakers without delay. For one I have felt that it costs a good deal to serve one's country. But all we ask, all we want is the confidence, sympathy, and hearty good will of our friends at home. This we feel we have a right to expect until we have been guilty of "shameful conduct" and become "miscreant poltroons." Then and not till then shall my pen remain dry.

Yours very truly,
Albert R. Sabin

Sabin submitted his resignation on December 24, 1862, and returned to his wife and Middlebury College where he graduated in 1863. He returned to Chicago and entered the field of education as a teacher in the Dearborn School. Concurrently, he was directing a choir in the city for $500 per year.[44] He continued through other schools in the city system, first the Newberry School, then the Franklin School, which was lost in the great Chicago fire of 1871, and the Douglas School. In 1872 Sabin was a teacher at Central High School. From that post he became Latin chair at Lake Forest Academy, returning to the Chicago public schools in 1881 as principal of the Kinzie School.

Six years later, Sabin became assistant district superintendent and in 1889 district superintendent. He returned to being a principal at the Audubon and Irving Park Schools, eventually accepting the post of principal of Medill High School, where he was still active at the time of his death. Besides his busy schedule as an administrator, Sabin found the time to author five school books; four in math, the other on spelling.

While in Chicago he was a long-term member of the Loyal Legion, an organization consisting of Union officers from the Civil War. Sabin's first wife died in 1891, leaving one son, Stewart, from the marriage. He remarried in 1893, to Helen Mackey of Fredonia, N.Y., and the couple had one son, Albert R. By the turn of the century Sabin's health began to decline. After being seriously ill for two weeks, he died at his residence on January 29, 1914, in his seventy-fifth year. The primary cause was Bright's Disease. Burial was in Chicago's Rosehill Cemetery.

Sabin was so respected in the school system for his years of service as both teacher and administrator, that in his honor the president of the Chicago school board ordered the flags of all city public schools to be at half-mast for ten days.

Camp Griffin burial
Illness took many lives in the first winter of the war, as inexperienced young soldiers learned the hard way how to survive, build shelters, and take care of their health while exposed to the elements on marches, on sentry and patrol duty.

Skirmishers in the woods
Sharp fighting by patrols in no-man's-land wildernesses was a daily part of regimental routine as the armies of North and South confronted each other in the countryside between Richmond and Washington.

Letters to Vermont

Chapter 3

In the Peninsular Campaign of 1862

"L.T.D."

Lewis T. Dutton, 5th Vermont Regiment

With the onset of war Vermonters flocked to join the regiments that were raising. The new soldiers never expected, however, that what lay before them was not only battle and the glory they were seeking, but the harsh adversity of camp life. This became reality for the men of the Vermont Brigade in the winter of 1861–62, when disease ran rampant and suffering was significant. Then, under the leadership of George McClellan, conditions changed, and it was on to Richmond, leaving the memories of camp behind. A new adversary awaited them.

Born in the hill town of Goshen, Vermont, Lewis T. Dutton[1] had a profession as a painter; he was a part–time botanist and cultivator of gladiolus in the Brandon region, according to family history. Dutton possessed some writing skills, for when the *Rutland Herald* needed a correspondent to report on the raising of the 3rd Vermont Regiment, he was selected.

Dutton's first three letters were in the capacity of an observer, possessing an eye for detail, of a scene being duplicated in numerous towns across the United States. Raised in the summer of 1861, the 3rd was to be Vermont's second three-year regiment[2] Arrangements were made to rendezvous at the fairgrounds in St. Johnsbury, soon renamed "Camp Baxter."[3]

Special Correspondence

The loveliness of the Passumpsic Valley. — Military matters in St. Johnsbury. — Encampment of the Third Regiment. — Charge of Chief Justice Poland in reference to Treason, &c., &c.

St. Johnsbury

June 5, 1861.

It was pleasant, as I passed up the charming Connecticut and Passumpsic valleys, to notice the fine prospect for bountiful crops. And here I must remark, before proceeding to give information of the military movements in this section, that one who has never penetrated into the nooks and vales which nestle among the steep and abrupt hills of Eastern Vermont, can not form an adequate conception of the attractive loveliness of this Passumpsic valley, of which the undulating village of St. Johnsbury is the jeweled crown and glory. The meadows so luxuriant of staple fruitage, the woodland on the clean hill side, and the deep green of the early summer foliage, mounting up and covering irregular but beautiful terraces, such as only the great Architect of nature can form, until, like the waves of ocean of similar hue, it seems to break in graceful billows over the tops of the hills against the sky, all combine in a landscape fit for the painter's brush or the poet's pen.

The martial spirit on the east side of the mountains, evoked by the treason of the Southern States, has not abated in the least since the commencement of hostilities by the rebels, and if any thing, is on the increase. Having noticed in some of our State papers a statement that the military company which was being recruited here in St. Johnsbury had backed out — *seceded* — and refused to be inspected, I have since my arrival here, taken some pains to learn whether a report so discreditable to Caledonia County and to the Governor's own town of St. Johnsbury, has any foundation in fact. You may judge of my gratification on learning that not only has a full company been enlisted and inspected here, but that the town of St. Johnsbury sent some forty stalwart men to the recruiting station at Wells River, in Orange County to fill up the company there. This fact goes to show that St. Johnsbury and Caledonia County do not intend to suffer in comparison with other localities, in respect to furnishing the necessary bone and muscle, and life blood if need be, in this great struggle for constitutional liberty. I am abundantly assured that the patriotic inhabitants of Caledonia, many of them descendants of the brave and hearty "Scots wham Bruce ha' often led," stand ready to pour forth one, two, or three, companies, in addition to those already enlisted from these Highlands of America's Scotland whenever the country shall call for their services.

The Third Vermont Regiment will go into encampment at this place, on the Fair Grounds about one mile south of the village, as soon as the camp equipments arrive, which I am told will be in a few days. The probability is that the companies will be called together next week, and remain in rendezvous, perhaps several weeks, for instruction in regimental and battalion drill. I visited the Fair Ground to-day, and found the necessary preparations in active progress under the superintendence of Major Hyde,[4] who is a graduate of West Point. Instead of using tents, the troops will quarter in the extensive buildings belonging to the Fair Ground Company. The buildings are 240 feet in length, by some 40 in width, the centre building being two stories high, 40 by 40, and each of the wings, both in extension, being 100 feet in length. One of these wings is being extended 100 feet by a temporary building, making when completed, the entire length of the building 340 feet. Three tiers of bunks are being put in, one above the other throughout the entire length of the wings on each side, sufficient to furnish sleeping accommodations for 1000 men. The second story of the main building is to be used for officers and the officer's quarters. Tables for eating are to run through the centre of the wings between the *sleeping nests* of the troops, and a temporary building near by for the cooking department is being erected. I also noticed upon the Grounds a large new reservoir for water, to be supplied from an excellent spring on the hillside. In short, every reasonable provision seems to be making for the comfort of the men: and the Governor, who takes a special interest in the matter, is entitled to the thanks of the people of the State, for the solicitude and humanity which he exhibits in such a practical manner.

Col. G.A. Merrill who is Post Master of St. Johnsbury, will establish an office in the Quarter Masters building, for the distribution of letters and papers sent to members of the Regiment during the period of rendezvous, as also for the mailing of letters by them.

The County Court commenced its session here yesterday, Chief Justice Poland presiding. In his charge to the Grand Jury, Judge Poland briefly, but patriotically and in appropriate terms, made allusion to the treason of the Southern conspirators against the Government and the Union, and to the fact that Judges in various other Northern States had thought it necessary in their charges to Grand Juries to call attention to the law of treason, as applicable to such persons as may extend "aid and comfort" to the rebels, and the reason he gave for declining to enter specifically upon that topic was so justly creditable to our State, that I send you that portion of his Honor's charge for publication, giving his language as nearly as my notes will enable me to do.

3rd Vermont at St. Johnsbury
Before enlisting in the 5th Vermont, Dutton reported for the Rutland Herald *on the raising of the 3rd Vermont, pictured here at the fairgrounds in St. Johnsbury, before uniforms or rifles had been issued; a Boston tailor admired their physiques, saying, "I never put the tape on such a set of men as these."*

He said: "Within the last few months, and since a considerable portion of the people of the United States have placed themselves in a condition of open rebellion against the general Government, several published charges to Grand Juries have fallen under my notice, made by courts in States where the State authorities and the people generally are undoubtedly loyal to the central Government. In these charges, the Judges have felt called upon to instruct the Grand Juries of their several Courts upon a branch of the criminal laws, happily hitherto almost unknown in this country — the crime of *Treason;* and more especially, what acts in support and aid of open and treasonable organizations, by supplying them with munitions of war, or otherwise, would subject the persons committing such acts within the limits of loyal States, to the legal penalties against traitors. Notwithstanding the deplorable condition of the country, involved by the passions and ambition of unprincipled men in the horrors of civil war, and the painful and undeniable fact, that many persons within the limits of the still loyal States, lacking all the feelings of patriotism, or overcome by appeals to their cupidity, have involved themselves in the guilt, and subjected themselves to the punishment of traitors, by furnishing means to carry forward the trea-sonable object of those in open and active rebellion, still, I do not feel that there is the slightest need for the Court, but within the limits of this State, there is not a man who is disloyal to the flag of his country, or who could be induced to give support or aid to traitors who would tram-ple it in the dust. I shall, therefore, only make such suggestions as apply to topics of your ordinary official duty."

The demand for daily and other papers in this vicinity is unprecedent-ed, and is proof that the population is made up of intelligent and well informed citizens. Some one, curious in statistics, has shown that more papers and periodicals of various kinds are taken in Vermont than in any other State of the Union in proportion to the population. Nevertheless, the idea has got abroad to [some] extent, that our people are about as "verdant" as our emerald hills: but those persons who entertain that false notion might come amongst them and find profitable instruction in every household. Such a one would be apt, at any rate, to find in every house and hamlet, not only a newspaper, Bible, and copy of the Declaration of Independence, but something bearing a strong resem-blance to that glorious tri-colored flag of America, which floated over the army of the Revolution, and now, in later times, is known and honored throughout the whole earth — and he would learn, too, that there is a prevalent religious trust that God is in that flag, and that it *must* and *will* be victorious.

In haste,
D. [5]

The first companies arrived in St. Johnsbury on June 7, 1861. The remainder arrived over the next four weeks. Dutton was a keen observer.

June 26, 1861
Special Correspondence

Gov. Fairbanks and his Patriotism — Camp Baxter
Fine Appearance of the Troops — Proficiency in Drill
Popularity of Col. Hyde — Sickness in the Quarter Master
Positions of Companies in the Regiment
Essex County "Log Rollers" the "Pet Lambs" — Various Matters.

St. Johnsbury
June 23, 1861.

If I have not written before this, it is only because of the lack of material for an interesting letter. And in fact, I have only time at present to give a naked detail of facts, without embellishment, and must write in great haste to get my letter into the morning's mail, which closes in an hour. Writing at railroad speed, and without "breaks," as I must, I hope the printer and proof reader will take care that I do not appear worse than I deserve to.

During the past week the Governor whose activity and vigilance would do credit to a man in the prime of life, and which would elicit special commendation from every press in the State, were he a young man, has been giving his undivided attention to the outfit of the Second Regiment. And here let me say that the people of Vermont will probably never know the extent of the pecuniary and other sacrifice which has been suffered and borne by Governor Fairbanks in the great cause in which we are all engaged. It is not unknown that the great Fairbanks Scale Company of which the Governor is the senior partner, has branch houses in all the principal cities in the South. While there are honorable exceptions, it is not to be supposed that "confiscation," has left the Governor of the Green Mountain state unscathed. But notwithstanding his pecuniary disasters stared him in the face, he would have moved along as calmly and resolutely in the discharge of his high trust, as if he were to be rewarded therefore by a princely fortune. I will say no more at this time, but I do trust that justice will at last be done to a patriot worthy of the darkest days of the Revolution in 1776.

The several companies are making great proficiency in drill. Though left to shift for themselves the past week, I am happy to say that no time has been lost. I never saw a body of men more ambitious and devoted to duty than are the companies which compose the Third Regiment. Since they donned their new shirts, which arrived in camp on Friday, they pass around as nimbly as a new American coin, and when they get their uniforms and arms they will stand at a "premium." I am tempted to say further that Gen. Hopkins,[6] himself, whose practiced eye will mark a good soldier as far as a Minnie rifle will carry its contents, if he were commissioned for that purpose, could not go through the State and select a better appearing body of men than the Third Regiment will turn out to be.

The men are learning rapidly. They are drilled most thoroughly by competent teachers. Only one company is as yet taught in the manual of arms. Col. Hyde, who is commanding at Camp Baxter, is a general favorite with all. The good feeling which prevails, the fraternization of the several companies, the emulation which exists, is all mainly due to his efforts. He is *the favorite* of the Regiment. Modest, unassuming, yet vigilant, prompt and energetic. I do believe there is not a man in the encampment who would not gladly lay down his life for Col. Hyde. He was a class mate of the lamented Lieut. Grebble,[7] who fell so gloriously at Great Bethel,[8] and he speaks in the highest terms of his comrade. I noticed that a tear glistened in his eye, as he mentioned his heroic school fellow. I predict nothing but a brilliant career and rapid promotion for Col. Hyde, if his life is spared. It is probable he will be appointed major of the Third Regiment, though in certain contingencies he may have a higher post.

Quarter Master Baxter is sick and confined to his bed with rheumatic fever. Colonel Merrill, Secretary of Civil and Military Affairs, has been acting Quarter Master for the past week. It is rumored that Redfield Proctor, Esq., of Cavendish, will be Quarter Master in the event that Mr. Baxter does not recover in season to go to the seat of war.[9]

I learn the Springfield Company, Capt. Veazey,[10] has been assigned to the right of the Regiment, and that the Wells River Company, Capt. Corbin,[11] will be the color bearer. The Essex County Company will do to go alongside the New York Zouaves. They are noble men; stocky, hearty, brave, and fearless. They are mainly composed of "log rollers" from the woods of Northern Vermont, and are commanded by Colonel Nelson[12] of Ryegate who has a "military turn."

The utmost good feeling prevails in the camp. Sobriety, gentlemanly deportment and strict subordination generally characterize the conduct of all the men. The Regiment is a miracle in this respect. The Calais Artillery, Capt. Mooer,[13] is to take the place of the Vergennes company which departed last Tuesday to fill the vacancy in the Second Regiment occasioned by the disbanding of the Winooski Company. The Regimental Band, is expected here from Burlington this week, Adams,[14] Leader.

In great haste,
D.

As the regiment neared its date of muster — when it would be sworn into Federal service — Dutton returned to Rutland to file his final report on the activities of the 3rd Vermont. The regiment still lacked a colonel, a position not filled until it reached Washington on July 26. The regiment's eventual commander would be Regular Army captain and Vermont native, William F. Smith.[15]

July 16, 1861
The Third Regiment
Rutland
July 15, 1861.

Having just returned from the rendezvous of the Third Vermont Regiment at St. Johnsbury, where I have been remaining for some three or four weeks, I have thought that a few items concerning the Regiment from my pen may be not without interest to the readers of the *Rutland Herald*.

The companies are now all full and fully organized, and the Regiment is uniformed, armed and equipped, and in readiness to start for the seat of war whenever orders shall be received from the War Department. The inspection by Captain Starr, of the U.S. Army, who was detailed by the War Department for that purpose, commenced on Saturday last, and is doubtless ere this completed.

I have frequently heard it remarked by military men competent to judge, that all things considered, this Regiment will be better equipped and prepared for actual service than any that has yet left New England. The experience of the men in camp will be incalculable to them. The art of cooking, so essential to comfort and health, has not been neglected, while much attention has been given to imparting sanitary instruction to the men; a matter of the last importance. Statistics show conclusively that an overwhelming percentage of losses in actual service occur in consequence of disease, and that the killed and wounded in battle are exceedingly few in comparison. This is a fact worthy of the gravest study and attention, and it is matter for congratulation that the officers of the Third Regiment, who are generally men of superior intelligence, many of them having enjoyed a college education, are taking this subject seasonably in hand, and giving special attention to it.

The arms furnished to the Third Regiment are the very best that could be procured. No better can be found in the service. It is hard to realize the satisfaction and joy expressed by the men when they learned these arms had been procured; for they had supposed it would be impossible to get anything but the smoothbore musket altered to the percussion lock. The arms, which were purchased in New York, through the immediate agency of W.B. Hatch, Esq., of the firm Fairbanks & Co., are the long rifled muskets, with angular bayonets, embracing all the modern improvements, and are, I think, of English manufacture. The Governor and Gen. Davis[16] are deserving of much praise for the perseverance with which they have carried out their purpose to procure arms of this description; especially as it turns out that this is the *only lot* of the kind to be had in the country for several weeks. They were bought at from four to five dollars less per musket than Massachusetts had paid for arms of inferior pattern and quality.

I should not omit to say also, that in the contract for these muskets, made by Mr. Hatch, it was stipulated that if Congress should remit the duties on imported arms, the remission of duties on this lot should inure to the benefit of the State. Congress, having passed a bill remitting such duties, the cost will be reduced some four of five dollars per musket, thus making the contract an unusually advantageous one.

In addition to the equipments furnished the first and second regiments, the third is amply provided with horses, baggage and ammunition wagons, harnesses, saddles, ambulances &c. The horses have all been purchased, mainly in Caledonia and Orleans counties, and are at St. Johnsbury, some sixty-five in number, many of them matched, and including horses for the officers. The wagons and ambulances are probably completed at this time. Most if not all of them were manufactured at Concord, N.H. It is understood that no regiment will hereafter be sent into the field without this kind of equipments. I understand the War Department has requested Gov. Fairbanks to forward horses, wagons, and ambulances to the second Regiment now in Virginia, and that the Governor has directed General Davis to procure them without delay.

It would be unjust to omit all mention of the ladies of our State, in an article embracing particular detail respecting the outfit of this regiment. The hospital department has been fully supplied by men with all needed articles of comfort and even of luxury, and the supply is greater than the demand. And here I will say that I have been requested to state for the general information of ladies' relief committees, that before any further articles are made, information of what is wanted should be obtained by addressing inquiries either to Gov. Fairbanks, or to Gen. Baxter at Rutland, or Gen. Davis at Cavendish. The supply of Havelocks[17] particularly is already super-abundant. It should also be borne in mind that no purchase of raw materials should be made with the expectation that the State should pay for them, unless upon orders specially obtained.

All the field and staff officers have been appointed or selected for appointment, with the exception of Colonel. It is understood that the command has been offered to Col. Phelps of the first Vermont Regiment,[18] and the wish is universal that he may accept. Gov. Fairbanks is so solicitous that this fine Regiment should go out under an experienced and tried commander that I divine he has sent a special messenger to Newport News to urge upon Col. Phelps the acceptance of the Colonelcy. The Governor should receive no censure for any reasonable effort he may make in that direction. The appointment would be hailed with great satisfaction throughout the State, and by none more than by every man in the third Regiment.

Should Col. Phelps, however, decline, it is rumored that Lieut. Stoughton,[19] late of the U.S.A.,[20] son of Hon. H.E. Stoughton of Bellows Falls, and a graduate of West Point, will be prominently considered in connection with the command. He is highly endorsed by the War Department as a thorough military scholar and an excellent officer. If I am not mistaken he was last year entrusted with the command of a small body of men in a military expedition to California, and was specially commended for his faithfulness, energy and prudence.

In regard to the appearance and morale of this Regiment, enough, perhaps has already been said. That it is a body of men who are capable of knowing and do know and appreciate the nature of the great contest in which they will soon actively engage; that their self respect and their respect and love for Vermont, will inspire them to the performance of deeds of valor, such as every Vermonter will be proud to name; that they will follow the flag of our country wherever it leads, in the darkest hour and in the thickest of the fight, no one will question who has looked upon them and mingled with them from day to day. As they will go forth with the prayers and benedictions of all the people of these hills and valleys, so may we not hope that a merciful God will take them under his special care, and so guide them in the day of trial, and amidst the rattling hail of the contending armies, that whatever may be their fate on the field of battle, the glory of having died, (if such must be the fate of any) faithful to the flag of the Union, and of having something to the perpetuity of our institutions, may be theirs. Heaven speed them on their mission of patriotism!

   D.

P.S. Since writing the above I have learned that the regiment had not been ordered forward this morning, and that new cases of measles have occurred within a day or two, making from fifty to seventy cases in camp, a condition of things which may possibly delay the departure of the regiment for a few days.

Lieutenant Colonel Gabriel Rains mustered the 3rd Vermont into the Federal service on July 16, 1861, and six days later the unit departed Camp Baxter for Washington. Lewis T. Dutton returned to Brandon, but not for long. After the Union defeat at Bull Run on July 21, Governor Fairbanks issued a proclamation to raise two more three-year regiments from Vermont. These would be designated the 4th and 5th Vermont Regiments. When the 5th Vermont commenced recruiting in August, a company of men from the Brandon region answered the call to duty. Among the ranks stood Dutton, who enlisted as a private in Company H and was mustered into the army on September 16. The regimental descriptive rolls listed Dutton as twenty-three years old, five foot six and three-quarter inches tall, light-complexioned, with auburn hair and blue eyes.

When the 5th arrived in Washington on September 25, it encamped near the 2nd and 3rd Vermont regiments. Joined in October by the 4th and 6th Vermont regiments, the five units formed what would become known as the "Vermont Brigade." They moved to a new campsite, soon to be known as Camp Griffin,[21] a place of much disease and death for the new soldiers from Vermont.

Dutton's first letters as a soldier are written from Camp Griffin. He gives an accurate description of camp life as these novices learn about soldiering and eagerly await the first combat experience. Dutton's hatred for the South was echoed by many other Vermonters.

December 27, 1861

Our Army Correspondence

From the Fifth Regiment

5th Vt. Regt, Camp Griffin, Va.

Dec. 20th, 1861.

Knowing the heartfelt desire your readers have to hear from their friends in Virginia, I herewith subjoin the following items concerning camp life.

Days and weeks have rolled away since we came to this place, and there are no more signs of a battle to-day, than there were the day we came here, which was on the 9th of October. We have many times been drawn up in line of battle, expecting of course that the enemy was upon us. But none came. Finally after a while, this became an old story, and instead of "falling out," and forming into line of battle at every alarm given, it was first ascertained whether the enemy were marching upon us, or whether our pickets had fired upon a harmless Secesh pig. For a time the various bipeds[22] suffered severely, but after a while their imagination abated somewhat, and the peaceful foe became less troublesome.

I have said that there were no signs of a battle. Yet we are preparing for one. Scarcely a day passes over our heads but that we have one or two company drills in the forenoon, and a battalion or division drill in the afternoon, which continues from about one o'clock until sun set. Yesterday on picket — no sleep through the night; — to-day, on division drill, and ere night comes, our wearied limbs fail to execute gracefully the many maneuvers we are compelled to go through with: "to form a square by rapid maneuver," "Right and left face," "Forward march!" The square being formed, the next order is "Reduce, Square!" The square being reduced, we are then prepared to execute further orders. These things being accomplished, then comes dress parade, which ends the programme, the day being gone. The next day the same drill is resumed. I need say no more, but will give a portion of Senator Lane's[23] speech on the subject:

"Ours is an army of volunteers, who must not be judged by the rules applied to regulars. You cannot drill it into that mere machine Martinets considers the perfection of efficacy. The citizen soldier is an individual; no amount of discipline can destroy his individuality. Four months of industrious drill is ample time to prepare such troops for effective service. The prospect of action must be ever present as an incentive. Inaction is the bane of the volunteer. These opinions I express with confidence, for I have had a large personal experience in the management of volunteer soldiers. The training of two distinct regiments during the Mexican war, with subsequent labors in Kansas, and the campaign of the last spring and summer in Missouri, have given me a practical knowledge on this subject entitled to consideration. The regiments that fought and won the battle of Buena Vista, were not as well provided as the Army of the Potomac, and not better drilled. Sir, I have witnessed the drill of that army; and I am satisfied that it has reached the maximum of discipline attainable by volunteers, and that every day of inaction now tends to its demoralization."

I fully coincide with the above. Drill is a good thing; but too much of it without action, is dispiriting.

To-day twenty-eight of our brave soldiers *lie beneath* the sod. And had we continued as active as when first we came here, many more would have been numbered with the dead. Death is certain; but by proper care our lives may be prolonged. There is no way whereby we may escape death. If we rest from our labors, and shun any exposure possible, death will snatch us away.

Letters to Vermont

The 5th Vermont on parade
After a few months at Camp Griffin in 1861, incessant drills and parades for inspection shaped the 5th Vermont into a disciplined force, eager to fight the Confederates, who were considered traitors to the country.

December 21st — Just as the above word "away" was written, we received orders to "fall out" and form into line of battle; but ere the line was formed the order was countermanded, and in less than ten minutes, we received another order to fall in, and with pickaxes, shovels and axes. The very moment the line was perfected, an order came to "ground arms." No sooner said than done. The next order was "fall out for guns and cartridge boxes, and forty rounds of cartridges." The line again being formed, the next command was, "Right, face! Forward, march!" Headed by the Vt. 2d, and followed by the "bloody 5th,"[24] the brigade moved rapidly westward. Arriving at Lewinsville, we halted, and loaded our pieces. We then proceeded nearly westward for about two miles, then turning directly to the right, I suppose in the direction of Dranesville. After journeying four or fives miles farther we again halted, probably eight or nine miles from camp. By this time the sun had nearly disappeared. In about ten minutes we received the command, "About, face! Forward, march!" and at about eight o'clock we arrived safely in camp.

To-day, intelligence reaches us to the effect that quite a battle had been fought at Dranesville.[25] Sixty rebels were killed, nineteen wounded and ten taken prisoner. On our side the loss was ten killed, and five wounded. Our men also captured several horses, and more articles of clothing than could be brought away. The struggle was with McCall's division,[26] and the booming of cannon told us that something fearful was going on. But ere we had left camp the loud booming had ceased; and the battle was over. Had it continued a short time longer, they would have heard from the "old Green Mountain Boy."

To-day, after the severe march of yesterday, all hands of us, except those on picket last night, have been out on fatigue duty, preparing a place for winter quarters; trimming trees, piling brush, &c. We shall probably move in a few days. It is but a short distance from this place, yet the labor is none the less. We have been furnished stoves by government. If you wish to form a correct idea of them, you have only to turn a funnel upside down. They prove quite beneficial.

The Band of the Vermont 2d, has gone home. On the eve of its departure several pieces were executed, one of which was "Auld Lang Syne." It had a pleasing, yet solemn effect upon the ear. It was a noble band.

Our company has received numerous articles from home. Gloves, stockings, shirts, &c., besides numerous eatables, such as sweet cake, maple sugar, &c. Indeed it looks rather inviting after subsisting so long upon bread and meat. Our Sutlers have numerous articles, but the price is so exorbitant that we don't like to purchase very freely; although at a private dwelling, an excellent meal is furnished for 25 cents.

Our Colonel[27] has a very bad hand, and the Lieut. Colonel[28] acts in his stead. We seldom behold a man with an eye as keen as his. His military appearance entitles him to credit. We think with him to lead us and if engaged in an action, the rebels would think that a Napoleon had risen. We are bound to

"Wade through slaughter to a throne.
And shut the gates of mercy on the rebels"
We must conquer, for
"Our cause it is just,
And *conquer* we must"

We must learn the South a lesson: — a lesson that they will never forget; and that is "to let well enough alone."

I will worry the patience of your readers no further, but will close, hoping that traitors may see their folly and turn from it, and that peace may once more be restored.

Yours for the Union and for Peace.
D.

January 17, 1862
Our Army Correspondence
Letter from Virginia
Co. H, 5th Vt. Regiment, Camp Griffin, Va.
Jan. 13.

You doubtless imagine this section of the country quite thickly settled. It being an old State one would naturally be of this impression. But quite the contrary. The villages of Lewinsville and Falls Church contain but a dozen buildings. Add on the different roads they are so scattering that if the inhabitants dwell therein they could hardly be called neighbors. At a distance of five or six miles from this place, and in the direction of Vienna there is a Church, and I am sure that it would be no disgrace to any of our mountain towns in Vermont. But there are only three or four buildings anywhere near it. It must be a silent church.

The soil of Old Virginia is a red marl, and two or three days of rainy weather makes the roads almost impassable. For the past two or three days our camp quarters have very much resembled a mortar bed. The clayey sections of Vermont, in my estimation have no parallel with the marl pits here. Yet the soil is quite good, especially for corn. Wood abounds in plenty, and the water is better than one would suppose by viewing the soil.

As pay day is close at hand, there is considerable speculation going on one way and another. A handbill has been issued warning soldiers not to be duped by a certain "allotment law," written, I should judge by some sutler, in hopes that they may succeed in getting most of the volunteers' pay for their own benefit. The following is the circular:

"SOLDIERS BEWARE,"

"The government seeks to place your hard earned dues beyond your own control, by a system called the ALLOTMENT LAW. The money you so allot never comes into your possession, and [the government] is, for the whole term of your enlistment evidently considering you *not capable* of managing your own affairs. It has been supposed you were fighting for freedom! and not to be enslaved. Your decision in the matter for the first pay governs each pay hereafter."

Should a certain bill in Congress be passed which is pending before the House and Senate, sutlers, after the first of February will be found missing.

It seems that the "ghosts of Dixie," are nearly as well posted in the movements of our army as we are ourselves. And is it any wonder why they should not be? As long as citizens are permitted to cross our lines, and go back undisturbed, how easy a matter it is for them to conceal about their person a newspaper or two, and if they are searched there might be an agreement made between themselves and the Secesh soldiers so as to receive Washington papers frequently.

There are two or three "fair faces" in our regiment who do the cooking for certain officers, rather out of their sphere, it would seem. It brings to memory the following verse:

> They say the time is coming soon,
> A day not far remote,
> When women will to Congress go
> And be allowed to vote.

When the time comes that they participate in the action of Congress then one could have no objection to their appearing upon the battle field.

Concerning the "onward movement" now talked so much about by editors, senators, soldiers and citizens, I agree with the good sense of your correspondent from Plymouth, signed Z.[29] Nevertheless, if we should have the choice of going to Richmond or on picket, I think the majority would move on to Richmond. At any rate we are ready to march at the command, and if we only had three or four more General Lanes, and as many John Browns, we would blot out Secesh before they had time to consider life and death.

If opportunity offers, and if anything transpires worthy of note you may perchance hear from me again.

Respectfully yours, D.

While at Camp Griffin, the Vermont Brigade was afflicted by many diseases, causing the sick rolls to grow daily. Regimental surgeons diagnosed pneumonia, diarrhea, and typhoid. At one time twenty-five percent of the brigade was incapacitated by illness. Not until the onset of warm spring weather did the number of sick decline.

While the men watched their comrades succumb to disease or enter hospitals, they drilled incessantly and speculated on when the army would move. McClellan, their commander in chief, waited.

February 10, 1862

Our Army
Correspondence
Letter from Dixie Land

5th Vermont Regiment, Dixie

Feb. 4th, 1862.

Life in camp has of late had some trials here. Rain, sleet, snow, freezes and thaws — mud in quantities and to almost any depth. Thus it has been for the past two or three weeks. No drill, yet our life is a busy one. It costs something and requires labor to eat, sleep and keep warm; especially if on picket.

At this juncture of the crisis every heart beats high, in anticipation of a stir. Five or six months picketing without any essential change in affairs, is rather a dull monotony with the soldier. As every one has an earnest desire to see their native land, and behold the once familiar faces, it is not at all strange that we become a little uneasy, for our present situation is a disagreeable one. Notwithstanding this, our enemy are none the better off in this respect; therefore we may as well eat, drink, and be merry, for tomorrow we may gain the victory.

Those who have a thorough knowledge of the book of books, are aware that there was once a rebellion in Heaven; and why such a rebellion should break out in a world of beatified spirits is beyond my comprehension. At any rate there was a certain angel now known as the Devil, who rebelled against the kingdom of heaven and was driven down to hell. Thus should the traitors of the South be served. This glorious government trampled upon by such a band of rebels, who fain would destroy, or attempt to destroy the throne of heaven, had they wings or means of getting there, should be dealt with roughly. Mr. Editor, you must not judge me too harshly, but I am of the opinion of Gen. Lane.

Our regiment awhile ago, in addition to their regular uniform, wore a new kind of an overcoat, called the Virginia overcoat. It consisted of a barrel with a hole cut through one end just large enough to thrust the head through, the other end being entirely open. It was not a very convenient article of clothing; however, many wore it, until at length the story comes that McClellan[30] finds it out, and sends word that he wants no more of his men barreled up alive, but wait until they are dead. The coat has since been thrown off.

Speaking of the comfort of our pickets, I would add that for the past few days the village of Lewinsville has been occupied as a reserve, making it quite comfortable, especially for officers. The health of our regiment is not as good as when I wrote you before. The long continued rain, the now and then fall of snow, have converted Old Virginia into a mortar bed. And our present camp ground being but a little better than "Dysentery Hollow," Camp Advance[31] is very destructive to one's health. Being a little greasy too, the position I occupy in writing cannot be compared favorably to an editor's sanctum. And the setting of type, differing so widely from handling the musket, can never be appreciated by your humble servant. But our country must be protected. The sword must be a substitution for the pen. We have unsheathed it, and thus let it remain until the victory is gained.

> "Our country now and ever!
> Land of the good and free!
> What daring hand would sever
> The ties of Liberty!
> Let him be known as traitor,
> And traitor shall he be;
> Who would insult this nation
> Must first himself be free.
> For some are slaves and cowards —
> Their names a thing of shame,
> To endless time our Union
> Will but increase in fame.
> Fight comrades, for our Nation,
> For Freedom's holy light;
> In union is salvation,
> God will protect the right."

D.

Our Army Correspondence

Letter from Virginia

5th Vt. Reg., Dixie's Land

February 11, 1862.

I promised to write you again if the opportunity offered, and if anything of importance transpired. Well, nothing of very great importance has taken place in this section of country, except a lucky and spirited dash of Cameron's Dragoons[32] upon the rebel pickets. They were stationed in a building, a small reserve. None of the dragoons were killed, but two were wounded. One rebel was left dead in the house, and thirteen taken prisoner including a Negro who ran away from his master. He states that when the battle of Dranesville took place the slaves were all taken beyond Manassas. And the money in his possession was deposited in a bank until after the fight was over. The slaves then came back, and the money was lately restored to the owner of the slave property.

The Peninsula
below Williamsburg
Union forces were sustained by supply depots, forts, and seaports on the Peninsula, as the land between the James and York rivers was named.

The captured rebels were rather poorly clad, but had good fire arms. One of them stated that it was his chief desire to pick off our officers. He fired at the Captain,[33] but failed in his deathly rebellious desire. Upon this the Captain wheeled his horse about and sent a leaden messenger in response which told well, but failed to blot out his Secesh sentiments. Both were wounded by the shots. At this they dismount from their horses, jump through the windows of the building with drawn swords, and by killing one the remainder yield up their arms. In the melee the Captain struck one of them with his fist and injured his feelings very seriously. He states that if he is ever taken prisoner, (the Captain) he deserves pity, for he knows his name and will communicate it to their camp. The prisoners were taken to Gen. Smith's[34] headquarters and politely escorted to Washington. They have since captured three more and a baggage wagon. The rebels hate these Dutch cavalry men[35] in the extreme. They are too cunning and fearless for them.

The defeat of Zollicoffer — the Union victory in Tennessee,[36] sadly depress the rebel hydra headed monster of this wicked rebellion. Lo! they are just beginning to realize their gloomy situation, and soon they will howl like the ravenous wolves of the western prairies.

Those who have read of the aerial voyages of Prof. John La Mountain[37] may be interested in learning that he is employed by government to watch the movements of the rebels about Norfolk, Centreville and Manassas. His gas works are situated about four miles from Alexandria. When he ascends in his balloon he is accompanied by an artist who sketches everything of importance, which is communicated to Gen. McClellan, and of course kept secret. I am told that he receives every pay day the snug little sum of one thousand dollars, or five hundred every month; a handsome remuneration, yet the danger he is subject to entitles him to every dollar. Professor Lowe,[38] who made pretensions to cross the big waters, attempted to prove that no John La Mountain is employed by government; that he assumes a fictitious name; but there are too many Orwell[39] boys in this section of the country, his acquaintances, to be foiled by such attempts at gas works. Proof sufficient.

The health of our regiment is a little better than when I last wrote you. Forty-one have died out of the regiment. Yesterday fifty-six were examined at the regimental hospital who have applied for discharges, but probably not one-fifth of them will get a discharge. It seems as though that those who have done no duty since they have been in the service, and are not like to for months to come, ought to be discharged from the U.S. service, and not left here to die, without even a friend to mourn one's lonely fate.

Letters to Vermont

February 12 — For the past two or three weeks there has been a thin covering of snow upon the ground, but not more than about two inches at any one time. The mud freezes up during the night, but thaws out again in the course of the day.

We are now having battalion and company skirmish drills. Col. Smalley, who by the way is an active military man, leads us out for an hour or so and then dismisses us promptly. We are also practicing target shooting, and occasionally blank cartridges are used.

Two or three weeks ago accidental shooting of the thumbs took place frequently, whilst on picket. I have known of three thumbs being shot off in a single night, two of whom belonged to our regiment and one to a New York or Pennsylvania regiment. At other times one and two have suffered the loss of a thumb, but of late the accidents have been less frequent.[40]

This morning Washington papers state that our men have taken possession of Roanoke Island,[41] hope it may be so.

Yours, &c., D.

March 1, 1862
Our Army Correspondence
Letter from the 5th Vt. Regiment
Brightening Prospects
Six more Rebel Pickets Captured by the Cameron Dragoons
22d day of Feb. in Camp — New Batteries — The Weather.
Camp Griffin, Va.
February 24, 1862.

At last the dark cloud that has so long obscured the political horizon is clearing away — the prospect as well as the aspect is cheering. Victory after victory has caused a terrible sensation throughout the whole rebel kingdom. The chuckling over the Burnside fleet[42] has altogether ceased, and now they stand

"With open mouth and staring eyes,
Like one descended from the skies."

Their prophets have proved false to them, and now their once happy anticipations are frustrated. Their hopes are crushed, and forever. Their shortsightedness has proved their ruin; and a lesson may be learned from this, that to leap before you look is dangerous.[43]

In my last, I made mention of the capture of several rebel pickets by the Cameron Dragoons. They have since captured six more. Several escaped by jumping from their horses and taking for the woods. One horse was killed and one or two others wounded. One of the rebel prisoners received a severe wound in the left side. Being at Headquarters at the time they came in, I can give you a brief sketch of Rebel soldiery. None of them had on uniforms, except one who wore an overcoat taken at Bull Run from a Maine regiment. Their clothing was of a rough texture, and not much of that. Two of them had no hats or caps, probably lost at the time of their capture. They were quite talkative when they found out no one intended to injure them. One of them, a very intelligent-looking chap, seemed less inclined to utter his views concerning their condition. Yet enough was learned from them to convince us that they were not in the best of circumstances. Upon their persons were found several letters which fully confirm the report that they were leaving Manassas and Centreville, and that drafting[44] had commenced in good earnest. They also stated that they had received no pay since July last. One of them had a two-dollar bill on a Tennessee bank, the only thing in the shape of money in his possession, except five or six Confederate postage stamps. These were exchanged for ours. Also their Secesh buttons upon their outer garments were exchanged.

At the time of the capture of the thirteen rebels a Negro boy came in, who ran away from his master — and at the time of the capture of the last six he was also taken, but let loose again. The Negro boy on seeing his master, more pleased on account of his escape than seeing him, remarked, "How do you do, Massa?" "Well; how came you here?" The boy, with a grin on his phiz, replied, "O, I found my way here." In the course of the conversation, the Negro boy used the following language, "Well, Massa, I have taken more comfort since I came here than I did all the while I lived with you." He also stated that his master was a staunch Secesh, and is in possession of about a dozen slaves. But to me it seems a little strange why he should be allowed to roam at large. The fact is, there are too many of a like stamp not far beyond our line of pickets — in my opinion doing more damage than all the rebels caught at the time he was. If this is a war for money, and if a certain clique wish the war to continue, on account of their moneyed position, this course is the way to do it; but if it is a war of confiscation, a war for peace, then I say confine all who are the least suspected of being traitors, or at least make them take the oath of allegiance. This is my style, and what true patriot is there that differs with me in this particular? It is peace that we want, not war for the sake of money. Then let everything in our power be done that can be done to shorten the war. "For behold the day cometh when all nations shall be judged," and "blessed are the peace makers" — not peace-breakers.[45]

On Saturday, the 22nd day of February, Washington's birthday, our regiment had a universal celebration of their own. Although in the morning the different regiments composing our brigade were marched to our old Camp ground, they listened to the reading of Washington's Farewell Address, besides having a brigade dress parade, which has taken place once before — quite a novelty indeed. On returning to our new Camp ground a little excitement was gotten up in the shape of fun, in which the Lieut. Colonel participated. A pole was greased, and ten dollars placed upon the top of it. Two dollars and a half were offered to any one who would climb half the distance, but no one won the prize. The next operation was a foot race by the different officers of the regiment, and the four who touched the pole last were to pay one dollar each. At the word desperate struggles were made of course, to reach the pole first.

Refreshment off-duty
Exorbitant though prices might be at the stores of the civilian sutlers who sold spirits, delicacies, and sweets to the troops, most soldiers gave grudging respect to the merchants for often risking life and fortune to follow the army and provide wares that government quartermasters did not.

Our Lieut. Colonel led the van, but somehow failed to touch the above mentioned pole. Next at his heels was a Captain, who fell full length, in time to reach the four dollar pole. Thus they came one after another, now and then striking it, but the majority failed to do so, knowing that if they touched it not they would lose no dollar. The joke passed off pleasantly, all sharing in the merriment. The next thing on the programme was a foot race by the corporals and privates — these being chosen from each company. First prize, $3; second do, $2; third do, $1. The first prize was won by a Corporal in Co. F, the second prize by a private in Co. D, and the third by a Corporal in Co. E. The next operation was a foot race by the privates, having a sack drawn over their persons. Prize one dollar — won by one from Co. E. The next thing was a five dollar greased pig, purchased at Washington for the purpose. The whole regiment joining in the race, soon caused "porkie" to come to a dead halt. The ones that caught him were to take him for their booty. He was captured by several from the following companies: One from Co. H, two from Co. G, one from Co. F, and one from Co.C. To close the exercises of the day, a football strife[46] took place in the regiment, between the right and left wings. The right wing drove the left into the woods, and was declared victor.

Thus passed the 22d day of February, 1862 — and never will the 5th Regiment forget the day.

Encamped upon our old Camp ground is a new battery; and should the rebels hear from us, or find us approaching the city of Richmond, they will be pretty apt to hear from several other new batteries.

The weather continues about the same as when I last wrote you. This morning it rained, but now it has ceased, and a chilly breeze sweeps over the field and forest, and such a drying up of mud one seldom sees. Speaking of the rainy weather, I have only to remark, that as long as God *reigns*, we must expect rain. For it is said that it "shall rain upon the just and unjust."

As ever, yours,
L.D.

As spring approached, the Army of the Potomac defending Washington gained in strength, discipline, and morale under the command of General McClellan. The Vermonters recovered their health. To many of the disgruntled, McClellan appeared loathe to advance against the Confederate forces, commanded by General Joseph E. Johnston, encamped at Manassas.

Finally, the Union army made preparations to move, and the Vermont Brigade departed its Camp Griffin quarters, destination unknown.

Our Army Correspondence

A Trip from Camp Porter to Alexandria.

5th Vt. Regt., Alexandria, Va.

March 16th, 1862.

Two days ago I sketched you a few lines, stating that we expected to leave momentarily, and that everything was in readiness for the march; but it so happened that we did not leave until next day, and a very unfavorable day it was, I assure you.

We left camp about 7 o'clock, a.m., marching by way of Vienna, Falls Church, and thence to this place direct. We arrived at this place at about half past 3 o'clock p.m., (the 5th Vt. Regt.) As our Regiment was the only one that took this route, our advantage in speed was not so much interrupted as the remainder of the regiments which took up a line of march another way and altogether.

But the characteristic feature of that day's march was the steady fall of rain which wet us to the skin. Having on at the time an overcoat, dress coat and fatigue coat, you may "calculate" that the extra luggage of these garments, soaked full of water, beside the remainder of our clothing, — the knapsacks, haversacks, bad roads, &c., was almost double what it would have been had we marched the day before. And what was worse still, was the night. Our wet and weary limbs would have failed us had we not kept up a strong and determined will to reach our journey's end.

But, Mr. Editor, we were not as badly off as a great many others of our brother soldiers. Our Colonel — who, by the way, *is a Colonel* in every respect — deserves much credit for what he did for us — the 5th Regiment.

On arriving at the suburbs of this city, he started immediately in search of a building where he might shelter his men for the night. In a few moments he returned, and to the joy of all brought the glad tidings that we could be protected from the cold rain of the night by marching into the heart of the city, where we are now quartered. It is a large brick building, a meat market. Besides, he purchased wood; and all at his own expense. Long will Col. Smalley be remembered by the boys of the 5th. Our company is also much indebted to our Captain[47] for his considerate kindness in furnishing us with certain "creature comforts."

It is expected that we shall go aboard of a boat in a day or two, the destination of which is to us entirely unknown. Further particulars when opportunity presents itself.

Yours in hope of success.
L.T.D.

Battlefields east of Richmond

The campaigns of spring and summer 1862 brought Union troops under McClellan to the doorstep of Richmond, but the Seven Days' Battles at Savage's Station, Frayser's Farm, Malvern Hill and others stopped the invaders, who had advanced up the Peninsula from bases near Yorktown.

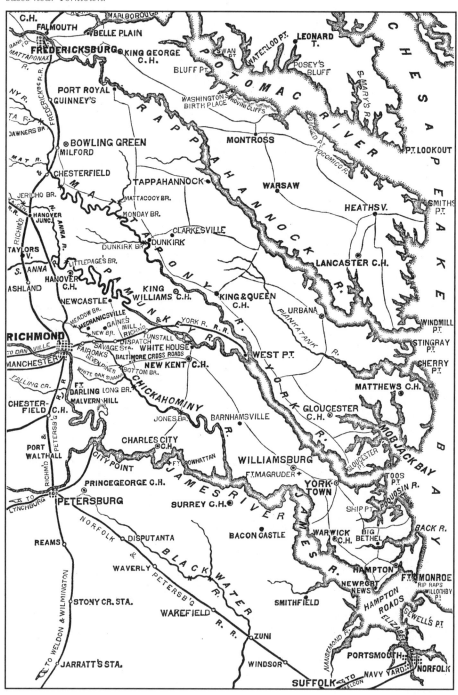

McClellan's goal was the capture of Richmond, the Confederate capital. The Union strategy was not a direct advance south from Washington, but the shifting of almost the entire Army of the Potomac by ship to Fortress Monroe on the southern end of the Virginia Tidewater Peninsula[48] opposite Norfolk. McClellan calculated that Confederate forces would be caught unawares, allowing an unimpeded march up the Peninsula to Richmond. Intelligence reported roads there were excellent in all seasons, but Confederate counter-movements and McClellan's extreme caution, combined with roads made muddy by spring rains, slowed the Union advance. The Union army also discovered its path blocked by Confederate works at Yorktown and along the Warwick River. McClellan did not realize his 120,000-man army was being stymied by a force one twelfth its size.

Confederate General John Magruder executed maneuvers and ruses to disguise his shortage of numbers. McClellan erected siege lines and conducted small probes against the enemy lines, expending valuable time. One of these probes involved three regiments of the Vermont Brigade at at Lee's Mills. The engagement, on April 16, won the Vermonters notoriety for their fighting ability. Dutton described the army's early advance and engagements.

May 3, 1862

Our Army Correspondence

Letter from Yorktown

Breaking up of Camp — Orders for Two Days' Rations
Our March to Young's[49] — Next Day's Proceedings
The Vermonters in a Fight — The Weather, &c., &c.

Camp Near Yorktown, Va.

April 27, 1862.

On the 3d day of April we were marched the distance of about a mile, by flank, through mud and ditches, near by a fort on the James River, where we halted, and commenced pitching our tents; but ere this was accomplished, we received orders to be in readiness for a march next day, at 6 P.M., and with two days' rations in our haversacks. As we drew near said Mills, a spyglass view was taken of the place and the strength of the enemy ascertained. At this we were drawn up in line of battle, and marched some distance in the woods, over fallen trees, underbrush, and the like. On we rushed, through a small clearing, and thence to the enemy's works. A few rods from their earthworks, is a steep bank and trees felled in every possible way; and such a tumbling down hill I never witnessed before. I recollect stepping on a log at the top of the hill, and also picking myself out of the mud at the bottom. Not heeding this, I rushed on with others, and in a moment's time we were all over their comfortable quarters, ransacking every nook and corner. In many instances meat was found frying, biscuits cooking, &c. We only had one man wounded in the affair, a private in Co. G.[50] Here we encamped for the night, but early in the morning we resumed our march; and a rainy day it was, too. As we neared the enemy's fortifications, at Yorktown, skirmishers were sent out, batteries planted, and several on both sides killed. Since that day, we have camped and decamped several times.

A few days since, the Vermont Third charged upon one of their rifle-pits, drove them out, killing many of them, and losing between thirty and forty on our side in killed. Two companies were sent across the pond, and two left behind for a support. After this the Sixth became engaged in the contest; but as the enemy had received reinforcements by the thousand, it was not thought best to contend with the "ghosts of Dixie" at such fearful odds. This latter disaster may be well enough, but I "can't see it." It may not by some be considered a disaster, but to me it seems quite a serious one.[51]

White House Landing

Great quantities of supplies for the Union forces under McClellan were collected at White House Landing, Virginia, for the coming campaign that would be known as the Seven Days' Battles, an unsuccessful advance on Richmond's outer defenses.

Letters to Vermont

.The Vermont troops, I notice, are very highly spoken of for their bravery; but as much may be said of the Massachusetts, New York or Maine regiments, and in fact I believe the Northerners will fight better than the Southrons.[52] They are engaged in a better cause. There are many incidents I might relate, but time and space will not permit.

The weather here for the past two weeks has been very disagreeable, raining most of the time. The roads are not so much affected by the rains as when we first came here. Logs have been cut and placed one upon another, until they finally show themselves above the mud.

Hoping for a speedy termination of the war.

Yours, &c.,
Ell Tee Dee

Just as the Union siege guns were set to open fire on the Confederate fortifications at Yorktown, the just-arrived Confederate general, Johnston, emptied the works and began a deliberate fighting retreat toward Richmond. The outnumbered Magruder's resistance and ploys had delayed the advance of the Union forces a full month. McClellan followed the rebel withdrawal, and his lead units encountered the Confederate rear guard at Williamsburg. A sharp engagement ensued, with the Confederates resuming their withdrawal.

May 16, 1862
Letter from Williamsburg
Camp near Williamsburg, Va.
May 8th, 1862.

Yesterday I sketched you a few lines, and this morning searched for the post office for the purpose of delivering it, but on reaching the post office found I had lost it, therefore I make a second feeble attempt at writing. I shall only state a few incidents, as you probably know more of what has taken place within the past two or three days than we do ourselves. There are plenty of rumors about camp, but as they are not generally credited I shall borrow no further trouble.

The rebels in evacuating their strongholds placed percussion shells in the ground for the purpose of blowing up our men, but without much success; however, I learn that two men were killed and seven or eight wounded by one of them; after this they were dug up and a guard placed around them.

In taking up our line of march into the enemy's country what sights we behold! Deserted camps and as many as thirty or forty tents in a place, telegraph wires left undisturbed, dead horses lying here and there, wagons scattered all about, some broken down, others partly burned up, while many of them are in working order. Provisions were also left behind. Thus they fled until they reached their last fortifications, — then they were driven from them like sheep before a pack of hounds, panic stricken, demoralized and maddened. In retreating from this place they threw their small arms into the muddy roads for the purpose of getting their artillery over, and then they were compelled to leave behind several of their big guns, many of which were spiked. The above is doubtless true, as many of our boys have seen, or reported to have seen, a great number at one place.

Observation balloon under fire
A tethered hydrogen balloon rises high above McClellan's Union headquarters, its observers able to see far over the battlefield to watch the movements and positions of the armies; this sketch shows Rebel shell fire bursting around the balloon.

Letters to Vermont

The number of men killed and wounded on our side is very large, but the loss on the other side must be two to one. For two days our men have been at work burying the dead, yet the woods are strewn with dead rebels, killed while retreating. In passing over the battle field I witnessed a very solemn site. Many had their heads blown to pieces, others were riddled completely, and those that were wounded and remained on the battle field all night suffered intensely, as it rained nearly all the while. Ah! it was a ghastly spectacle! It brought to my mind many instances connected with the life of Napoleon Bonaparte. But if people will commit treason, and put their own feet into the fire, they must suffer.

If Magruder has surrendered who comes next?[53]

Respectfully, Ell Tee Dee

The capture of Williamsburg on May 5 and the continued Union advance opened up the prospect of a new supply depot at White House on the Pamunkey River. The depot was named for the plantation house standing on the property, which belonged to William H.F. Lee, eldest son of Robert E. Lee. The property possessed a rich heritage, for a prior owner had been Martha Dandridge Custis and it was here George Washington courted the widow to make her his wife.

With the depot established, the Federal army had access to a rail line which led directly to Richmond, thirty miles distant. Supplies could be moved forward easily. The Vermont Brigade continued to be part of the Union advance. Soon, the army could hear the chimes of church bells in Richmond.

May 30, 1862
Letter from McClellan's Army
White House Hospital, Va.
May 24th, 1862.

For several days we remained at this place — the White House — but on the 19th the army again moved forward. Not being able to follow the regiment, I with several others from the regiment took up a line of march for this place, the hospital. There are probably one thousand men stationed here in tents; besides there are several boats or floating hospitals upon the Pamunkey[54] filled with those who are less capable of caring for themselves. Some have fevers, others have a severe cold and a bad cough; most, however, are worn out, and only require rest and suitable food to set them right again. Our supply so far has been rather

Burning White House Landing

Once the headquarters of General McClellan and the base for the Army of the Potomac's enormous supply fleet, White House Landing on the Pamunkey River was abandoned and burned as the Union force withdrew from Richmond in the campaign and repulse that became known as the Seven Days' Battles.

Lewis T. Dutton — In the Peninsular Campaign of 1862   93

scanty and irregular, although at times we get our fill. Probably in a few days things will be so far arranged that better care will be taken of the many and the unwearied soldier. Already we have received pillows, bed quilts, and bed ticks — furnished, of course, by some Relief Association.

Yesterday report reached us, that our men had once more taken up their line of march for Richmond. The distance from this place to where our advance is camped is fifteen miles — only eight miles from the boasted Rebel capital. Indeed another march will bring them upon the very verge of their undisputed city.

Yesterday some fifteen rifle repeaters left this place for the scene of action. They are a small cannon, throwing a ball about the size of the Springfield rifle. They are drawn by one horse, and shoot so often as 60 or 100 times a minute. They are operated by a crank, and the execution of such a machine would be fearful, if brought to bear upon a large body of men.[55]

Every few moments can be heard the fearful booming of cannon in the direction of Richmond — probably our gunboats, or perhaps a few large siege guns have been pointed in the direction of the rebel mass now running wild and frantic through the streets, except those who are left to guard and fight the Yankees, and if possible, save their *cause* and their *Capital*.

Probably before this reaches you, you will have a full account of what has been going on in the direction of Richmond to-day.

The weather is unpleasant. It has rained for some time.

Yours,
Ell Tee Dee

Shortly after Dutton wrote this letter, rebel General Johnston assaulted two Union army corps encamped at Fair Oaks and Seven Pines. The attack forced McClellan to halt the advance. He soon received intelligence that a new Confederate commander was on the field, for Johnston had been seriously wounded. The new officer was Robert E. Lee.

For nearly a month, the opposing lines barely moved. Then, Lee took the offensive. On June 25, Lee began what became known as the battles of the Seven Days. He first attacked the portion of McClellan's Army of the Potomac that was north of the Chickahominy River, hoping to destroy it in piecemeal. He failed to achieve this, but McClellan withdrew his army south of the river, burning the supply depot at White House and the plantation house. Lee remained in hot pursuit.

On June 29 the Vermont Brigade was involved in action. At Savage's Station, the brigade was attacked by a Louisiana brigade. The fighting was hard, especially for the 5th Regiment, which suffered 201 casualties. The Brandon company, H, had its captain wounded and thirty-five killed and wounded from its ranks. Among the wounded was Lewis T. Dutton.

Newspaper accounts listed him as wounded in the chest and shoulder and captured by the enemy. His service records, however, confirm he was not captured, but retrieved from the battlefield and evacuated to the Camden Street Military Hospital in Baltimore. There, on August 19, 1862, he died from his wounds.

Friends from home took charge of his body, and brought it back to Vermont for burial in the Goshen Cemetery. He lies with family members, his grave marked by a plain government-issued marble headstone stating his name, company, and regiment.

In close proximity to the cemetery is a monument, dedicated in 1901, commemorating Goshen's Civil War soldiers. Lewis T. Dutton's name heads the list.

Savage's Station abandoned by the Union
Driven back by the Confederates during the Seven Days' Battles, Union troops were compelled to abandon and destroy their supply depot at Savage's Station, leaving thousands of wounded, dead, and dying, in and around the military hospital, which continued to operate, though captured by the enemy.

Landing of troops below New Bern

Union soldiers wade ashore from troop transports in February 1862, advancing to assault Confederate defenses near New Bern, a port town on the North Carolina coast.

Cedar Mountain

After Stonewall Jackson defeated a Union force near Cedar (or Slaughter's) Mountain in August 1862, Reed's Massachusetts regiment operated there, on the eastern edge of the Blue Ridge Mountains, trying unsuccessfully to trap Jackson.

Federal hospital at Hilton Head, South Carolina

The Union constructed this general hospital at Hilton Head in May 1862, by which time most of the South's Atlantic coast had been captured, with the exception of Charleston.

Chapter 4

A Transplanted Vermonter in the 21st Massachusetts

"E.R.R."/"America"

Edwin R. Reed, 21st Massachusetts Regiment

Vermonters were not a stationary people in the 19th century. Thousands emigrated westward to seek new careers and fortunes. Many of these same individuals or their sons served with honor in Union regiments from their adopted states. Not everyone who left Vermont emigrated west; some remained in New England. The 21st Massachusetts Regiment became the new home of one of these transplanted Vermonters.

One of the soldier correspondents to the *Rutland Herald* was Edwin R. Reed, who enrolled in Company A, 21st Massachusetts. Born in North Clarendon in 1835, Reed had moved to Orange, Massachusetts, where he earned his living as a mechanic, repairing machines and tools. The twenty-six-year-old Reed stood five-feet-eight inches tall, had fair hair and blue eyes. He enlisted in the 21st Massachusetts on July 19, 1861, and was mustered in on July 30. His three-year regiment, made up primarily of men from Worcester County, departed for Maryland on August 23.

The 21st Massachusetts Regiment's training started at its camp on the grounds of the U.S. Naval Academy in Annapolis, Maryland. In May, the sixteen-year-old Academy had been moved from Annapolis to a more secure location in Newport, Rhode Island. The buildings and grounds were perfect for training. Along with learning soldiering at Annapolis, Reed developed a case of rheumatism that would plague him the rest of his life.

Letter from Annapolis
Naval School Academy
Annapolis, Md., Oct. 14, 1861.

Thinking that perhaps you would like to hear from a Vermont boy, I will write a few lines. I belong to the 21st Mass. volunteer regiment, but my native State is Vermont, and the Rutland Herald comes regularly to our camp, being sent to me by my friends in Vermont. We are stationed here for the purpose of guarding the Annapolis and Elk Bridge railroad, it having been torn up by the rebels. General Butler[1] came up and took possession of the road, laying the track over and putting a strong guard along the road to prevent a second attack from them. The engine was also taken to pieces, but Mass. furnished men for the emergency and the engine was soon in running order, but all of this was done last spring. Now there is perfect order here; there are now twenty-five thousand troops here; they are going on a secret expedition.[2] Sherman's battery[3] is also here. One of our men showed me the flag which was completely riddled with shot in the Bull Run battle. The man that showed me the flag was also wounded, seven shot striking him in the breast and face: he says he is good for seven more of the same sort. I visited the State House a short time since. The State House was built by the English and is built very tastefully, each room being neatly ornamented. The room where Washington resigned his commission is as it was when he resigned, there is also a very large cannon here used by Lord Baltimore.[4]

The Academy ground contains twenty acres and there are 50 buildings on it. Government uses a part of the buildings for Hospitals; there are some three hundred sick at this place. We have been here now some seven weeks and there has been but one death in that time. We have also had some prisoners here, the Baltimore members of the Legislature, also some of the prisoners taken by General Butler at Fort Hatteras. There are five steamers here at this station to take the troops on the expedition now forming; they came up the Bay last night.

Since leaving Mass. we have had four of our regiment killed; two were run over by the cars[5] at Philadelphia; a Lieutenant was killed while trying to run the guard. Another one (a corporal) was shot by a sentinel for not giving the countersign. One had his hand shot through, and one had his arm cut off by the cars.

Yours, &c.
E.R.R.

While at Annapolis Reed heard news of the capture of Port Royal, South Carolina, which was greeted with great fanfare. The 21st Massachusetts remained in camp protecting the rail line through the city. Most trains to Washington traveled this route to avoid problems in pro-secession Baltimore, where there had been anti-Union rioting.

November 19, 1861

From Annapolis

Naval Academy

Annapolis, Md., Nov. 11th.

The news received last night was of the most cheering kind. The report made to Col. Augustus Moore,[6] commander at this post, was to the effect that the fleet had succeeded in all their undertakings, and there was a general rejoicing among the inhabitants and soldiers in the action. Our Band played Yankee Doodle, the Star Spangled Banner, and other pieces of a similar kind.

The statement in the Northern papers that our regiment (the Mass. 21st) had gone with the expedition, is not correct. We have been here at Annapolis for nearly three months, and I think we shall stay here until the first of April, at least that is the talk now among the officers of our regiment. We have had some hard guard duty to do since we came here. There is considerable responsibility resting on the command of this post. If the rebels could get possession of this place and the Junction, they would cut off all the communication between the North and South, for the reason that the Potomac is blockaded.

Many of our men are sick on account of having such severe and laborious work to do when we were at the Junction (Company A); we were up night and day for a long time, but now they have relieved us and the Michigan first regiment are there, and we only guard from this place to the Junction.

The expedition now forming at this place bids fair to be as large as the one sent before it. There are several thousand troops at this place ready to start as soon as the government gets the vessels here. I should judge that they had forty thousand boxes of hard bread here now.

Our sick in the hospital are improving.

Yours truly,
E.R.R.

Whether caught up in the excitement of the times or from the Thanksgiving celebration, Reed changed his pseudonym for the next several letters, now signing off as "America."

November 28, 1861
Letter from Maryland
Post Naval Academy

Annapolis, Md., Nov. 22, 1861.

Our Thanksgiving passed with us here same as it would at home had we been there. Company A, 21st Regiment Massachusetts Volunteers, bought eight turkeys and several gallons of oysters, and went in for a New England Thanksgiving supper, and you can be assured that when we sat down to eat our supper there was still something lacking. Had we been by the side of the loved ones at home we should have been contented, but that could not be. While the fixings were doing, we visited the camp of the 25th and 27th Massachusetts regiments. New York and Connecticut are sending their troops here to go in the expedition. Two

Union troops at Annapolis
The Naval Academy at Annapolis, Maryland, was moved out at the start of the war, and Union recruits on their way to the front frequently landed here for brief stays and training before being sent to other camps and forts.

of the steamers that went with Sherman's[7] expedition are now here, and the probability is that the second expedition will soon start. The men are very anxious to be moving. But to return to our Thanksgiving dinner. After partaking of the good things, the Chaplain, Rev. Mr. Ball, read the Proclamation of Gov. Andrews,[8] and made a few remarks, and then we were dismissed to our quarters. After roll call at 6 o'clock we adjourned to a large hall which was formerly used as a library, and danced until 9 o'clock, when we returned to our quarters and went to bed, thinking that we had a good time. There was but one thing at the dance which was left out, that we wanted, and that was ladies.

There are three Vermont boys in our hospital. I saw them this afternoon, and they were glad to see a Vermont boy, but their eyes glistened when I showed them three copies of the Rutland Herald. One of them, a young fellow from Brandon, told me that one of their company was employed as a spy, and had three times been into the enemy's camp and found them sleeping. The fellow's name is Button,[9] and is from Swanton, Vt. These young men are anxious to get back to their regiment, and will probably be sent back next week. They belong to the 5th Vt. regiment. It is now time for the Dress Parade, and I must close.

America

The 21st Massachusetts lingered in camp, though rumors were flying about a pending expedition, though the destination was unknown. During this time Reed witnessed the stark division between officer and enlisted man.

December 12, 1861

Letter from Maryland

Post Naval Academy

Annapolis, Md., Dec. 8, 1861.

December is now upon us but we have not suffered any from cold weather. There has been no snow here yet, and most of the time it has been very pleasant and warm. There are about ten thousand troops here, destined for the expedition south, under Gen. Burnside[10] and Commodore Porter,[11] when to sail not definitely known. Most of the officers prefer more comfortable quarters than the tents, and fill some of the Hotels to the almost exclusion of others. Very stringent measures are adopted in regard to these military gentlemen. The Provost Marshal's guard patrols the city at all hours of the day and night and requires them to produce a pass from headquarters when not known to the officer of the guard. This produces considerable inconvenience occasionally,

an officer being compelled to leave a lady on the street during a delightful promenade, and make his way to camp, or be confined at the headquarters of the Provost Marshal. Still more severe are they with the
Privates. An officer when he feels inclined can enter any drinking
establishment and enjoy himself at the bar with his fellows, but the
poor private, no matter what his social position was before he entered
the army, is treated as an inferior being altogether and promptly refused
anything of an intoxicating nature. This is a wise measure if it was general. Certainly so wide a distinction should not be made in a volunteer
army where perhaps there are many in the ranks superior in social position and intelligence to many of the officers.

The small pox is rather on the increase. We have some eighteen that
are now in the hospital sick with that disease, and many of them, no
doubt will never see their homes again.

We are now doing some heavy drilling and it takes the tuck out of us.
We start in the forenoon laden down with our knapsacks, haversacks and
our other equipments and march five miles out, then drill one hour in
Battalion drill and by that time we are ready to go back to our quarters
and by the time we get back we are ready to take off our knapsacks and
lay them down and lay ourselves down also.

We are having considerable company here now, the Legislature having
come together it brings them in from all parts of the country, and they
are having good times.[12]

Yours truly,
America

Just after New Year's, 1862, orders came to break camp and board
waiting vessels. The men looked forward to some fighting, but
where it would occur remained unknown. All they could glean was
that they were on the "Burnside Expedition," an operation named
after General Ambrose E. Burnside, its leader and planner.

January 16, 1862

Our Army Correspondence

From the Burnside Expedition

Steamer Northerner

Ft. Monroe, Jan. 11, 1862.

As all incidents of [the] soldier's life are of interest at home I write a
few lines concerning the Burnside expedition. We embarked on Monday,
Jan. 6th, and expected to steam down the stream immediately, but
Monday night came and passed as did Tuesday and Wednesday. When

Thursday morning came we were ordered to sail and the anchor was cheerfully raised and off we started. During the night the fog was so thick that we came to anchor about forty miles from Fortress Monroe, and the next morning we started on our journey again, arriving at this place at 4 o'clock. We passed by the Rip Raps and the ships of war left here to blockade. Sewalls Point[13] is in full sight, and it seems impossible that a shot can be sent from here to that point, but Sawyer's gun[14] does the work. The large Floyd[15] gun is in plain sight. It is very singular that all expeditions start from here only on Sunday. We leave here to-morrow (Sunday) for some place unknown to us.

General Burnside came aboard this morning and assures us that we should not stay here many hours, but that in less than seven weeks he would have our regiment, the 21st Mass. volunteers, at Annapolis, Md., but how he can tell is more than I know. He seems to be the right man in the right place, if a person can judge by looks and actions. Gen. Reno[16] is the commander of the second brigade, the 21st Mass. regiment having the right of the brigade, the N.Y. 51st being on the left. Massachusetts is well represented in this expedition having 5 regiments, the 21st, 23d, 24th, 25th and 27th.

The men are all anxious to be at the rebels, and well they should be. We have been stationed at one place four months, and had begun to feel uneasy and as if we did not have an equal chance with other regiments. Our Lieut. Col.[17] has command of the regiment, Col. Morse[18] being appointed to the command of the Naval School Academy at Annapolis.

The Vermont Cavalry were at Annapolis when we left and will probably spend the winter there. I was at their camp just before starting on the expedition, and found them all feeling cheerful and contented, although they did not find the army just what they expected. I must now close as the mail leaves for the Fortress in ten minutes.

Yours truly,
America

Expeditions did not always move quickly, as Reed and his comrades discovered. Weather played a major role, especially in joint army-navy operations. Eventually, the men learned their destination was Roanoke Island, which commanded the passage into North Carolina's Albemarle Sound. Control of the island would effectively close off several Confederate ports to Atlantic shipping. Reed's letters shed light on this expedition against the island and coastal towns of North Carolina. Vermont regiments took no part in it.

Caught fatally on the sandbar
In January 1862, as a Union invasion fleet under Burnside moved through the entrance to North Carolina's Hatteras Inlet, the heavily laden steamer City of New York *foundered on the bar, its captain and crew escaping only after forty hours clinging to the rigging until the waters calmed enough for lifeboats to reach them.*

Our Army Correspondence

Letter from the Burnside Expedition

Steamer Northerner, Pamlico Sound[19]

Feb. 1, 1862.

Since my last letter, we have moved many miles, but not in the direction many supposed we should. We left Fortress Monroe with very pleasant weather, but many hours had not passed before we were having a fine wind. It soon increased to a gale, and the men became sick and turned in for fear of falling overboard should they stay outside or at least I calculated that to be the trouble, as they reeled some.

We passed a fearful night off Cape Hatteras, one that will never be forgotten by your correspondent. There was great danger of our going in among the breakers. We got well nigh among them. The captain of the boat was determined to shove us over the bar or on to it, when the General sent and had him arrested. The ship was turned back, and we ran back twenty–five miles and came to anchor. I am not inclined to be very timid, but I must say I felt rather funny that night. It was said by those who ought to know that the captain of the boat was drunk, and I think he was, or he never would have run the steamer within twenty

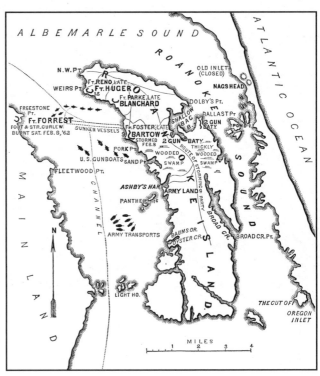

Positions on February 8, 1862

Among the few Northern military successes in the war's first year was the capture of Roanoke Island in North Carolina's Albemarle Sound, part of a flanking movement against Confederate defenders of the naval yards at Norfolk, Virginia.

minutes of destruction as he did. Such men are put into (or at least it seems so) the most responsible places. Had the captain had his own way, we should not have been in Pamlico Sound to-day. The City of New York went to pieces in plain sight of us.[20] She could not be got off the bar. We have had some considerable sickness since leaving Annapolis, having lost two by fever, out of the 21st Massachusetts Regiment. January 15, Col. Allen and Surgeon Weller of the 9th New Jersey Regiment, and the first mate of a ship on the outside, came to make us a visit. When leaving, the Colonel said he must go and see his men, and off they started in a surf boat. It was overturned, and all three drowned. The remains of Colonel Allen and Surgeon Weller were recovered, but the mate's could not be recovered. Col. Allen and Surgeon Weller's bodies were buried on the shore. They received the respect due them, by both officers and men. Our privates, some of them, are buried from the after part of the boat.

We have been on board of the steamer almost a month, but long before you receive this, we shall be on the soil of North Carolina. I will not endeavor to say where we are going, but will say we are headed towards Roanoke Island this morning. Probably before this reaches you, the telegraph will have informed you of our leaving this place. We have had some little excitement. The rebels send up a gunboat to look after us occasionally, but they run like fun when one of our gunboats goes out to give them a salute. Yesterday a sail hove in sight out towards Roanoke Island, when one of our boats took after it, and overtook it and fetched it back. It proved to be a boat belonging to the southerners, loaded with wood. Three men were on the boat, and are here in confinement, and the wood will be used for our benefit. A rebel deserter was picked up some days ago. He reports fifteen thousand rebels on the Island, and twelve gunboats there to give Goldsborough[21] a reception.

In order that the soldiers may get their mail, letters should be directed as follows:

Mr. —— ——,

Co. ——, —— Reg.

Burnside Expedition,

(1st, 2d, or 3d Brigade, whichever Brigade they may be in,)

via Fortress Monroe, Va.

There are three Brigades in Burnside's division. Our ships have all arrived, and we shall sail from here probably Monday morning. But I cannot write more now, as the mail leaves for Fort Hatteras as soon as they can get the letters.

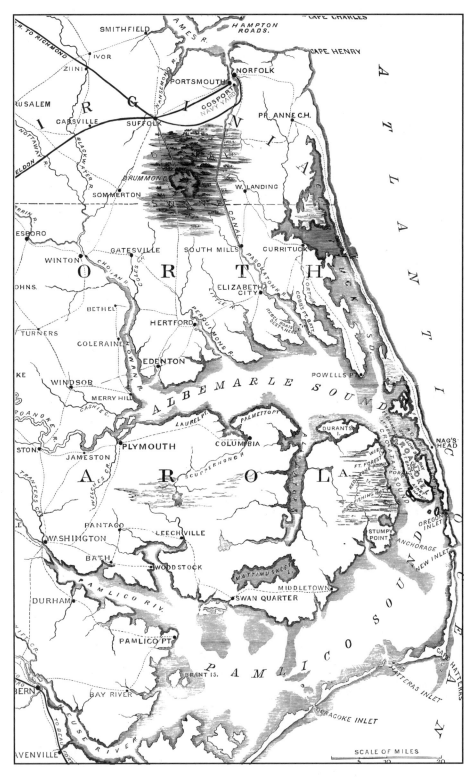

P.S. There is one thing more that I would like to have our friends know about, and that is our living. We get hard-bread and coffee and salt beef three times a day. We also get one quart of water per diem. So you see we do not get the same feed here that we did at Annapolis. I will also say, I have gained in flesh just fifteen pounds since we left Mass., but I think I have not gained any on board of this craft.

You may expect to soon hear from me, or at least as soon as we land.

I am, respectfully, &c.,
America

Roanoke Island, Burnside's first objective, was inadequately defended by the Confederates. While the U.S. Navy bombarded the enemy fort commanding a vital channel, the army landed unopposed on the island on February 7. Reed was among those who set foot on firm ground for the first time in more than a month.

The next day, Union forces started their advance up the island, encountering some Confederate resistance and difficulty in traversing swamps. They met a roadblock which required flanking, and the 21st Massachusetts led the way. The regiment successfully skirted the Confederate lines and with a rush captured an enemy battery. The Confederate defenders broke and streamed to the rear. The Union advance continued and occupied other abandoned works.

When the Confederate retreat reached the northern end of Roanoke Island the troops found no boats to carry them to safety. The garrison was trapped, and the Confederate commander had no choice but to surrender. In one day, Burnside's forces had won a skirmish and captured approximately 2,500 prisoners. Federal casualties totaled 283. Roanoke Island had fallen. Morale soared in the Union ranks.

North Carolina Atlantic coast (left)
In early 1862, the Southern coast had many worthy targets for the Union, none more promising than North Carolina's Albemarle and Pamlico sounds — within reach of the Federal base at Fortress Monroe, and with New Bern and Roanoke as prizes.

Our Army Correspondence
Letter from Roanoke Island
Camp Burnside, Roanoke Island
February 8th, 1862.

As I am at liberty this evening I will improve the time in writing. I begin that the war is coming to an end *sometime*. If the rest of the *regulars* (the name that the rebels gave to our regiment at the battle of the 8th) do as well as we have, the fighting cannot last long. We have disposed of all the prisoners with the exception of the sick and wounded. They still continue to stop, and many of the poor fellows will stay a great while. I saw the prisoners that left to-day. One of them said to me: "take care of yourself, and be assured that if ever I get back home I shall never be taken prisoner again, for I shall not enlist into Jeff. Davis' army, for I don't like his money after seeing Uncle Sam's money." But some are still *gritty*, and declare that if they get back they will enlist again. Some of the prisoners have gone to Elizabeth City.[22]

Mr. Editor, I wish you could see the place where the battle was fought. Come to go over the ground, it is singular that we got into the position we did. An officer asked me who informed us how to take the position and how we got through the swamp. I told him we Yankees had various ways of finding out such things, and the swamp was nothing to speak of, as the mud and water was only about four feet deep. "Well," said he, "the best engineers in the country pronounced the swamp impassable, and d—d if I was not fool enough to believe it." We took two fellows prisoners who were spies. When we were in Annapolis one of them was there selling stationery; he was here acting as Brigade Quartermaster.[23] He was sent to New York. The other was a tobacco merchant on a small scale; he was also sent to New York. I think they ought to hang them. If they don't I would resign if I was not a *low private* in the front *ranks*. General Burnside said to the boys today that he would not detain them here long, as there was plenty of shooting to do. I thought to myself that I had rather be excused if there is to be as hard fighting again as we had before. But, however, if I am ordered, I shall go for the good reason that I could not avoid it, but I am now detailed in the hospital. Our men in the hospital are doing well. Only two or three in the building out of 57 wounded soldiers are dangerous, and only two that will lose a limb. Two died with consumption.[24] Preparations are being made for the expedition from here as fast as possible; but I must now close, as the roll will soon call.

Yours, &c.,
America.

In the next three weeks, while Union soldiers conducted small forays around Albemarle Sound, the navy swept away the last enemy naval opposition. Confederate forces gathered about New Bern, an important port on the Neuse River. It was here they expected Burnside to attack next.

During this time Reed was still detailed to light duty in the hospital, and he witnessed the unforgettable aftermath of the bloody skirmish on Roanoke Island. The young soldier did not tell the readers that he himself was on the mend. Apparently, Reed had sustained a hernia in the left testicle while moving ammunition.

March 19, 1862
Letter from Roanoke Island
General Hospital, 2d Brigade, Roanoke Island
Feb. 28, 1862.

From the fact that this letter is dated at the General Hospital you are not to infer that I have a leg or an arm amputated or broken. I am merely detailed as a wardmaster to attend to the wants of the wounded in this place. One poor fellow by my side lying on his bunk, has both legs amputated; they were struck by a canister shot and shockingly mangled, but the brave man before the battle is the same brave man after the sad calamity; hardly a murmur do we hear from him. On the left of this man lies a young man some eighteen years old, with the right leg amputated below the knee. On the right of this man is an elderly man with his left leg amputated. In front of the three lies a young man who had his left leg amputated to-day, after suffering several days with the hopes of saving the limb. He was hit by a shell. This Hospital is for the wounded alone. We have forty-seven wounded here, among whom is one Captain, one Sergeant, five corporals, and the remainder are privates. They are from the Massachusetts 21st regiment, the New York 51st, and the 9th New Jersey. We have lost five since we came into this building, making the whole number 52, the 21st Massachusetts regiment losing three out of the five. It seems very strange to me that more were not killed and wounded under the terrible fire of the enemy from their masked batteries.

One of the Georgia soldiers told me after the surrender, that their orders were to give no quarter nor receive none, but fight to the death. What a contrast. Our orders in this respect were that when quarter was asked to give it. Before this you have probably heard of the naval forces taking possession of Elizabeth City, therefore I will say nothing about that affair. I have so many calls from the poor wounded fellows, that I

Letters to Vermont

Final assault by Union troops at New Bern
After a forced march, Union soldiers routed the Confederates from their defensive works near New Bern, North Carolina, on March 14, 1862, capturing the city soon afterwards.

cannot write more than three minutes at a time without hearing the call of "Mr. __ , I want my wounds wet, may the nurses put some cold water on them?" I hear another call and I must close.

Hoping to be in Vermont next July, to see the friends, I am

Respectfully, &c.,
America

For the next four months Reed did not communicate with the *Rutland Herald.* Many events occurred during the letter writing lapse. New Bern had fallen on March 14, after a pitched battle. The outnumbered Confederates made a stalwart defense, but Union forces won the day. The 21st Massachusetts led another successful flanking movement against the Confederates and captured more artillery pieces. Outflanked, the Southerners had no alternative but to abandon New Bern. Burnside won the battle, but sustained twice the losses of the Confederates.

In April, Union forces captured Fort Macon and Beaufort, North Carolina, sealing off another harbor. In the next months, the 21st Massachusetts was involved in a successful engagement at South Mills, northwest of Union-held Elizabeth City. The entire campaign was rough on the regiment.

Reed was spared from the fighting, for he remained on duty at the General Hospital on Roanoke Island through March and April, then found himself a patient in the hospital in May and June. His illness permitted him a furlough north in June and he made a point to call on the *Rutland Herald* office during his unexpected sojourn to Vermont. While visiting, he presented the paper's editor with a Bowie knife he had captured on Roanoke Island. The paper later described it as "an ugly looking weapon, heavily made with a blade about thirteen inches in length and in the hands of an expert in a hand-to-hand encounter, we should judge would be a dangerous weapon." Reed received gracious thanks from the paper for his gift, and the knife was regarded by those in the office as "a representative of Southern chivalry and the 'divine institution.' " Reed's furlough expired shortly thereafter and by June 30 he was back in North Carolina detailed to hospital duty as a nurse. This assignment proved short. He soon re-established his correspondence with the *Rutland Herald.*[25]

Army Correspondence

Letter from Newbern[26]

Camp Andrew,
Newbern, N.C.

July 1, 1862.

Your valuable paper comes duly to hand, and is read with much pleasure. We are encamped about two miles from the city in a healthy locality for this country. After I arrived here, I thought it quite unhealthy, but have, after looking thro' the other camps, come to the conclusion that Camp Andrew is one of the very best. I had hardly arrived in camp before I was detailed to the hospital. There are numbers about getting their discharges, and all who are not able to march 20 miles per day are ordered to go to the hospital in Newbern city. We have been to-day ordered to pack our knapsacks and be ready to march in eight hours for some place unknown to the soldiers; but the destination is probably Goldsborough. We take nothing but our two blankets and gun and equipments, and three days' rations. We also take sixty rounds of cartridges. I escape carrying anything but my blankets. Our knapsacks are to go on one of the transports. It seems too bad that we are obliged to wear our thick woolen clothes this time of year, but such is war.

I yesterday visited the battle-ground[27] and it seems almost impossible that any force could take the place. There were two breastworks, each one about a mile in length, mounting eighteen large guns, the last breastworks mounting 13 large guns, commanding the field as well as the shipping. It is very strange they should give it up; but you know I told you the rebels could not stand the cold steel; yet the battle told on our regiment — the 21st Massachusetts — fearfully.

They are just forming for dress-parade, and our company — Co. A, — turns out 32 men. We started from Worcester with 101 able-bodied men. Think of that, you who are at home enjoying life and all its pleasures!

Yours respectfully,
America

With insufficient strength and an inadequate supply line to advance further inland into North Carolina, Burnside received orders to take two-thirds of his expedition force to Virginia to support McClellan's advance against Richmond. Rumors reaching both McClellan and President Lincoln strengthened the belief the Confederates were gaining reinforcements and would soon outnumber the Army of the Potomac. The 21st Massachusetts, Edwin Reed included, embarked from New Bern and headed northwards.

For some reason Reed returned to his original pseudonym for the remaining letters.

July 16, 1862
Letter from Newport News
On Board The Schooner *Scout*

Newport News, Va.

July 12, 1862.

I find myself with Burnside's troops at this delightful place, Newport News. It is most certainly a splendid camping ground. We found on our arrival here but one company of cavalry and the 7th Massachusetts Battery; but the hospitals are being filled up with the sick and wounded from Richmond. They have good accommodations for the sick and wounded—better than any general hospital that I was ever in, and I have been in a good many here in the South. Our regimental hospital is on this ship (the Scout), a transport belonging to the government.

The stream here is filled with shipping. I have counted some three hundred vessels of all kinds. We are to be reinforced from Annapolis, with _____ thousand soldiers, that will make Burnside's division amount to some _____ thousand troops, and *if he could get the President to say, March your men into Richmond, he would start at once.* He has good Brigadier Generals. Gen. Reno of our Brigade is a man of determination. I was pleased to hear the remarks that Gen. Reno made at Camden, N.C.,[28] when our forces went there. The 57th Penn. Regiment were thrown out as skirmishers by order of their Colonel.[29] When Reno came up, he asked the Pennsylvania colonel where his regiment was. The reply was, that he had thrown them out as skirmishers. Reno's answer was, "Skirmishers be d—d," then turning around he said to Col. Clark[30] of our regiment, (the 21st Mass.,) "Charge on that d—d rebel crowd!" and they did, with a will, driving them like chaff before the wind. I verily believe that Gen. Reno had rather go into battle than to sit down to a good dish of oysters. It is hotter here at this place than I ever experienced in the North or South, and I was in Maryland the hottest months of last year.

The steamers are moving around in a very mysterious manner to-day, some going up the James River, some moving out towards Fortress Monroe, some coming from up the James River and from the Fort. Those from the Fort are loaded with something that looks very much like hard tack, so called by the men, instead of calling it by its proper name (pilot bread); others are loaded with "salt horse," or more properly, salt beef.

I have got a small piece of the old ship *Cumberland* that was sunk by the *Merrimack*,[31] also a piece of wood from the *Congress*.[32] Our boys amuse themselves by making rings from these pieces of wood. They make some splendid rings from bones which come out of the beef; but I must close by saying that I hope soon to be in Richmond.

Yours truly,
E.R.R.

Reed's wish to be in Richmond would go unfulfilled. McClellan remained in his position at Harrison's Landing on the James River and continued inactive. While on detached duty in the hospital, Reed grew frustrated, wondering if the war would ever end.

July 29, 1862
Army Correspondence
Letter from Newport News
Camp Simeon, Newport News, Va.
July 24, 1862.

It is now one o'clock in the morning, and as I sit watching the poor sick fellows I have wondered whether their friends at home are thinking of their suffering; but I have no need to wonder for I know they are. Each day we bury three or four poor fellows. The hospitals here are filling up very fast with soldiers from McClellan's army.[33] The poor fellows are well cared for. We have faithful nurses, among whom are a few ladies. When they first come they are very tired, but they soon get over that and take hold with a will, and do everything in their power for the sick and wounded. Most of the hospital buildings are fixed up in good shape.

There has been continual roaring of heavy guns up the river all night. To-morrow we shall hear of an engagement of some kind.

Yesterday I spent some time at the steamboat landing. There were boats coming in and boats going out, some going up and some going

Virginia, from the Blue Ridge to Fredericksburg

As part of a new corps commanded by Burnside, Reed's 21st Massachusetts left the Atlantic Coast in the summer of 1862, heading for Northern Virginia, eventually engaging Robert E. Lee's army at Centreville in the Second Battle of Bull Run, where Reed was taken prisoner.

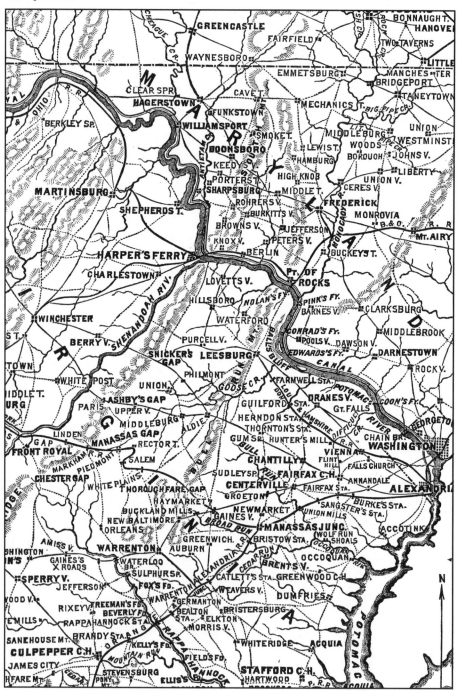

down the river. The troops are pouring into this place every day. Yesterday two regiments came in from north or south. There is going to be some terrible hot work before a great while, and you can depend that somebody is going to get hurt, for they have carried some large guns and several kegs of powder up the river towards the rebel city of Richmond. Yesterday we sent a battery up to Yorktown to look after the Federal interest in that direction.

How long is this war to last? Will it be over in a year, or is it to last longer, or shall we never see the end of the accursed rebellion? There should be troops enough in the field by this time to put it down. Why are so many troops lying idle when there is work to be done? I for one have seen enough of it. Why can it not be put down at once and have it done with? Richmond can be taken to-day as well as a year from now. The longer we wait the stronger the enemy become. Why not make a bold dash and have it [done] with? After all I suppose I don't know anything about the affair. We find out more about the war here on the James River through the papers from the North than we know or hear from those that are on the spot and have a hand in it. How do the editors get the news so soon?

I will now close, as the time has come to give the medicine.

Yours truly,

E.R.R.

While the 21st Massachusetts waited at Fortress Monroe, the regiment and the other units from the Burnside Expedition were incorporated into a new Federal corps, the IX. Burnside was appointed commander. The new corps received orders to proceed to the town of Fredericksburg, Virginia, the uppermost point of navigation on the Rappahannock River. From this position it could support the three Union army corps known as the Army of Virginia, under General John Pope. Reed definitely wanted to finish the war as soon as possible. The glitter of glory had been tarnished by hardship.

Letter from Fredericksburg

Camp Ferrero,[34] near Fredericksburg, Va.

August 7th, 1862.

Here we are smack upon the sacred soil of Old Virginia. We did not stop to enquire whether we could or could not, but landed at Acquia Creek,[35] and took the cars for this place — Fredericksburg, Va. We found two brigades here under the command of Brigadier Gen. Rufus King.[36] Since we arrived these two brigades have left, and the report is that they have met with some of Jackson's[37] men, and had a little brush with them. The rebels tried to burn the railroad bridge, but did not succeed, our men being rather too lively for them.

I will not undertake to tell you how many soldiers there are here, but our brigade landed on Monday, the 4th inst., and ever since troops have been coming in both night and day. What does it all mean? Something is to be *did*, and that very soon. We are under marching orders. Each officer is allowed only 30 pounds of baggage, privates only what they can carry comfortably. We are to take no tents — that means work.

It is very warm here, and should some of the northern folk come up to camp some day about noon, when the boys are all off duty, except the guard, they would stare some — I reckon. We dress very light, wearing only a *shirt*, until about 4 o'clock, when the hour for drill comes, then coats, pants, and other articles are put on. It is rather tough, but it must be done.

When we arrived here we had no tents for the sick. The Division Surgeon went up the road about a mile and took possession of a splendid mansion, belonging to a Mr. Wallace, a law partner of ex-Gov. Wise.[38] Mr. Wallace told surgeon Cutter, that it would be very unpleasant to have fever patients in his house; but the surgeon could not let the building slip through his fingers, and he took possession. Mr. Wallace is a rank hater of the North, and has two sons in the rebel army. There are plenty of his stamp in this vicinity. We are continually kept in our camp, and are under the most stringent orders that we ever were.

Mr. Editor, please send us a few more men so that we can go ahead and finish up this war. We have been here as long as we want to stop in any place, but if the Government will send us some more men we will wait a few days longer. I tell you, if I were at home and going to enlist, I should go into an old Regiment. *Take my advice, boys, and enlist in some old regiment*; but don't send out your men unless they are able bodied and can lay down in the mud or any place where they may be.

Those that cannot eat salt hoss[39] and hard tack, had better stay at home, for they will not be needed here in the army.

There is no boy's play in being a soldier now a days. We have heard some heavy firing to-day off in the direction of Richmond, what it is or what it will amount to, is more than we know of at present.

It is getting late, and I will close by saying all good night to you.

Yours truly.

E.R.R.

Events unfolded quickly in northern Virginia when Robert E. Lee let "Stonewall" Jackson have an independent command. The name of Jackson generated much excitement among the Union generals, for they never knew where he would strike. On August 9, 1862, Jackson met the Union force under the command of Nathaniel P. Banks at Cedar Mountain, south of Culpeper, Virginia. It was a bloody contest resulting in a Federal retreat. General Pope quickly moved to gather his scattered troops to pursue Jackson's force.

The IX Corps — including the 21st Massachusetts and Edwin Reed — immediately departed from Fredericksburg. Reed's letter provides an account of how adroit the Union soldiers were when permitted to forage on their own for food.

August 28, 1862
Army Correspondence
Camp near Cedar Mountain, Va.

6 miles from Culpeper Court House

August 17, 1862.

We are now encamped a little to the left of the battle field of Saturday. As soon as the battle commenced we were ordered forward from Fredericksburg. We started Sunday night at 6 o'clock, marching until four o'clock in the morning when we came to a halt. We laid ourselves down upon the ground and rested two hours when we were ordered to take up our line of march. We marched some 14 miles arriving at a station on the Richmond and Alexandria R.R.[40] when we took the cars for Culpeper, arriving at this place at five o'clock. We went into camp for the night. At three o'clock the next day we again started on our march, and came to this place, Cedar Mountain, where we are now encamped. We are only half a mile from the Rapidan river. When we came into this camp the men were ordered to stack their arms, they then broke ranks, and there being two plantations close at hand, the boys went in for their supper. One of them came over the hill with a load of chickens, another with turkeys, and another with a good fat sheep. One of the farmers had 400 nice sheep and last night there was not one of them left. I went out and got one myself and better mutton I never saw. We are living as well as any one can. This morning I went out and got six quarts of milk. Each one has taken care of himself so far on the march. I should say there were more than a thousand dollars worth of blankets thrown away on the march. Some of our troops are beyond the Rapidan already, and probably before night we shall be on our way towards Richmond. An order was read to us on dress parade, to the effect that if a soldier was shot at from any house, the building should be razed to the ground, and the inhabitants for five miles should be held responsible for the outrage.

Our Brigadier General has been promoted and is now Major General Reno and is in command of this division.

But I must close as the mail will leave soon.

E.R.R.

After the brief respite in the camp at Cedar Mountain the 21st Massachusetts set off on a hectic marching pace for nearly two weeks. The quarry was "Stonewall" Jackson, but he was not about to be drawn into a battle unless on his terms. Jackson eluded the Union forces until August 28, when he pounced upon a Union division that had moved too close to the Confederates.

The bloody, late-afternoon battle at Groveton was the start of the Second Battle of Bull Run. Jackson had disclosed his position, and General Pope gathered his forces to defeat him. For two days Jackson fended off uncoordinated Union assaults, and on the afternoon of August 30, Lee ordered a smashing counterattack by General James Longstreet, wrecking the Union lines. Federal units streamed in disarray back to Centreville.

The 21st Massachusetts participated in the battle, but Edwin Reed had been assigned to hospital duty, where he heard the sounds of the conflict and witnessed the retreat. His detached status, did not, however, keep him from danger. Enemy cavalry captured Reed on September 1. Rather than be burdened by prisoners, the Confederates issued paroles to Reed and many others. Parole allowed the prisoners to return to their own lines, go to a camp for parolees and await exchange for enemy soldiers who had been taken prisoner.

Reed's next letter details these events up to his arrival at the parole camp in Annapolis. He repeats some descriptions set forth in the previous letter, probably having no idea whether that letter had been printed, for it is doubtful that all the mail from the army was delivered during the fury of the campaign. Paroled prisoners were not treated with the greatest esteem, and Reed describes some of their frustrations.

September 19, 1862

Letter from Annapolis

Annapolis, Md.

Sept. 11, 1862.

It is now sometime since I have had the opportunity of writing to any of my friends in the north, but now I expect I shall have nothing to do but write. I will try and give you the outlines of our march from Fredericksburg, Va., to the Rapidan River or Cedar Mountain, and our march back to Bull Run. Some six weeks ago we started from Fredericksburg on a march for some place unknown to us. We started about 6 o'clock in the evening and traveled through the night, the mud being about a foot deep. We made only about seven miles and stopped for refreshments, which consisted of hard bread and cold water, and that is what we continued to have during our march south. We made a forced march to Culpeper Court House, arriving there the day after the battle at Slaughter Mountain.[41] From the Court House we went out about six miles to the battle ground, where we went into camp for two days. One night after nine o'clock we were ordered to fall in, with everything ready for a rapid march. Our goods that could not be carried were put in a heap and burned up to prevent their falling into the enemy's hands. We then started, following the mountain road; we had proceeded but a short distance before it became evident that the enemy were in front of us as well as in the rear. We passed within forty rods of Stuart's[42] advanced cavalry picket, and passed them safely, but from that day for sixteen days, until I was taken prisoner at Centreville, we were under a constant fire from their artillery and musketry. The enemy shot from their artillery pieces anything in the shape of iron. I saw the air at one time filled with short pieces of railroad iron, and when they hit a person they would tear him all to pieces. We stopped for two hours rest at White Sulphur Springs, and two sweeter hours' rest I never experienced. We then took up our line of march, and it seemed as if every man would fall before we had gone one mile, but we traveled on. You will recollect that all this time they were at every place where they could place a battery to any effect, pouring in their iron hail upon us, and we would reply with ours; but still we kept picking our way along towards the famous Bull Run Mountains. Well, all I can say is we arrived at Bull Run with most of our division (which by the way was Maj. Gen. Reno's) in time to have a hand in those battles, where in my opinion we lost, killed and wounded, something between 6,000 and 10,000 men, and after all we had to retreat. I stayed at Centreville by order, and by what I saw I judge the number of our killed and wounded larger than theirs by a good deal. I was taken by Gen. Longstreet's[43] cavalry, taken to their camp and allowed to lay my weary bones down to sleep; but got nothing to eat; so that night I lay down hungry and thirsty, hoping morning would soon come. Morning came at last, and with it a sad prospect for anything to eat. The cavalry got their meals, which consisted of flour and fresh meat, but I could not purchase any for money. I then asked for some in the name of humanity, but got none. I then picked up a piece of tainted pork and ate it with good relish. We then were marched back to Centreville, where they made out our parole papers and gave us an escort out of their lines. About nine o'clock in the evening we got outside, and we were so fatigued that we lay ourselves down on the ground and slept until morning. We then got up and found the rebels had advanced their pickets to Fairfax Court House during the night, but we pushed along, and finally got into our own lines, and about nine o'clock in the evening we arrived in Washington, where we reported ourselves to the proper authority. We were worn out and foot sore when we arrived there, and told the provost marshal so, but he sent us tramping off some two miles to the Soldier's Home.[44] After leaving his office I gave out and could not go further. We stopped. A gentlemen came along and inquired into our case. We told him as briefly as possible, and he kindly got a carriage and sent us to the Soldier's Home, defraying our expenses, as we had no money, the rebels having taken our canteens, our haversacks, and what little change we had. We were three days with scarcely anything to eat. The next day I went to the war department, and found that I could get no pay at present. I find the paroled prisoners are all in the same fix, and something must be done for them. They have been quiet a good while, and the time will soon come when they will have their pay or go home without leave from the government. I think something ought to be done for them, as many of them have eight months pay due them. There are now some 3500 prisoners[45] here, and still they come. There are some Vermont boys here, and all the New England States are represented. New York has a large number here. I cannot say how many of the Vermont boys there are, but some thirty or forty I should judge. Our regiment has some forty men here, all taken within two weeks. It has only about one hundred and ninety men now, and some five weeks ago the number was seven hundred and fifty men. We lost our Lieut. Colonel,[46] who was shot dead. Our Adjutant and Major were taken prisoners, and several of the Captains and Lieutenants were killed and others badly wounded, leaving us with no officers to speak of. But I must close this as I am nearly sick.

Yours truly,
E.R.R.
Co. A, 21st Mass. Vols.

Even after the losses in North Carolina and the Manassas Campaign the 21st Massachusetts continued fighting, engaged at the bloody Battle of Antietam on September 17. Reed remained a paroled captive in his own country. He was permitted to await his exchange at home in Massachusetts, but his health had deteriorated so that he could not rejoin the regiment if he were exchanged. At Boston, on March 26, 1863, Reed secured a discharge for disability for "Chronic Hepatitis, accompanied with Diarrhea of long standing" and pulmonary disease.[47] He headed home.

Edwin Reed returned to Vermont and married Sylvia Manley in 1867; they had one daughter, Winifred. A resident of Benson, he secured the position of postmaster, which he still held in 1887 when he first applied for a disability pension. Only a small pension was granted, although the rheumatism forced Reed to use a crutch to move about. In the late 1890s, he moved to Somerville, Massachusetts, where he died on April 16, 1910, at the age of seventy–seven.

Colder than Vermont
Northerners knew how to keep themselves warm in snug huts they built, but men still had to stand guard duty in harsh weather, go out on patrol without shirking, and make sudden marches to meet reports of the enemy advancing in force — usually false alarms; more than one Vermonter thought the Virginia winter could feel even colder than their own.

Field officers and staff of the 12th
With Colonel Asa P. Blunt seated at center in front, the staff and field officers of the 12th Vermont pose for noted Vermont war photographer George H. Houghton, who joined the troops in 1861, recording all aspects of life on campaign, from camp to battlefield.

Letters to Vermont

Chapter 5

With the 12th Vermont Regiment

"B"

Unknown Soldier, 12th Vermont Regiment

On July 1, 1862, Lincoln issued a call for an additional 300,000 volunteers, and Vermont immediately forwarded five more regiments to serve nine-month enlistments. The men, who represented all portions of the state, settled quickly into the regimen of camp life and guard duty protecting Washington.

After McClellan's disastrous Peninsular Campaign with its high losses, and recognizing the need for more men in the Western Theater of war, President Lincoln asked the Union states for another 300,000 volunteer soldiers. Times and spirits in the North had radically changed since the summer of 1861, however, when men had flocked to enlist. By mid-1862, enthusiasm had decreased drastically as people viewed the casualty lists in the papers and saw the crippled veterans returning home. Enlistees only trickled in, so Lincoln and Congress devised an alternative plan.

Under a 1793 Federal law, the president could call up state militia. Congress enhanced the law by adding provisions to implement a draft if a state's quota went unfilled. With this act in hand, the Federal government called for 300,000 state militia to serve nine-month terms. It was expected that within this time the rebellion would be defeated.

Vermont authorities, who had just completed the raising of the 10th and 11th volunteer regiments for three-year terms, hoped they would not be subject to a compulsory militia call-up. Anyway, Vermont could not have filled the required quota of 4,898 more men by calling up the members of established militia companies, because these companies had been reduced by so many members already having enlisted in the volunteer regiments. That August, Vermont called for volunteers to fill the militia companies. By September 20, a sufficient number of volunteers had stepped forward, avoiding conscription in Vermont.

One company, which had maintained its membership, was the Rutland Light Guard. Though the members had changed because of transfers to the previously raised regiments, its ranks contained some veterans of the 1st Vermont. It received the designation of Company K, 12th Vermont Regiment. The 12th was a near copy of the 1st Regiment, with seven of the companies having served back in 1861. Captain Walter C. Landon commanded Company K, for its previous captain, Levi G. Kingsley, was appointed major.

On October 4, 1862, the regiment was mustered into the federal service, Colonel Asa P. Blunt[1] commanding. By October 10, the unit was encamped in Washington, and twenty days later brigaded with the other four nine-month Vermont regiments, which had recently arrived. The 12th, 13th, 14th, 15th, and 16th Vermont regiments were designated the Second Vermont Brigade.

The name of the correspondent who signed himself as "B" remains an enigma. From his letters it can be determined he served in Company K, from Rutland, but ten soldiers in Company K had a surname beginning with the letter "B." Thus, "B" will remain an unknown correspondent, but he is as eloquent as the others in his description of a soldier's life. His first letter is from Camp Vermont, southeast of Alexandria, Virginia, in the vicinity of George Washington's estate, Mount Vernon. The 12th had arrived here on November 3.

From the 12th Regiment
Camp Vermont

Nov. 14th, 1862.

I have been hoping that some more worthy scribe than myself would write a communication for your columns, from the "12th," which numbers among its ranks so many friends and relatives of the patrons of the *Rutland Herald*. Surely some one ought to keep our anxious friends informed of "things of note" which occur in this camp of ours, on the "sacred soil" of Virginia. I believe no one has yet ventured the undertaking, and you will pardon me if I make myself the humble medium of communication for the present time with those who have always taken such a kind interest in the fortunes and welfare of the "Light Guards." And let me ask of our friends to always continue the interest, for I assure them that nothing serves better to strengthen the resolution, and encourage the patriotism of soldiers, than the kind and affectionate remembrance of those at home. There is always enough in a soldier's life to depress and discourage him, and if it was not for the thought of dear ones at home who were anxiously watching his course he *would* become at times disheartened. If you at home could see with what eager interest all letters and papers from home are perused, you would not fail to write often and long and interesting letters.

It is a beautiful morning. One of the balmy mornings of the sunny south. One can hardly realize that the "melancholy days have come; the saddest of the year," and if it were not for the withered verdure of the fields and the changing foliage of the forest, one would imagine that spring had just opened, and "was giving rich promise of the coming summer." All is busy about the camp, and in the happy countenances of the men, the privations of a soldier's life seem far off. And indeed we ought to be thankful that we are so comfortably situated, with so good a prospect of comfort for the winter. Our camp is situated on ground gently sloping south, and overlooking the camp of the remainder of the brigade. It is elevated ground; 100 feet above the Potomac, I should judge. By stepping a few paces back of camp, we have a fine view of the river, and the broad bottom or interval land upon its banks. Alexandria may be seen situated on the hill having the river for its base, only two miles distant; and Washington some nine or ten miles to the north, can easily be seen from the hill behind our camp. I noticed when in Washington that, be wherever I would, if I could look about, the capitol building was the most prominent object to be seen. It seemed to overshadow all others, and forms the center for all. It is the same when viewed at this distance. It appears of even more massive dimensions

The 12th at Wolf Run Shoals
Guarding a strategic Occoquan River ford called Wolf Run Shoals,
Company B of the 12th Vermont pitched tents among trees that soon were
cut down for building materials and firewood.

than when viewing it from under its walls. Mt. Vernon is only five miles from camp, and can be seen from our line of pickets. It is only two miles from the line at some stations, and many of the boys have already availed themselves of the opportunity of visiting it while doing picket duty. It seems a fit resting place for our National Father — so calm and peaceful, and with a fitting respect for its memories both parties in this war have left it undisturbed. The visitor can pay his homage at the tomb of Washington unmolested by the clang and clash of arms.

This must have been a beautiful section of Virginia before war had devastated it. As one stands upon the upland and looks down upon the broad valley of the Potomac, stretching far away southward, with its rich and fertile soil and adorned by the mansions of those who were the F.F.V.'s.,[2] and thus perceives around him the dwellings deserted and dismantled, the large orchards, and avenues of ornamental shade trees all cut down and destroyed; large forests of magnificent growths of oak and chestnuts, prostrated for army purposes, and the whole country desolate and almost deserted, no one could desire a worse retribution for Virginia than he sees has already befallen her from the march of opposing armies.

Building huts in the rain
With the approach of Northern Virginia's cold, wet winter, there was no time to lose when troops went into permanent encampment: huts with chimneys had to be built, and these soldiers of the Army of the Potomac undertook the task with the experience of hardy campaigners.

Letters to Vermont

We visited a few days ago since the former residence of Col. Kemper[3] of the rebel army. It had been a fine brick mansion, consisting of two wings joined by a long colonnade. The grounds had been tastefully adorned and commanded a fine view of the valley, one of the finest situations I have seen. Now it is nothing but a deserted ruin. The rooms have all been despoiled of their furniture and fixtures. Even the doors, windows and flooring have been taken away, and it looks sad and desolate enough. It has been thus with many of the dwellings, and hardly a plantation has escaped without more or less devastation.

The health of the regiment is remarkably good, only a few are in the hospital, and none from our company. Our camp is in a healthy location, with good pure air, with a good spring of water, and a running stream beside it. Our Colonel is beloved by all, and most worthily so, for he unites in himself those qualities which make a commander loved and respected by his men. He is an excellent disciplinarian, yet kind, and attentive to the wants of his men. He is a perfect gentleman in every respect. The Major has already gained for himself the respect and affection of the regiment, and our company may well take pride in having furnished so good a field officer. Our company officers it is needless to say do all they can to aid and improve us. Capt. Landon is always careful of our wants, and anxious to serve us in the best way possible. He has the confidence of us all. Our other officers too are well fitted for their positions, and under their guidance the company progresses finely in the discipline and duties of soldier's life. The men are contented, and bear whatever privations they are called upon to suffer, in a patient, philosophical manner, knowing that it will do no good to complain and having no disposition to do so. We live upon "hard tack"[4] part of the time, and it would cause many a smile from our kind friends at home if they could see us "munching" our hard crackers and water. It is almost Thanksgiving season in Vermont, and I hear many wishes daily expressed that we could be at home to enjoy it with friends. Our prospect of "salt beef and hard tack" for Thanksgiving contrasts strangely with the bountiful tables that are always spread upon that day in Vermont. We trust that you will all hold us in kindly remembrance, as you gather around the family circle on that day, and you may think of us as being with you in spirit abroad in the flesh.

I have already extended my letter beyond rational bounds and will not trespass upon your patience any longer.

Very truly yours, &c.,
B.

The brigade remained at Camp Vermont for more than a month. On December 12, under the command of newly appointed Brigadier General Edwin Stoughton,[5] it marched to Fairfax Court House to set up its winter encampment. For the next three months this site would be the brigade's home. Life in a garrison camp allowed free time, and "B" went with a number of his comrades to visit the Chantilly battlefield.

December 30, 1862

From the 2d Vt. Brigade

In Camp near Fairfax Court House

Dec. 25th, 1862.

"Camp Vermont" is "no more" to us save in the pleasant memories of the past. Two weeks to-day, as we were on picket duty, the unexpected order came for us to move onwards. Pickets were hastily drawn in at evening, knapsacks packed, letters written, rations drawn, and all the "*et ceteras*" performed. A few hours' rest, and the bugle sounded its morning call. A hasty breakfast, tents struck, and the brigade were moving before Aurora had fairly risen from her "dewy spangled couch."

5000 men filing in a line of nearly a mile in length, over hills and through valleys, is an imposing spectacle, and might well have been gratifying to any Vermonter, for in those ranks were many of Vermont's best sons.

A long march was before us, and frequent rests were given to make it as easy as possible. The men stood it well, and night found us beyond Fairfax Court House, pleasantly encamped in a small pine grove, with our shelter tents pitched, fires built, and our suppers cooked. A good night's rest, and we awoke refreshed, and in good spirits; a little foot sore and with stiffened limbs to be sure, but still able to do good service if necessary. The brigade has since been employed in doing duty at Centreville, being held there as a support for the cavalry pickets beyond, each regiment going out for four days, and being relieved in turn by the other regiments.

Last Sabbath we again changed our camp, moving about a half mile farther on, for the sake of being nearer wood and water. We are now encamped beside the woods, well protected from the winds, and altogether better situated than we have yet been. The boys have been at work with a hearty good will clearing the camping ground, stockading their tents and making themselves comfortable in various ways. If we are not moved soon, we shall be pleasantly situated that we shall be very happy in seeing any of our Vermont friends here.

Gen. Baxter[6] has already visited us, and it seemed very natural to see him once more. Present prospects would indicate that we are to remain for some time, but of course we are liable to move at any moment. Christmas has nearly passed, and a strange one it has been for many, I ween; passed amid scenes so different and associations so varied from those with which we are usually surrounded on this holiday. It has been a day of recreation for us, and well improved has it been.

Off duty in wintertime

A warm hut, good companions, and a pipe were well appreciated by these Company B soldiers in the long hours in camp between rounds of duty, marching, and inspection parades.

A party of us have just returned from the battle ground of Chantilly[7] where our Christmas has been passed. A sad though interesting manner of spending it, amidst so much reminding us both of life and death. Our object in revisiting it was two-fold: partly to gratify our curiosity, and partly for the humane purpose of caring for the still unburied dead. Having partaken of a hasty breakfast, we started out under the guidance of one of our party who had already visited the ground. The weather was foggy, and, as often happens in such cases, we lost our way. To lose one's way, however, on such occasions, only serves to enliven the party, and give zest to the walk; so we quietly retraced our steps, and started anew. It is only three miles from camp, but the sun pointed almost noon before we found ourselves entering the woods, which skirt the eastern side of the open field where the battle was principally fought. A solitary grave, with its small wooden head-board, marked "J. Fellows, Louisiana Tigers, killed September 4th, 1862," was the first indication that death had been there.

As we walked on, the trees on every side showed abundant proof that the bullets flew thick as hail on their death dealing errands. Emerging from the woods, the battle ground lay before us. A pleasant field of 20 or 30 acres, of gently swelling ground, skirted on the east and north by woods, with its pleasant farm house on the south. It did not seem, to look over it, as though death and destruction had so recently been there in such horrid forms. We were not long in discovering the traces of the conflict. Only a short distance from the woods in a narrow gully, a number of bodies had been rudely thrown, with nothing but a scant covering of earth which the rains had already washed away, leaving their bleached skeletons partially exposed. We gave such burial as our means afforded and passed quickly on. A little further on in the edge of the woods, we found the skeleton of some poor fellow lying at the roots of an old oak tree, wholly unburied. His accouterments were beside him, even to his shelter tent. His musket stock had been shot away, and lay beside him. It furnished the only identification, being marked "J.B.H." Alone and unhonored he died; who shall answer for it? A bountiful supply of mother earth was all we could give him, and we passed on.

A line of rail fence runs through the center of the field, and here was where our line of battle was formed. The ground was thickly carpeted with the bitten ends of cartridges, showing how bravely our men stood their ground. Further on, in a long row of cedars, the rebels formed their line, and scattered fragments of their accouterments are thickly strewn around.

We wandered over the field for an hour or two, picking up here and there a memento of the battle ground, and doing what kindly services we could for the unburied dead. We turned homeward with more thoughtful countenances, feeling sick at heart with the sight of such war's horrors. Whoever, hereafter, visits the battle ground of Chantilly, will not be shocked by such sights as we saw, I trust, but can view the ground with more pleasant feelings, and carry away with them more pleasant thoughts.[8]

Very truly,
B.

The peace and quiet of camp was broken when word reached the brigade of a raid conducted by Confederate General "Jeb" Stuart and his cavalry. The Second Vermont Brigade stood ready.

January 7, 1863
Army Correspondence
12th Regiment, in Camp near Fairfax Court House, Va.
January 2d, 1863.

Although but few days have elapsed since I wrote you, they have been exciting ones for our regiment, and an account of the "almost a battle," in which we were engaged, may be of interest to your readers.

Sabbath evening, just as we had eaten our suppers, the order to "fall in," was suddenly given. Orders were given to hold ourselves in readiness, in light marching order, with two-days rations in our knapsacks. Various rumors were of course indulged in as whereabouts we were going. All was excitement about camp; blankets were quickly rolled, and haversacks well lined with pork and hard tack, soldiers' best rations when on a march. Soon the regimental line was formed, and at a quick pace — almost a "double quick" — we started, where? No one seemed to know, but the impression prevailed that a long march was before us, and many murmured at the rapid pace we were taking. As we filed along through Fairfax, and turned down the Alexandria road, it was said "we were on a rapid retreat," then that "the rebels were between us and Washington." The painful uncertainty was, however, in a measure, soon relieved; for as we passed beyond the Eastern limits of Fairfax village, a sudden turn brought us into the field behind a long range of rifle pits, when the command "halt," was given, and our line of battle formed. A prospect of immediate action was before us, for scouts reported that a force of several thousands rebels were only a few miles off. Companies B and G were detached as skirmishers, and occupied a position in the woods on the hill, some one hundred rods farther down the road. The 13th were on the left of us, and the 14th on the right; while the 2d Massachusetts battery, of 4 pieces, held the road. Positions being taken, and the lines having been formed, then was time to inquire what was the cause of this sudden movement. On inquiry, I learned that a detachment of Stuart's cavalry had crossed the river at Dumfries,[9] and were reported to be moving this way. The force was estimated at 8000,[10] and as we had no cavalry force here to oppose them, it was left to the infantry to take care of them. Exactly where they were was not known, nor whether there was a force of infantry with them.

We soon found out, however, where they were, for an aid of the General came galloping down the road with the report that they were directly behind him, and he had only escaped by fast riding. The order to load was promptly given and quickly executed, and we lay upon our arms waiting the attack. A moment more and the clatter of hoofs accompanied by a fierce shout, or rather a yell, told us that our skirmishers had been discovered. Almost simultaneously a volley of a hundred muskets told us that they been well received. Everyone expected to see their column rising over the hill, but a messenger soon reported that they had been repulsed and fallen back.

Large fires were soon seen some distance off, and Gen. Stoughton rode down the road to ascertain what they were. As he came back the battery was brought into position, and at his order, several shells were thrown in range of the fires. They quickly disappeared and scouts reported that the enemy had taken another road to the left of us. Our regiment was then ordered to the western part of the village, and again formed in line of battle, where we remained until morning dawned once more, when we returned to camp well wearied and hungry, and glad that our watching was over.

This being in line of battle all night, in momentary expectation of being attacked, is not the most pleasant of duties; especially during such a cold night as that was. We had the satisfaction, however, of having done our duty and done it well, too.

It was a bold raid on the part of the rebels, but can have done them little or no good. If they had been able to get down to Fairfax Station, they might have captured a quantity of Government stores, but it was too well guarded. Our cavalry are in pursuit of them now, but I hardly think they will find them. They have probably escaped within their own lines before this. As trophies, we have taken two prisoners, with their equipment, and killed one of their horses. How many were wounded by the volley fired at them is not known, but some of them must have been. Although they fired a number of shots at our skirmishers, none of them were injured.

We have "smelt gunpowder" if we have not felt it, and from the conduct of the men no apprehensions need to be felt that they will not do their whole duty if ever brought into action. The regiment was in command of Lieut. Col. Farnham[11] and Major Kingsley at the time, both of whom were cool and self possessed, and inspired confidence in the men.

Wednesday evening we were again ordered to be in readiness to march, and expected to march that evening, but reinforcements having arrived, we have not yet been called away. It is reported that Jackson[12] has crossed the river with a large force, and is endeavoring to get in our rear. I do not think we shall remain in our present camp much longer, and anticipate lively times ere long. In whatever circumstances we may be placed, I am confident company, regiment and brigade will account themselves with credit, both to themselves and our much loved State.

B.

Feeling like veterans after the Stuart raid, the brigade received orders to shift their encampment. Three regiments moved to Fairfax Station, a vital rail stop, and the 12th and 13th Vermont erected camps at a ford on the Occoquan River known as Wolf Run Shoals. Here, a main highway crossing the river required protection.

January 27, 1863
Army Correspondence
Twelfth Regiment, in camp at Wolf Run Shoals
[No Date]

As I predicted in my last letter, we have again changed camps. The Army of the Potomac has once more commenced an onward movement, and this time, let us all hope, there will be no retrograde one until Richmond is ours. Slocum's corps which has been encamped hereabouts since the repulse at Fredericksburg,[13] have again gone to the front. Siege guns and batteries have been sent forward, and troops moving in every direction during the present week. Everything betokens active operations at the front,unless the bad condition of the roads prevents. Operations must be retarded for a few days, at least, by the heavy rains which have fallen during the past two days, rendering the roads almost impassable. The weather looks more promising now — a few days of sunshine will dry up the mud, and then the new campaign can be opened with good prospects of success. Orders came for our brigade to be in readiness to march on Monday afternoon, and Tuesday morning our regiment, together with the 13th, struck tents and took up our line of march for this place. Good marching was done too, for we came the

Battle-tested and well-drilled
Having stood their ground in a strike by rebel cavalry under Stuart, the 12th Vermont turn out with the confidence of veterans before their tents near Wolf Run Shoals; Union staff officers considered Vermont regiments among the best disciplined in the army.

"B" — With the 12th Vermont Regiment 141

distance of twelve miles, over a rough frozen road, in about four hours. We came just at the right time, too, for it commenced raining shortly after we arrived, and has been raining ever since. Our duty here is to guard Wolf Run Ford, and already a company from each regiment has been sent down to the ford, a distance of nearly a mile. They will encamp there, while we are held back as a reserve, to support them in case of the enemy appearing. The 14th, 15th and 16th are at Fairfax station, guarding the supplies there, so that our brigade is once more separated. We are encamped at present in quarters of a cavalry regiment, which left the morning we arrived, but shall change our camping ground for a better one, in a grove of pines, as soon as pleasant weather returns. We are living on short rations, as the road from the station is almost impassable. 100 men have gone out this morning to cut a new road in some places, and to repair the old one in others, and in a few days we shall be as comfortably situated as before.

Capt. Landon has left us for the present, but a few days will return him again.[14] You have doubtless seen him in Rutland ere this. The health of the company and regiment is good, and the men keep up good courage during these uncomfortable days.

Will write again when we get settled, and anything of interest occurs.

  B.

Little happened in camp over the next two weeks as the weather continued wet and cold. The health of the men remained good, but exposure to the bad weather brought on the first symptoms of pneumonia and typhoid fever. When the weather was poor, however, the threat of enemy attack lessened, and "B" had time to contemplate his philosophy toward the war.

February 12, 1863
Army Correspondence
From the 12th Regiment — Feeling in the Army
Condition of the Regiment, etc.

12th Regiment in Camp

Feb. 3d, 1863.

Stormy weather in camp — rain, snow and mud; roads almost impassable; army movements totally impeded, the new campaign broken off, just at its commencement; the very elements against us; shadows of dissensions in the North beginning to darken the horizon; our rulers and statesmen in Washington continuing a vacillating and hesitating policy: leading men at home in the different states animated with partisan zeal

and blind party prejudices, rather than with that lofty and fervent patriotism which can alone rescue us from anarchy and ruin; an army of
more than half a million men rapidly wasting away with disease and
inactivity: whither is the war ending? When and how will it end?

During the past fortnight of almost continual rain or snow, with here
and there a day of sunshine succeeded by a night of storm, there has
been abundant time to think over and discuss all these dark and discour-
aging phases of the war. Little knots of men gathered together in their
tents, seeking ways and means to while away the dreary hours, naturally
talk over their situations and the prospects of the cause in which they
are engaged. Earnest discussions are engaged in; sound sober sense falls
from the lips of these young men of the nation. It would be well perhaps
if more heed were given to the views of this half a million men, unmoved
by the clash of party strife at home, and expressing only the opinions
derived from sober thought of the "why and wherefore" they left home
and friends; opinions founded upon the motives which actuate a patriot,
and from a duty point of view.

Hospital huts of the 12th
Log and canvas structures, such as these housing the regimental hospital,
were thrown up quickly wherever the soldiers encamped for more than a few weeks.

We hear it said that the "army is discouraged," that they "consider the struggle hopeless and useless," and desire "the war to cease." It is not so. They are not discouraged with the war. "The Cause" is as sacred to them, and they are as ready to fight for it as when the first gun of Sumter proclaimed to them that the time had arrived to do battle for their birthright — their God-given liberty. The soldier still sees, above the bickering of party strife and the trammels of party power, the holy cause for which he is fighting. He understands by making it his faith. He is confident of the result. He understands clearly the issue. He is not fighting for any particular party; for any particular institutions; for any particular ideas; but for the one great and noble idea of liberty itself.

But this dragging in of politics and political measures; this ambition of self-aggrandizement which actuates so many; and this lukewarmness of many in the cause, throws a shadow of discouragement over the whole army. To thus degrade our noble cause, is it not enough to discourage a patriot's heart? Let those at home do their duty. Let them cease their strife for personal aggrandizement, and devote their energies to the prosecution of the war, and all will be well. The soldiers will do their part. Let those at home do theirs, and we shall hear no more of a "demoralized and discouraged army." The war may then continue for years, but the right will triumph at last. The principle of liberty cannot be conquered. We are fighting for that, and we shall be successful even though the nation perish.

Vermont has hither done her duty nobly. Her soldiers have done theirs. Let her continue to act nobly in future and she may rest assured that they will not falter in their work.

I trusted to have been able ere this to write you of our advance still farther towards the front; but the weather has ruined the campaign. We are situated as when I last wrote you, with the exception of having changed camping ground for a better one in the woods. We shall in all likelihood remain here some weeks. The roads are in too bad a condition for an onward movement. The changeable and damp weather is telling badly upon the health of the regiment. The health of our company remains good. All are in good spirits, and are anxiously awaiting the return of sunshine. This morning it snowed but tonight the wind has changed, and is quite cold. I trust there is pleasant weather before us.

"*B.*"

The 12th Vermont encamped at Wolf Run Shoals until June 25. Two days earlier it had received orders to join the Army of the Potomac, which was marching towards Pennsylvania in pursuit of Robert E. Lee's army. On July 1, as part of the Union I Corps, it just missed the action at Gettysburg. The 12th Vermont arrived near the battlefield early in the morning of July 2, and along with the 15th Vermont was assigned to guard the corps's wagons, which relocated to Westminster, Maryland. The other three regiments of the Second Vermont Brigade fought with great distinction in the Battle of Gettysburg.

After the previous letter there is no further correspondence from "B" in the pages of the *Rutland Herald*. Perhaps he received a discharge for disability, or died in the spring disease outbreaks, or was discharged with the remainder of the regiment when its service ended on July 14, 1863.

John C. Williams
14th Vermont Regiment

***Refreshment "saloon"
in Philadelphia***
*Union troops being transported to the
front by train rested at Philadelphia,
where they were welcomed by patriotic
citizens with bands, drinks, cheering,
and "kind and generous treatment,"
according to Williams, who said the
Vermonters responded with "repeated
cheers and 'God bless you.'"*

***Stoughton's
headquarters***
*The commander of the
Second Vermont Brigade
was Edwin Stoughton of
Rockingham, left,
pictured here as colonel
of the 4th Vermont
during the Peninsular
Campaign; brother
Charles, the regimental
adjutant, is at center,
Lieutenant Colonel
Henry Worthen at right.*

Chapter 6

Tales of the 2nd Vermont Brigade

"J.C.W."

John C. Williams, 14th Vermont Regiment

The five nine-month regiments raised in Vermont were joined into one brigade. When they enlisted, the men of the 2nd Vermont Brigade little expected that their greatest hour as soldiers would occur just days before their term's expiration. It would come at a small Pennsylvania town named Gettysburg.

When Vermont began raising the nine-month regiments in 1862, Danby-born John C. Williams answered the call. He left his farmer's trade and enlisted in Company B, 14th Vermont Regiment, mustered in as a corporal on October 21.

The eighteen-year-old Williams stood five foot six and a half, with brown hair and blue eyes. His older brother, Martin, joined at the same time. John Williams had written to the *Rutland Herald* before the outbreak of the war.

After mustering in, the regiment immediately departed for Washington, proceeding via rail, steamer, and rail again. Train cars were packed and uncomfortable. Williams's first letter was mostly paraphrased by the editor.

November 15, 1862
The 14th Vermont Regiment

We are in receipt of a letter from "J.C.W." of Company B, 14th
Vermont Regiment, descriptive of the journey of the regiment from
Brattleboro to Washington, and its subsequent movement from one
camping ground to another, up to the time the letter bears date —
November 9th. The regiment at that date was encamped two miles south
of Alexandria, and had received orders to go into winter quarters there,
for which purpose they were about to construct log houses. Our correspondent's account of the fare and accommodations of the regiment at
New York, on its transit through that city, corroborated all the other
accounts we have received or seen. He says the regiment was "misused
in regard to its refreshments and had no accommodations whatever.
We gave no cheers for our treatment was not such as to demand them."
(*Where* was our state all this time?) From New York the regiment proceeded by boat to Port Monmouth, getting aground in the Strait and
being detained about two hours thereby; and from Port Monmouth to
Camden by railroad in the night, suffering from want of fires in the cars.
At Philadelphia their treatment was so kind and generous as to call forth
repeated cheers and "God bless you" from the regiment.

Here we pause long enough to say our Legislature has done what will
meet the hearty commendation of our volunteers as well as of their relatives and friends — the people of Vermont — in passing a resolution of
thanks to the city of Brotherly Love, for its noble and generous [care].

At Baltimore soldiers who came through it the same night in which
soldiers [?] were mobbed[1] but owing to the change which has been
wrought in that city since the commencement of the rebellion, the
14th Vermont, says our correspondent, "met with only cheers and
flags."[2] From Baltimore they proceeded the same night to Washington,
arriving about noon on Saturday, and thence marched about nine miles
to Arlington Heights. There they remained about three days, exposed a
portion of the time, from want of proper tents, to rain and wind; when
they were ordered to Capitol Hill, about ten miles distant, on the
Maryland side of the Potomac, where the other Vermont regiments were
stationed, and where they received better tents. On the same night of
their arrival, they were ordered to march again, this time to Camp
Seward, Arlington Heights, Va., about a mile from Camp Chase. The five
Vermont regiments were ordered there at the same time. After five days
sojourn there, the 14th was ordered to its present camp.

The health of the regiment was good, it not having lost a man at the
time our correspondent wrote, the muskets with which the regiment

was armed, at first, were condemned, and have been exchanged, and the regiment was doing picket duty at the date of the letter. The 12th, 13th, 15th, and 16th Vermont regiments were encamped near them. Snow had fallen there in the depth of four inches, and the weather had been cold.

"I do not think," confided our correspondent, "there is any danger of the enemy coming near us at present, but whenever we do meet them, we consider ourselves ready."

The editor did not often paraphrase any of Williams's future letters.

November 27, 1862
Army Correspondence
Headquarters Company B,
14th Vt. Reg't, Camp Vermont, Va.
Nov. 22, 1862.

Nothing has transpired to disturb the usual quietude of our camp since I last wrote you. Our regiment returned from picket duty yesterday. We did not have a very agreeable time of it, in consequence of the heavy rain, which continued the whole time we were gone. The picket line is about five miles from our camp, and one mile this side of Mount Vernon. There are cavalry pickets four miles beyond this line. Our regiment guarded the extreme left of the line which extends down to the river. We were exposed all the time to the drenching storm, without any shelter other than bough tents,[3] through which the rain would pour about as badly as it did in the open field. I will assure you it was not a very comfortable time for us, being exposed for three days as we were to the rain and mud. We arrived in camp alright however, save an accident which happened to one of Co. C, by a comrade in arms, whose gun was accidentally discharged, the contents entering the shoulder in front and coming out at the back.

I will mention an incident or two. Companies B and G, and part of Company K were ordered to the extreme left of the line under the command of Lieut. Blakeley[4] of Company B. We had not been there a great while before the reports of two guns were heard, the signal of the approach of the enemy. Lieut. Blakeley ordered us to form into line immediately, and prepare to give the enemy a warm reception in case they should indeed appear. But it proved to be some hunters who had carelessly discharged their pieces near the line.

I think Elias Baker[5] of Company B, will make the best shot of any man in the regiment. A wild duck came flying along and alighted in the stream near by where the reserve was stationed. Two of the boys fired their pieces at it, scaring it up without hurting it. But Baker, drawing his "Manhattan" revolver from his pocket, shot the duck through the breast, while at a considerable height in the air. Our log houses are being constructed very rapidly. The weather has been extremely fine here, with the exception of the rain mentioned above.

A member of Company H died this morning. I learn that it is intended to send him home. His name I believe is Nash.[6] We are waiting anxiously to hear that Burnside[7] has successfully entered the rebel capital. But the boys of the 14th are not forgetful that they may become involved in a fight in connection with the present movements. The whereabouts of the rebel army is unknown to us. He may make his appearance in a quarter least expected. But I think Washington is secure from all danger. It is defended by a reserve corps of a hundred thousand true and loyal men.

Yours, &c.
J.C.W.

Train at Union Mills
Vermont troops guarded train stations and bridges, such as the ones at Union Mills, Virginia.

On November 26, the 14th Vermont marched to Union Mills, Virginia, to picket along Occoquan Creek and Bull Run and to assist in guarding the nearby railroad. The threat of Confederate attack was ever present.

December 6, 1862
Army Correspondence
Headquarters, 14th Vt. Regiment
Camp near Occoquan Creek, Virginia
Nov. 30th, 1862.

Perhaps you have before this heard of the movements of part of our brigade. The 14th, together with the 13th and 15th Regiments, received orders on the 24th inst., at about eight o'clock in the evening, to get ready to march at a moment's warning. At about nine o'clock the regiment was ordered to fall in, and but a few moments elapsed before the 14th was in line, every man in light marching order[8] and supplied with one day's rations. It was a very dark night, and rained slightly. Col. Nichols,[9] after thanking us for our promptness, ordered us forward. We halted awhile at Col. Blunt's[10] quarters, and then, forming in with the 13th and 15th, took up our line of march for some place unknown to any one in the ranks. It being very dark and muddy, our march was very slow. We marched until about four o'clock in the morning, when the column halted and was ordered to stack arms and rest. We built a fire to dry ourselves and lay down to rest, making ourselves as comfortable as possible. When daylight came we found we were within six miles of Fairfax Court House, and at eight o'clock in the forenoon we resumed our march, our place of destination being still a mystery to us. We halted again one mile the other side of the Court House to take dinner, after which we again took up our line of march. At Fairfax Station we again halted and pitched our tents such as we carry when on the march. We rested well that night, being fatigued by our marching. At about ten o'clock the next morning we resumed our march, each man supplied with one day's ration of hard bread.[11] We marched until about noon, when the regiments separated, the 14th being ordered to its present camp, and the 13th and 15th off in another direction, towards Bull Run. The first night of our arrival here the 14th was formed in line of battle about midnight, firing being heard near by which signalled the approach of the enemy. You can hardly conceive with what alacrity the regiment formed; our officers praised us highly. The firing proved not to proceed from the enemy, however. We have part of a battery of artillery with us, and also a squad of cavalry which go out scouting every day. The 1st

Mass. and 26th Penn. are encamped not far from us. We are encamped on the road over which Sickle's brigade passed a week ago. He has passed on to Fredericksburg. We are in sight of the Bull Run field, where that ever memorable battle took place.[12] The object for which we came here is not known to me. The weather is mild and comfortable. We are put on drill every day, so as to perfect ourselves as far as possible in the art of war. The war will never be found wanting.

Yours, &c.
J.C.W.

The 14th Vermont, having completed its assignment, returned to Camp Vermont on December 6, and suffered through the foul winter weather.

December 11, 1862
From the 14th Regiment
Camp Vermont, Virginia
Dec. 6th, 1862.

Thinking that the friends of the 14th would be very glad to hear of our movements and well being, I hasten to address you a short letter. We are back on our old camp ground again, and we hope to stay through the winter. It really seems like home here. Our movements to the front did not amount to so great a deal as far as I can see, but I do not profess to know the object of it. While encamped near the Occoquan, we performed picket duty; our pickets extending up Bull Run creek meeting the pickets of the 13th and 15th Regiments, which were encamped at Union Mills, six miles from us. False alarms are very frequent to soldiers stationed near the enemy. Our regiment was formed in line of battle twice while there, the boys falling in very promptly both times, and showing themselves ready to meet the enemy. Our regiment captured a number of prisoners whom we judged to be spies. They were sent on to headquarters.

We hope we were remembered by friends at home on Thanksgiving day. Our "hard tack" was greatly in contrast with the tables usually set in Vermont at that time. Rail fences[13] were very handy there [Union Mills], and if the orders had not been strict on "lifting" things, Rebel chickens would have come handy also. Our company had just come in from picket duty on Thursday, the 4th inst., when an order came for the regiment to get ready to march in ten minutes, each man to be supplied with three days rations. And when it was made known that we were going back to Camp Vermont, shouts of joy were heard all through the camp. It was finally decided not to start until the next day, and at 2 o'clock a.m., our regiment being relieved by the 125th New York, we moved off. Before we had marched a great way, it began to snow quite hard. The distance to Fairfax Station was 7 miles. Col. Nichols ordered the battalion to march in two ranks, and giving the companies the privilege of falling out and resting, commencing at the head of the column and then falling in the rear of the battalion on its moving past them. By this means the regiment was to be kept on the move, and still give us the chance to rest. But the companies on the right not falling out as often as they should, companies B and G did not have a chance to rest until we got to the next station, which made it rather hard for us, inasmuch as we had to carry our knapsacks and other equipment.

On arriving at the station, we found the 13th aboard of the cars, bound for Camp Vermont also. Cars were procured for the 14th; some of the boys, however, got on the baggage train with the 13th. It was about dark when the remainder of the 14th reached Alexandria, having to wait until after the 13th went through. By this time the ground had become covered with snow. Our tents had all been to Fairfax Station, so that we were left without shelter in case we should go up to our camp, the distance being two miles. Some of the boys sought shelter in the city; and others, through the kindness of the boys in the 12th and 16th, were kept over night. By noon the next day the boys had all got into camp, and the tents coming, they were all pitched before night. I do not think we shall move again this winter.

The field officers of our regiment are all very much beloved. There is not one of the boys but what speaks well of them all. They are doubtless the right men in the right place. The weather is quite good at present.

Yours, etc.,
J. C. W.

On December 7, 1862, the Second Vermont Brigade saw the arrival of its official commander, newly commissioned Brigadier General Edwin Stoughton. The twenty-four-year-old Stoughton had been colonel of the 4th Vermont Regiment. Five days later the brigade vacated the comfortable quarters at Camp Vermont and left for Fairfax Court House.

From the 14th Vt. Regiment

Fairfax Court House, Va.

Dec. 15, 1862.

Our Brigade received marching orders on the 11th inst., about four o'clock P.M., to be ready to start at five A.M., the next day, each man to be supplied with two days' rations. We had previous to that, and for the second time, received orders to go into winter quarters at Camp Vermont. At three o'clock the next morning the bugles sounded, calling us up to prepare for the march. Our camp was again a busy scene. At half-past five the 14th was formed into line, this time each being in heavy marching order.[14] Lieut. Col. Rose[15] taking the command, we were ordered forward, the 12th, 15th and 16th preceding us, and the 13th bringing up the rear. We marched in this order about four miles, when the regiments ahead halted, the 14th filing past them and taking the lead. The day was pleasant, and it was a very favorable time for a march. We arrived at Fairfax Court House about four o'clock in the afternoon, and camped a half a mile north, where we remained that night, and till four o'clock the next day, when we moved to our present camp, which is about half a mile south of the Court House. The 1st Vermont Cavalry were at Annandale as we passed by. The distance from Camp Vermont to this place is called twenty miles. It was a fatiguing march, fifteen miles being the average distance which an army moves in a day. General Sigel[16] left here last week with fifty thousand men and also General Banks'[17] old corps of forty thousand is passing through here, en route for Fredericksburg, from Harper's Ferry. A part of his corps camped here last night. I know not exactly the object for which we were ordered here, but I suppose that it is to guard this section, in place of Sigel's army. The army that is passing through here I understand is going to reinforce Burnside. We found sixteen hundred cavalry here when we arrived, which were guarding the place. I learn that Camp Vermont was occupied by other troops soon after we left, who will have the benefit of our labours in case they should go into winter quarters. The weather is very fine at present. The health of our regiment is good.

Yours, &c.,
J.C.W.

Williams was describing some of the movements by the Army of the Potomac preceding the Battle of Fredericksburg on December 13.

In the new camp the men fell immediately into the established camp routine: picket duty and drill. In his next letter the editor of the *Herald* decides to paraphrase once again.

December 25, 1862

The 14th Regiment.[18] — We have received a letter from this regiment, dated Dec. 20, stating that the 2d Vt. Brigade are still encamped near Fairfax Court House, the 14th, 15th and 16th regiments being on the south side, and the 12th and 13th regiments on the north side of the village. Their tents and baggage had arrived by rail, and the camp had resumed its usual condition of quietude. "Our present business," continues the letter, "is to do picket duty. A regiment goes out every five days. The 12th is out now. Our turn has not come yet, but we expect it will soon. The first review of this brigade by Gen. Stoughton came off day before yesterday, near the camping ground of the 12th and 13th regiments. Yesterday, about one o'clock in the afternoon, orders came for us to be ready, in light marching order, to start at a moment's warning. The boys all got ready, and awaited further orders for about an hour, when the orders were countermanded, and changed into orders for battalion drill.

In possession of the mill
In the spring of 1863, Vermont troops posed for George Houghton's camera at Ford's old mill near their camp at Wolf Run Shoals on the Occoquan River.

The weather has been quite comfortable, with the exception of a day or two which were as cold as the weather usually is in Vermont, without snow. The weather being so fine, accounts, I think, for our staying here so long, as we generally receive marching orders just before or during a storm. We do not get much time for play, for company and battalion drill, together with other exercises through the day, take up nearly all of our time."

Army Correspondence
Fairfax Court House, Va.
Jan. 1, 1863.

Since I had wrote you the 14th has been out on picket to Centreville and was gone five days. When and where, they expected to have an engagement with Stuart's[19] cavalry which was said to be in that vicinity for which purpose a supply of ammunition was sent out and the men all ordered into the forts. The enemy, however, did not show himself in that quarter that day. On Sunday, the 28th, it was discovered that that rebel chief, Stuart, was within our lines with a large force of cavalry, and intended making a dash into this place. Our cavalry picket from here were driven in to Fairfax Station and stated that the enemy cavalry had made an appearance in that quarter, and were pushing to this place. Accordingly preparations were made to give them a reception. Our regiment was relieved from picket by the 15th, and had been in only a short time, when on Sunday, about 5 o'clock p.m. it was ordered to be ready at a moment's notice. About 7 o'clock in the evening, we were ordered forward at double speed. We expected to march to the Station, but went in another direction towards Alexandria, and halted about half a mile beyond the Court House. The 15th was sent to the Station.[20]

Our force consisted of four thousand infantry, a battery of artillery and a squad of cavalry. The battery was drawn in fine behind breastworks, supported by the 13th and part of the 12th and the remainder of the 12th and the 14th were sent out by companies to watch the various roads, videttes being sent out ahead in every direction. We had been in these positions but a short time when the enemy's cavalry made their appearance, driving in the pickets and coming unexpectedly upon two companies of the 12th, upon whom they charged. The two companies fired a volley at them, killing two horses, and captured another horse and two prisoners. None of our boys were harmed. The squad that charged fell back to where a larger force was stationed in the woods and built fires. Gen. Stoughton sent a flag of truce there, stating that he would like an interview with Gen. Stuart who replied that he would correspond in the morning. Gen. Stoughton pursuing an immediate interview, ordered a few shells to be thrown among them, which made them "skedaddle," and they were not seen or heard of again last night.

This same force of cavalry was at Dranesville the next day. Gen. Stuart was in command himself. His intention was doubtless to surprise us, but he found the Vermont boys awake. Gen. Stoughton had so disposed us that we should have cut the enemy to pieces if he had come up. Stuart has found out what we have got here, and that the Vermonters are ready for him.

The health of the regiments is quite good, and the weather is comfortable. The boys of the 14th are all in good spirits, and ready for any emergency.

Yours, etc.,
J.C.W.

Though soldiers regularly wrote of the regiment's health, they seldom mentioned their own conditions. Williams neglected to inform the readers he had contracted a severe case of pneumonia during February. He recovered, but the debilitation would hinder him in later years.

On March 1, 1863, Williams requested a reduction from his corporal's rank to private and accepted a transfer to Company K. There, he assumed the position of drummer, a post that had been vacant since the unit's inception.

A major event occurred in the brigade on the night of March 9. That rainy evening a small party of Confederate cavalry under Captain John S. Mosby infiltrated the Union lines and entered Fairfax Court House undetected. Mosby captured Brigadier General Stoughton, asleep in his bed, and hustled him off to Richmond. No losses were sustained by the Confederates, and the incident was a great embarrassment for the Union. Colonel Asa Blunt of the 12th Vermont became acting brigade commander. Williams makes no comment on Stoughton's capture except for noting the regiment was involved in digging more entrenchments to repel any Confederate attacks as ordered by Colonel Blunt.

In late March the 14th shifted the camp's location from Fairfax Station to Wolf Run Shoals on the Occoquan River, where a strategic highway crossed.

April 6, 1863
Letter from the 14th Vt. Regt.
Camp Near Wolf Run Shoals Va.
March 29, 1863.

Thinking the friends of the 14th would be glad to hear of our late movements and our whereabouts, I address you another letter. The boys were very glad to receive marching orders on the 23rd, for our camp at Fairfax Station was getting somewhat monotonous. We had remained there three weeks without being called out in line of battle once. During our stay there the 14th was put upon drill most of the time when the weather was favorable, with the exception of the last two weeks, which were devoted to digging rifle pits with which the station could be defended in case an attack should be made. Orders came to be ready to march at seven o'clock, A.M., the next day. Accordingly tents were struck and the regiment in line ready to move off at the appointed hour. We were hard up for field officers at the time of our move. Col. Nichols was absent, being in Washington at the time orders were received. Lieut. Col. Rose was unable to march with us, in consequence of bruises received by being thrown from his horse the night before. Major Hall[21] was not very well, having a few days before returned from home, where he had been sick for some time. The command then devolved upon Capt. Gore[22] of Co. A, but he being sick, it fell upon Capt. Thompson[23] of Co. B., to act as Colonel. We arrived here at ten o'clock A.M., the dis-

Camp of the 14th Vermont at Wolf Run Shoals
The 14th Vermont left this camp on the Occoquan River in mid-1863, when the Gettysburg campaign opened with Lee's Confederate army advancing north, threatening Maryland and Pennsylvania.

tance being seven miles. Our present camp is but a few rods from the 12th and 13th. We have plenty of picket duty to perform at this place. False alarms are as frequent here as ever. On the 28th firing was heard on the picket line; soon the long roll was beaten and the 14th was in line with its usual alacrity. Companies B and G were sent out as skirmishers to ascertain the cause of the alarm. It was found that the firing was made by some straggling pickets who had been relieved that morning and were returning to camp. Last night news came in from headquarters that a force of rebel cavalry was lurking around in the vicinity, and might attempt a raid during the night. Preparations were made to give them a warm reception in case they should show themselves, but no alarm was given. The place is strongly fortified by rifle pits or breastworks, behind which the artillery is placed commanding the ford. We could keep three times our number at bay easily. Another promotion has taken place since we have been in this camp: 1st Sergeant Sheldon[24] of Co. H to be 2d Lieutenant of Co. K, vice[25] Fuller[26] resigned. The weather is very changeable yet, rain and snow still continuing to fall every day or two. We never have more than one fair day at a time. The health of the regiment remains quite good. The boys are all in good spirits and do not intend to be caught napping.

Yours, &c.,
J.C.W.

The 14th Vermont remained at Wolf Run Shoals as the other Vermont regiments were shifted around the region. On April 20 the brigade received its new commander, George J. Stannard. The new brigadier general had been promoted from the colonelcy of the 9th Vermont Regiment and now replaced the captured Stoughton, whose appointment had been withdrawn from consideration.

May 19, 1863

From the 14th Regiment

Camp Near Wolf Run Shoals, Va.

May 11th, 1863.

Perhaps another letter from the 14th at this time may not come amiss. About a month ago the Second Brigade received orders to take the field, for which purpose we were soon prepared. Since then we have held ourselves in readiness to march at any time, and especially for the last two weeks — having been under orders to move at a moment's notice. We expected to have been participants in the late battle at Fredericksburg,[27] but in consequence of the important position we occupy here, and the essential duty we are performing in keeping up this picket line we could not be there. We shall probably stay where we are for the present, at least, for Gen. Hooker[28] does not desire any more troops to his command, whose time will be out so soon as ours during his summer campaign.[29] The 14th is the only regiment here now, the 12th having moved to Warrenton about a week ago. We hear now and then, of people at home, who are finding fault with us. They say we are not doing anything, that we are living too easily. But ignorance only, can be the mother of such absurd talk. No sensible person, who understood the importance of the duty our brigade was doing keeping up a picket line of forty or fifty miles, in the heart of the enemy's country, would be heard to utter such words. But we expect nothing different from those who are determined not to help the cause of Freedom, and who are trying by putting forth every effort to destroy and discourage all means employed to finish this fratricidal strife.

Our A tents[30] were taken away from us soon after we were ordered to take the field, which left us with nothing but fly tents.[31] Gen. Stannard[32] and staff visited our camp yesterday. His head-quarters are at Union Mills. We cannot complain of nothing to do, for we are put upon drill about every day. The regiment is now learning the skirmish drill and bayonet exercise, a knowledge of which is invaluable to well drilled troops. Col. Nichols is determined to have the 14th second to none, and so are we. The weather is extremely warm here now. The health of the regiment is good, and the boys are in good spirits.

Yours, &c.
J.C.W.

By May, the Second Vermont Brigade found itself stretched to the limit. The five regiments now picketed fifty miles of territory, where a force of 16,000 Union troops had been in position a year earlier. Mosby and his raiders remained a constant threat.

In June the situation changed radically. The battle at Brandy Station, on June 9, determined that the Army of Northern Virginia was moving north toward Maryland. General Hooker's Army of the Potomac started off in pursuit, and the advance elements of the army passed over the ford at Wolf Run Shoals. Eventually, almost the entire army passed by, day after day, in long columns that extended for miles. For the time being, in expectation of its nine-month enlistment soon ending, the 14th Vermont remained observers of the spectacle.

Lee's army moves north

In a calculated maneuver to bring on a decisive battle with the Union army, Lee moved out of Northern Virginia and advanced through Maryland and into Pennsylvania, with Meade's army in pursuit; both were heading for the crossroads at Gettysburg.

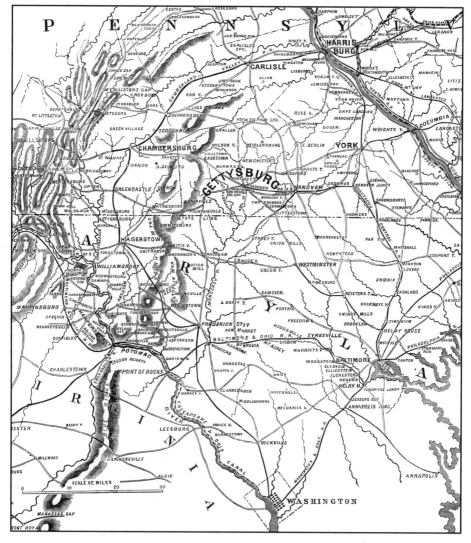

Williams: "It took four days and nights for the column to pass."
*Expecting to be mustered out that summer after serving their nine-months' term,
the men of the 14th Vermont watched column after column of the Union Army
pass by in the counter-move against Lee's advance northward; the 14th soon
would follow and be in the thick of the coming battle.*

From the 14th Regiment

Headquarters, Co. B, 14th Vt. Reg't

Camp Near Wolf Run Shoals, Va.

June 18, 1863.

During the present startling aspect of affairs, the friends of the 14th may again be desirous of knowing that we are still acting in this great drama.

It can be said with truthfulness that the 14th is now in front. The movements of General Lee[33] have compelled [the Army of the Potomac] to fall back towards Washington. We [were] apprised of that fact on Sunday, the 14th. This being one of the principal routes to Fredericksburg, a part of the army passed here. The center column of the army, composed of the 2d, 6th and 12th corps, together with the reserve artillery of forty batteries, passed here. It took four days and nights for the column to pass.

The 1st Vermont Brigade passed here on Tuesday. The brigade stopped here two hours to rest. We had a fine chance to see our old friends, and to give these heroes of many battles, a hearty shake of the hand. The officers and men appeared to be in fine spirits, notwithstanding the forced march which they had endured. The brigade halted near Fairfax Station until this morning, when they have again moved on. The 14th is now in a very exposed position. There was no picket lines between ours and the Rappahannock, which now leaves us in front. I do not know whether it is the intention to keep this picket line here, under present circumstances or not. It is my opinion, however, that inasmuch as this is the outer picket line in the defenses of Washington, that we shall not move from here until we are obliged to. There has been various rumors afloat, but it is evidently a fact that General Lee is advancing in force up the Shenandoah Valley. Yesterday heavy cannonading was heard in the direction of Thoroughfare Gap.[34]

The Government is making speedy preparation to check the raid into Maryland, and it is hoped this desperate act of the rebels will result in their annihilation.

The regiments of our brigade remain in about the same position as when I last wrote you. The general impression is now that the second brigade will have a chance to be tried in battle. If so, we are determined to keep up the good name which the Vermont troops have already so nobly earned. The 1st Brigade has won a name which the State as well as themselves may be proud of; and, although we have been called by some "nine-monthlings, hatched on two hundred dollars bounty eggs,"[35] we understand the use of the bayonet and if we ever have a chance to meet the foe, we shall not falter.

The weather for the past six weeks has been extremely dry, not having had any rain during that space of time.

Our brigade was again paid off on or about the first of the present month, up to the 1st of May. Our regiment still remains healthy. The boys of the 14th are all in good spirits, and ever ready for any emergency which is the true character of the Green Mountain boys. More anon.

Yours, &c.
J.C.W.

On June 23 the Second Vermont Brigade was ordered to join the Army of the Potomac as it proceeded north through Maryland. Two days later it broke camp and followed behind the rest of the army. In six more days the men marched 120 miles in hot June weather, reaching the battlefield of Gettysburg at sunset on July 1, too late to participate in the first day's actions.

The battle at Gettysburg was not a planned affair for either side. Lee had chosen to invade Pennsylvania to reduce the pressure on war-torn Virginia and to seek a major victory which might convince Great Britain to support the Confederacy. When Lee learned of the pursuit of the Army of the Potomac, he selected the road hub of Gettysburg to unite his scattered forces. The July 1 battle opened between Confederate advanced elements and Union cavalry. The unanticipated engagement soon blossomed into a full-scale battle.

Williams was with his regiment at the Battle of Gettysburg, but his role is unclear. According to pension records, he suffered greatly on the long arduous march into Pennsylvania.

The 14th Vermont played a minor role in the action in front of Cemetery Ridge late on July 2, but on July 3 it was at the forefront with the 13th and 16th Vermont regiments in pouring a terrible flanking fire into Pickett's Division as it made its famous doomed charge. The Second Brigade won its share of glory, just days away from its discharge. The soldiers could say proudly they had fought in one of the most crucial and bloodiest battles of the Civil War.

After Gettysburg, the 14th Regiment returned home, its term of enlistment expired. His body weakened by fatigue, John Williams contracted typhoid fever immediately after the regiment received its discharge on July 30. He survived the fever, but its effects com-

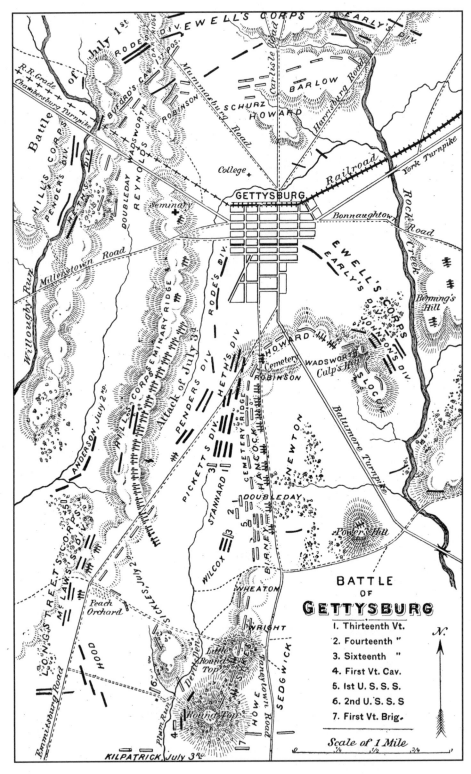

Battle of July 1st

R.R. Grade
Chambersburg Turnpike

HILL'S CORPS

RODES DIV.
EWELL'S CORPS
EARLY'S DIV.

OAK RIDGE
BUFORD'S CAV.
WADSWORTH
ROBINSON

Carlisle Road

BARLOW

Mummasburg Road

SCHURZ
HOWARD

Harrisburg Road

PENDER'S DIV.
HETH'S DIV.
DOUBLEDAY
REYNOLDS

College

Railroad
York Turnpike

Seminary
GETTYSBURG

Bonnaughton Road

Rock Creek

Millerstown Road

Willoughby Run

EWELL'S CORPS
EARLY'S

RODES DIV.

HILL'S CORPS
SEMINARY RIDGE

Attack of July 3d

PENDER'S DIV.
HETH'S DIV.

Benning's Hill

JOHNSON'S DIV.
Culp's Hill
SLOCUM

HOWARD
Cemetery
WADSWORTH
ROBINSON

ANDERSON July 2d

PICKETT'S DIV.
3
STANNARD
2
WILCOX
5
CEMETERY RIDGE

DOUBLEDAY
BIRNEY

NEWTON
HANCOCK

Baltimore Turnpike

Power's Hill

LONGSTREET'S CORPS
Mc LAWS DIV.
SICKLES, July 2d

WHEATON

WRIGHT

Peach Orchard

HOOD

Devil's Den
Little Round Top

SEDGWICK
HOWE
Taneytown Road

Emmitsburg Road

Plum Run

Round Top

KILPATRICK July 3d

BATTLE OF GETTYSBURG

1. Thirteenth Vt.
2. Fourteenth "
3. Sixteenth "
4. First Vt. Cav.
5. 1st U.S.S.S.
6. 2nd U.S.S.S
7. First Vt. Brig.

N.

Scale of 1 Mile
0   ¼   ½   ¾   1

bined with the earlier pneumonia to greatly diminish his ability to perform manual labor. He applied for, and received, a two dollar monthly invalid pension, effective July 31, 1863.

His disabilities might have limited him, but Williams maintained a busy life after his return to Danby. In 1864, he published a memoir of his service in the 14th Vermont, entitled *Life in Camp*. He worked as a store clerk, school teacher, superintendent of the Danby town schools, town constable, town clerk, tax collector, was a cheese manufacturer and managed to do some light farm labor. In 1868 he married Nora Colvin. Two years later he wrote a detailed history of Danby. His lung problems worsened, and in 1879 he was granted a two dollar increase to his invalid pension.

In 1884, Williams and his wife moved to Minneapolis. They remained there only a year and then continued west to Denver, where he found employment as a clerk in the Registry Department of the Denver Post Office. Then, in April 1894, while picking up mail sacks, Williams suffered a severe hernia. Because of this additional disability, his pension was increased to twelve dollars a month. In December 1895, his wife Nora died at age forty-four. They had no children.

Two years later the fifty-three-year-old Williams married twenty-three-year-old Bertha Knox of Denver, and in the next six years the couple had three children.

Williams's ill health continued to trouble him. Tuberculosis developed in his lungs, and he died on October 18, 1908, at sixty-five. His second wife never remarried, but moved to California where she died in 1948, receiving her widow's pension all the while.

Pickett's charge at Gettysburg (opposite page)
On the final day at Gettysburg, July 3, Lee sent a massive frontal attack against the Federal center on Cemetery Ridge, with Pickett's Division charging at Hancock's Corps and Stannard's Second Vermont Brigade, which was just days away from mustering out of the service; in a daring move, the Vermonters advanced against Pickett's right and poured their fire into the Confederate ranks, which suddenly melted away, shattered.

John C. Williams— Tales of the 2nd Vermont Brigade   **167**

The decisive moment
Just to the left of this, the high water mark of the Confederate attack upon the Union center on Cemetery Ridge at Gettysburg, the largely untested Second Vermont Brigade fought gallantly in the repulse of Pickett's ferocious charge that resulted in Lee's decisive defeat.

**Meade pursues Lee
on the Emmitsburg Pike**
In the broiling heat of June 1863, the
endless columns of Meade's Army of the
Potomac executed a forced march toward
Gettysburg to prevent Lee's invading
Army of Northern Virginia from turning
and striking at Washington; the battle-
hardened 6th Vermont in the
First Vermont Brigade were among the
Union's best fighting men.

**The sweepstakes —
the grandstand — the finish**
For off-duty soldiers in huge Union
encampments such as this one at Falmouth,
Virginia, free-for-all horse racing of every kind
was the passion — almost an "epidemic," said
one reporter — with hundreds of contestants
and thousands of military and civilian
spectators, many betting on the results.

The 6th Vermont at drill
Looking smart and eager soon
after being mustered into service
in October 1861, I Company of
the 6th Vermont turns out for
drill and a company photograph.

Letters to Vermont

Chapter 7

From Battlefield to Campground with the Vermont Brigade

"A.A.C."

Albert A. Crane, 6th Vermont Regiment

The Vermont Brigade established a reputation for hard fighting, and all soldiers recognized its fighting prowess. But war was not constant battle. Soldiers spent much time in camp, where they constantly tried to overcome boredom. Albert Crane told the people at home how their boys lived while waiting for the bugles to sound the call to war.

Albert A. Crane was born in Bridport on December 13, 1836, the eldest child of Jesse and Amanda Crane. He was joined by seven other siblings: two brothers and five sisters. Jesse Crane, who had moved from New Jersey to Vermont with his brother, ran a successful farm and had a fine reputation as a Merino sheep breeder.

In 1859, Albert Crane entered Middlebury College in the class of 1863. After the Union defeat at Bull Run in July 1861 — proof the war was not to come to a quick resolution — President Lincoln issued another call for volunteers. Vermont responded by creating more regiments, and Crane left college to join up.

On October 3, Crane was enlisted by Capt. George Parker in Middlebury, becoming a member of Company A, 6th Vermont Regiment, for a term of three years. He was 24 years of age, five feet seven inches, with a light complexion, blue eyes, and light hair. The regiment was mustered into Federal service at Montpelier on October 15, with Crane as fourth sergeant in the company. After leaving Montpelier four days later, the regiment moved to Camp Griffin outside Washington on October 24, where it joined four Vermont regiments — the 2nd, 3rd, 4th, and 5th — to form the Vermont Brigade.

Crane did not immediately send correspondence to the *Rutland Herald*. He first endured the sickness that hit the Vermonters in the latter part of 1861 and early in 1862, and survived the actions of the Peninsular Campaign, where the brigade was bloodied. On August 21, 1862, he was promoted to second lieutenant in Company A. After the battles of South Mountain and Antietam, Crane was promoted again. His first lieutenant, Riley A. Bird of Bristol, was promoted to the captaincy of Company A, and on November 1 Crane took his position as first lieutenant.

The Vermont Brigade was not involved in the December battle of Fredericksburg, a stunning Union defeat, and went into winter quarters at Falmouth, Virginia. At the time of the Fredericksburg battle, Crane was on emergency leave for ten days to visit a critically ill sister in Vermont. He rejoined his regiment at Falmouth and had another leave in March 1863.

In May, the reinvigorated Army of the Potomac, under General Joseph Hooker, began a flanking movement around Lee's Army of Northern Virginia. The 6th Vermont remained fronting Fredericksburg with 26,000 other troops under the command of General John Sedgwick, whose orders were to capture Marye's Heights, the same fortified elevations which had held against Burnside's frontal assaults the previous December.

On May 3, while Lee was occupied with Hooker's army, Sedgwick made his move. The Confederate lines were now held by General Jubal Early's 10,000 men. In his first letter to the *Herald*, written four days after the action, Crane described the assault of the Vermont Brigade.

The region of Lee's 1863 invasion (right)
In a desperate gamble to break the North's will to continue the war, Lee drove northward into Pennsylvania in mid-1863, attempting to outmaneuver the Army of the Potomac and its two Vermont brigades; under Meade, the Union force hustled after Lee, keeping itself between the Confederates and Washington until the great battle was joined at Gettysburg.

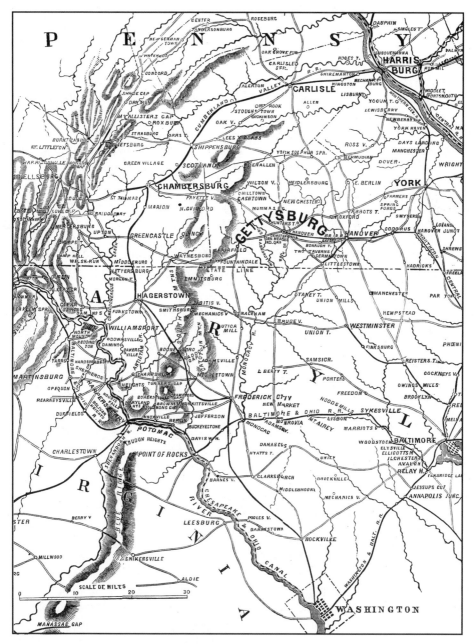

Camp near Falmouth, Va.
May 7th, 1863.

I briefly sketch for you the history of the Brigade, and more especially of the Regiment on the 3d and 4th of May.

The 6th Army Corps, to which the Brigade belongs, crossed the river during the evening of the 2d, and lying under arms during the night, at 4 o'clock in the morning of the 3d advanced to the attack of Fredericksburg. By taking advantage of several ravines, and under cover of our artillery, we had by eight o'clock reached a position near the city, and in front of the stone wall, and works which proved impregnable to our troops at the former attack. At about eleven, preparations for the assault having been completed, we advanced rapidly across the plain in front of the heights, the 2d and 6th Vermont Regiments being attached temporarily to the Brigade of Gen. Neil.[1] The enemy's artillery hurl their death dealing shell, plow our ranks, but still the advancing columns press onward and upward, until the stars and stripes wave over one after another of the enemy's works, and Fredericksburg is ours. But our task is not yet completed. We rest for a time, while Gen. Brooks' division[2] pursues the retreating enemy on the Gordonsville road, and engages him, but being checked after driving them a mile and a half, we are ordered forward to his support, and later are moved to the left, where we rest on our arms for the night.

The 4th of May opens with a quiet morning, but during the forenoon the rebel's artillery and infantry are seen moving past us to the left, and they have evidently been re-enforced. They move upon the heights at our left and rear, and take them with little opposition. We are now moved back to a position near the Gordonsville road. There is as yet little firing, and little is done until in the afternoon we see Gen. Anderson's division[3] coming to our front from the front of Gen. Hooker's army.[4]

We, (that is the Sixth Vermont) are at this time posted upon the slope of a hill at the left of the 1st Maryland Battery,[5] a noble Battery, manned by as brave a set of men as ever faced an enemy. This position commands a view of the broad open fields before us, over which the enemy's long grey lines are seen advancing. When they reach our front lines a terrific fight of artillery and musketry ensues, but our men, apparently overpowered, are forced to fall back, while the enemy, emboldened by success, press eagerly on. "Two second fuse,"[6] shouts the brave Captain of the Maryland Battery,[7] and about this time their line wavers, but they soon rally and are coming rapidly on. — "one second fuse," and soon "half second fuse, bring on the shells," cries the brave commander of the battery. They are close upon us, but still the men nobly serve their guns, and still our Regiments are ordered to lie down and hold their fire, though many are wounded by the shower of bullets which fall upon us from the right and left. But now the enemy are directly at the cannons' mouths. The battery is in danger, and is taken at double quick to the rear, its Captain shouting to us as he leaves: "Stand forth, boys; you are our only hope now." It is now time for us to act, and, rising, we pour a murderous volley into their ranks. "Forward charge!" is now the order of our commander, Col. Barney,[8] and in an instant, our unbroken line of bayonets is fronted to the foe, and with a shout we come on, but the grey-coated fellows not wanting the prospect of immediate impalement, turned en masse and fled, and then started a race, the like of which is rarely seen. It was the Green Mountain Boys versus the chivalry of Louisiana, as represented by the 7th and 9th Louisiana regiments of Gen. Early's Division. The chivalry had the advantage, however, in being a "little ahead," and in not being burdened with knapsacks. Yet we overtake large numbers of them, the rank and file throwing up their caps as they surrender, and the officers yielding up their swords with a dignity becoming men who had light[9] so bravely. We take as prisoner one colonel, three lieutenant colonels,[10] two majors, fifteen line officers, and two hundred and thirty-seven rank and file. After pursuing them about one-fourth of a mile it is deemed prudent to halt, as we would be entirely unsupported upon the field and Lieut. Butterfield,[11] aid to Col. Grant, riding up soon, informs us that the enemy are three-fourths of a mile to our rear, on both flanks, and we must retreat immediately, which is accordingly done. During the night with the rest of the brigade we cover the retreat of the corps across the Rappahannock. It was daylight, though fortunately foggy when the rest of us crossed the bridge at Bank's Ford.

A.A.C.

After the battle had ended and all was again at a stalemate, Crane could look back in retrospect at the struggle and his enemies. Though the Vermont Brigade had its successes, both at Fredericksburg and Banks' Ford, the rest of the Army of the Potomac had not fared that well. The Battle of Chancellorsville was Robert E. Lee's greatest tactical victory in the face of a numerically superior foe. The campaign, which had started so gloriously, ended in a dismal failure for Joseph Hooker, the Union commander, and reinforced the sense of the invincibility of Lee's Army of Northern Virginia.

June 2, 1863
From the Vermont Brigade
Camp of the 1st Vt. Brigade — Near White Oak Church
May 26, 1863.

It has been not a little encouraging to us here to see how soon and how firmly public confidence was restored at the North after the recent repulse of the army.[12] "Demoralization" throughout the country very quickly produces demoralization in the army, and the present healthy state of public feeling throughout the North cannot fail of exerting the most excellent influence here. I would not imply that we are in need of encouragement. On the contrary, so far as I am able to learn, (and I have enquired of those belonging to nearly or quite every corps) the best possible feeling prevails. The Vermont Brigade, which had not been at any time forced from its position, left the battlefield elated rather than despondent.

Fredericksburg is no longer a terror to those who have scaled its formidable heights, nor indeed to the rest of the army, since the recent movements have shown that we can force the enemy to leave it whenever it is desirable. There has been little or nothing added to the works at Fredericksburg since last December, thus showing that the enemy has long been convinced that the musket rather than the spade must decide this contest.

The same reckless fury with which the Confederate troops rushed to almost certain destruction at Fair Oaks, Malvern Hill, and elsewhere, was again exhibited in the recent contest. Their writers, I believe, attribute this to their patriotism, while ours regard it as the result of a too free use of whisky. There is another theory which I think more correct than either, viz: love of plunder. There is little doubt that their officers have encouraged this incentive to bravery and circumstances have greatly assisted them in this respect. In the earlier part of the war a soldier's knapsack contained almost as many notions as would suffice to stock a small country store, and it is as well known that at the first battle of Bull Run the rebel army secured a great amount of plunder. During the retreat from the Peninsula they met with similar good fortune, and "Greenbacks"[13] formed no inconsiderable portion of the spoil. It has unfortunately happened that the last two payments of the army were immediately preceding the first battle of Fredericksburg and the second battle of Fredericksburg and Chancellorsville. Thus it occurred that many who wished had no opportunity to send their money home and there are well attested cases where several hundred dollars were taken by rebel soldiers from the bodies of individual officers. When we consider the worthlessness of their currency, and their total want of the luxuries and almost the necessaries of life, it can easily be seen what an incitement to bravery must be the prospect of robbing our well paid soldiers.

The appearance of the prisoners captured affords little encouragement to those who hope to starve the South into submission. They were stout, healthy looking fellows, comfortably though coarsely clad, and said they had enough to eat — if they had not, short rations are certainly conducive to health. Last autumn they were really in a most destitute condition — one third of those taken during the Maryland campaign being barefoot — and probably next October will find them in the same condition.

It was amusing to notice that they were at first quite anxious in reference to their treatment by us officers, in some cases, insisting upon a promise of good treatment, before giving up their swords. One of the most intelligent of them told me that stories were current with them similar to those with us, in reference to cruel treatment of prisoners, and he supposed with as little reason. None but low, abandoned wretches, principally foreigners, he said, were ever so base as to ill treat a prisoner.

A.A.C.

Relative quiet existed in northern Virginia and western Maryland after the Chancellorsville campaign until Lee commenced his advance in early June north to Pennsylvania. Hooker set off in pursuit, but was replaced on June 28 by General George Meade. On July 1 the armies met at Gettysburg and the battle raged, with total casualties for the two forces amounting to more than 51,000. After marching more than thirty miles on July 1 and 2 under a broiling sun, the Vermont Brigade, along with the rest of the VI Corps, served as a rear guard during the battle. The brigade repulsed an attack by Lee's rear guard at Funkstown, Maryland, on July 10.

After Gettysburg, attention turned to another quarter, one quite unexpected. Implementation of the military draft ignited a spark in New York City and widespread anti-draft riots broke out. To quell the uprising the Vermont Brigade and other regiments were ordered to the city in mid-August. The hardened veterans of the Sixth Regiment were encamped at Tompkins Square, and Lieutenant Crane had temporary command of Company A. Regiments also were sent to other cities to enforce the draft.[14] The Vermont Brigade remained in New York City for a month. As New York cooled, Meade and Lee maneuvered in Virginia. In mid-September the brigade returned to the Army of the Potomac, and

The aftermath of a fight

A temporary resting place until the bodies could be reinterred in a military cemetery, these wooden headboards mark the fresh graves of men from the 6th Vermont who fell in a minor skirmish in Virginia.

in late November marched off into the Mine Run Campaign. Meade attempted to engage Lee in the region south of the Rapidan River, but was stymied by the Confederate entrenchments. This campaign proved very ineffective and unproductive, as Crane's narrative describes.

December 15, 1863
The First Vermont Brigade in the Late Advance
Camp near Brandy Station, Va.
December 5, 1863.

The experience of the Vermont Brigade, during the recent operations beyond the Rapidan, differed little from that of the rest of the army, but a few particulars may interest your readers.

We left our old camp near Brandy Station early on the morning of the 26th of November, after a tedious march crossed the Rapidan at Jacob's Ford about midnight, not until 10 o'clock at night were we able to eat our Thanksgiving dinner; but at that time I doubt not the soldier partook of his humble meal of hard bread, pork and coffee, with a keener relish than it knows to those who, at an earlier hour, sat at tables loaded with the choicest viands. Thus refreshed, we moved on and finally encamped, or rather halted, near the southern beach of the Rapidan, spread our blankets, and were soon asleep. Reveille is sounded at 4 A.M., accompanied by orders to take our breakfast and hold ourselves in readiness to march; but the morning passes without any movement. Skirmishing and cannonading are heard in front, when the 3d Corps, having crossed before us, is feeling its way forward. In the afternoon the firing rapidly increases, and we are sent forward some two miles or more, through what is very properly termed the "wilderness."[15] Approaching the battle-field we halt, but are soon thrown forward in very quick, and then in double-quick time, and form in line of battle in the woods at the right of those engaged.

It was noticeable that on approaching the field of battle, our course was at one time checked by the crowd of non-combatants, pioneers, waiters,[16] &c., &c., who were hastening to the rear with all possible speed. Few are aware of the large number of this class in the army, but when they muster their full force; that is, at any reverse or momentary alarm upon the battlefield, they sometimes seem to outnumber those with arms in their hands.[17]

As our part of the line is not engaged, and as we can see nothing, we have only to watch the progress of the battle by the sounds that reach the ear. We hear considerable musketry, sometimes a lively cannonade,

Mine Run and vicinity

After playing only a minor part in the Battle of Gettysburg in the summer of 1863, A.A.C.'s 6th Vermont spent many weary days marching and countermarching through the valley of Mine Run in Virginia, crossing and recrossing the Rapidan, often on the edge of battle, always close to Rebel defensive works and at risk of surprise attack by enemy raiders.

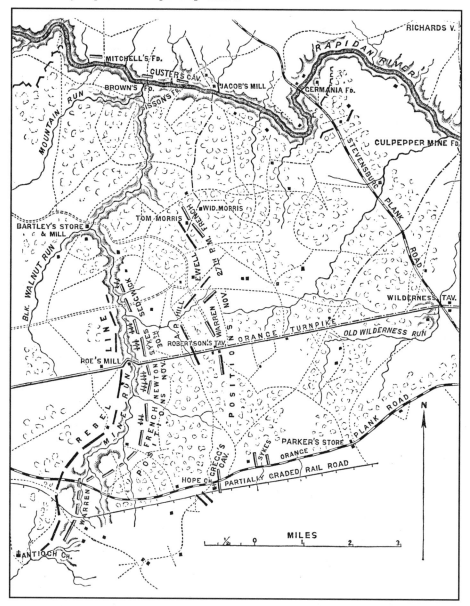

and a great deal of cheering or other yelling by both sides. We had supposed that the practice of employing noise to frighten the enemy belonged to the age of the spear and the shield, but is it practiced by both armies in this war and sometimes not without effect. I know of nothing more hideous than the demoniac yell of a rebel column advancing to the charge, and our boys are not far behind in this style of warfare.

Late in the evening all was quiet and we lay down to rest, but were aroused at one A.M., and were at once on the march, to join the 2d corps, as it was reported. At daybreak we halted for breakfast, but in a short time, with the 5th Vt. ahead as skirmishers, were in motion again. A drizzling rain soon set in, but still we moved on through the forest, crossing ravines, wading brooks and forcing almost impenetrable thickets, until at about noon we emerged from the wilderness, and saw before us the fortified lines of the enemy upon the hills on the opposite or left bank of Mine Run.

A little harmless skirmishing and equally harmless artillery practice, was all that would have been noticed by a casual observer upon the ensuing day, but it was evident that our generals were doing their utmost to ascertain the position and strength of the enemy, and the safest places to cross the insignificant, but rather ugly looking stream in our front. Night finds us quietly confronting the enemy, but late in the evening comes a notice that we must rise at midnight and cook our breakfast as another opportunity may not soon occur.

It is understood that we are to march to the right while the 5th corps takes our position, and that an attack is to be made at daybreak. We take our breakfast at the time appointed, and are soon in motion. As our course is near the enemy's outposts, strict silence is enjoined, yet the campfires of the enemy seemed to brighten up considerably soon after the movement commenced. We soon reached the position assigned us, and formed in three lines of battle, were ordered to lie down and sleep in our places, but on no account to build fires. The moon shone brightly, but the air was piercing cold, and while some spread their blankets and slept, many found it more comfortable to walk.

Day dawned but all was quiet in the valley of Mine Run, and we felt instinctively that there would be no battle. We spent the day in endeavoring to keep warm, and at night were glad to go back to our position of the day before, build fires and get supper. The next day passed quietly, though we heard the rumbling of wagon and artillery trains on the way to the Rapidan. At nine in the evening, our turn came and after a tedious night's march we reached the Rapidan at daybreak, at Germanna Ford, and passing two miles further on, halted for breakfast. The following day finds us again in our old camp at Brandy Station.

In conclusion, let me say that though the army would have welcomed an order to assault the enemy's lines, yet both officers and men believed that the rebels must have almost if not quite equal numbers with greatly the advantage of position, and all acquiesced without a murmur in the decision of the commander, that under such circumstances an attack was not advisable.

A.A.C.

The Army of the Potomac settled into winter quarters around Brandy Station. Crane's letters caught the essence of camp life and the emotions of the soldiers while they endured their third Virginia winter. Although more free time was available than during a campaign, discipline still had to be maintained. On December 18, Crane witnessed the execution of two Vermonters for desertion. No execution had been carried out previously in the brigade.

December 25, 1863
Execution of Deserters from Vermont Regiments
Camp of the Vermont Brigade
Dec. 19, 1863.

Yesterday for the first time, during this war, Vermont soldiers were executed for the crime of desertion. On that day private John Tague, 5th Vt. Vols., and private George E. Blowers, 2d Vt. Vols.,[18] having been convicted of desertion under aggravated circumstances, were shot to death by musketry in the presence of the Division.

At about three o'clock, P.M., the Division was placed in position at the designated point, forming three sides of a square enclosing the Commanding General with his staff. Soon after two ambulances, each containing one of the prisoners sitting beside the coffin closely guarded by a detachment of the Provost Guard, approached the Square. The detachment, twenty-four in number commanded by a Lieutenant, formed the detail to which was entrusted the execution of the sentence of death. The coffins were placed upon the ground by the side of two freshly dug graves, and the condemned persons took their place near them. A dirge was performed by the Band while the solemn preparations went on. Lt. Col. Stone,[19] acting Assistant General of the Division, then read the report of the proceedings of the Court Martial in each case, each one advancing a few paces and removing his hat, when his name was pronounced, and at the conclusion returning to his former position. They now knelt with the Chaplains of the 5th and 3d Vermont Regiments, while the latter offered prayer, after which, having conversed a moment with the prisoners, they shook hands with them and retired. The guard then took a position about twenty yards from and facing the prisoners who knelt upon their coffins while a Sergeant placed a target upon their breasts so as to cover their hearts. The guard was then brought to a "ready," the prisoners removed their hats, placing them upon a stake fixed in the ground near them, and brought their right hands to their hearts as a signal that they were ready; then followed with fearful distinction the words, "Ready, aim, fire," and with scarcely a groan both fell forward and instantly expired.

Tague maintained throughout an air of reckless indifference and even volunteered to assist in moving his coffin from the ambulance and to aid the Sergeant in adjusting the target. He was a desperate fellow, had deserted two or three times and was an inmate of the guard house nearly all the time while with his regiment. The other was evidently much affected by the awful fate awaiting him, but preserved a firm and resolute bearing to the last.

Thus closed a scene far more terrible than any of the horrors of war which it has thus been our fate to witness. Many a soldier who had never known fear in battle was awed to tears by the solemnity of the occasion. Yet there was no mawkish sympathy for those who had deserted a cause to which they had solemnly plighted their lives, and it seemed to be universally felt that their fate, though terrible, was just.

A . A . C .

During December 1863, army administration took steps to prevent the mustering out of troops in the middle of the next year's campaign. Regiments that had enlisted for three years in 1861 would have their terms expire, depriving the army of some its most veteran troops. To entice re-enlistments, a thirty-day furlough was granted to every soldier who signed on for another term of duty lasting to the end of the war. Men who took immediate advantage of this opportunity were hopeful to be home in time for the holidays, but the government stumbled.

From the Vermont Brigade

Camp near Brandy Station, Va.

Dec. 26, 1863.

Externally, all is very quiet here now, and were it not for an occasional tour of picket duty, we might forget that we were in an enemy's country or even that we belonged to an army at all. Winter, that paralyses the genial influences of nature, seems also to lull even the demon of war to temporary repose. The efforts, made last winter, to prevent a repetition of the "Quiet on the Potomac,"[20] resulted in a sad failure and winter campaigns are now regarded as worse than profitable.

But, although, for many days, not even the somewhat nervous cavalry in our front have disturbed us by the slightest alarm, yet the recent orders from the Department upon the subject of re-enlistments have produced more excitement in camp than would ordinarily precede a great battle. The possibility of spending the Holidays among their friends proved too much for those who have been "exiles from home" for more than two years, and could they have re-enlisted and received their furloughs as regiments which was at one time ordered, nearly all would have re-enlisted. The Fifth and Sixth with several companies from the other Vermont regiments engaged to re-enlist, and would have been already in Vermont had the Government let them alone long enough, but one order has countermanded another until the whole subject has reached a state of dim uncertainty, which is very perplexing to those who thought themselves certain of a sleigh ride in Vermont on New-Year's Day.

It now seems probable that the Government, not wishing to countermand an order almost as soon as issued, determined to smother it in a deluge of red tape and blank forms. Certain it is that the sublime art of "how-not-to-do-it" never before reached such a stage of perfection in this Army, not even when applied to the capture of Richmond.

As the case now stands, the Fifth Vermont is mustered into the service for three years unless sooner discharged, the muster to date from Dec. 15th, 1863; but the order under which they were re-enlisted has since been countermanded, and the *regiment* cannot be furloughed, while the men, I believe, decline to take a furlough unless given in accordance with the terms of their enlistment, by which the regiment was to go to Vermont for thirty days. But the soldiers are in earnest in this matter; two years hard service has not weakened their patriotism and of the Vermont soldiers I am sure that at least one half of those present who come under the terms of the order, will re-enlist in some manner, I am not well informed in respect to the regiments from other States.

A . A . C .

All the re-enlisted veterans deserving furloughs did receive them, but after Christmas. An additional incentive was offered to re-enlist more veterans. If a certain percentage of the men re-enlist-ed, the regiment would be designated as a "Veteran" regiment, a proud distinction of honor.

January 9, 1864
From the Vermont Brigade — The re-enlistments Change in Political Sentiments, &c.
Camp of the Vermont Brigade
[No Date]

Re-enlisting has ceased here for the present, and nearly all those who have re-enlisted, have received their furloughs. The following num-bers have re-enlisted in the different Vermont regiments, in the 2d, 100, the 3d, 148, the 4th, 168, the 5th, 250, in the 6th, 149, in all 815, being about three fourths of all the originally enlisted men in the brigade. As there are probably not more than twenty-five thousand men in this army, whose term of service will expire next summer, and at least half of those have re-enlisted, there is very little danger to be feared from this cause in this army at least.

The absence of the "veterans"[21] has given rise to the usual number of rumors of raids, "Lee moving down the Shenandoah," etc. The sending of a brigade from each corps to Harper's Ferry gives a coloring of truth to the latter report.

The holidays passed off very quietly here. "Commissary"[22] was dis-pensed of a little too freely, but generally the best of order prevailed.

Although the position of this army is scarcely any in advance of that occupied one year ago, yet the change in its morale is in the highest degree encouraging. There has also been a great revolution in political sentiments. This, though owing to various causes, is due in a great mea-sure, to the change in the character of the newspapers read here. Owing to the leisure afforded him, the soldier reads the newspapers much more than the same class of persons at home, and when this army read little but the New York Herald, it is easy to conjecture what its political faith, or rather want of political faith must have been.[23] But lately, the circula-tion and influence of the Herald have greatly declined, and for some time past the Washington Morning Chronicle paper, eminently loyal and scarcely inferior in either in size or ability to the leading New York dailies, has had a more extensive circulation in the army than any other paper. Nearly ten thousand copies of the Chronicle are sold here when the communication is regular. It reaches us as early on the day it is issued, thus being twenty-four hours in advance of the New York papers. The corps news agents also keep on hand for sale a great variety of periodicals, novels, etc., so there is no lack of reading matter here though it must be confessed its quality might be improved.

Those who wish to send anything to their friends here, need not hesitate on account of the risk involved, since communication, both by mail and express, is very safe and regular.

There is scarcely any sickness here at present, and the office of a Surgeon is almost a sinecure.

A.A.C.

Early in 1864, new recruits began to appear, bolstering the ranks of the Vermont regiments. The veterans proved willing teachers to the recruits. Their experience would prove useful in surviving disease and combat.

January 13, 1864
From the Vermont Brigade
Camp of the Vermont Brigade
January 9, 1864.

The advance guard of three hundred thousand men has arrived here. The first detachment of recruits for this Brigade came on the 5th instant and about the same number have reached here since that time. They are generally fine looking men and much larger than average of those now here. Few large or at least tall men remain in the old regiments. Very few deserted while on the way here. An unusually large proportion are French[24] but are none the worse for that. The French and Irish make good soldiers, but save us from the Dutchmen.[25] Take any shape but that.

It is surprising to see how soon these men become efficient soldiers. Associating constantly with those to whom every service is familiar by the time their first uniform has lost its brightness, they are almost as reliable as their more experienced comrades. Time and training can alone insure proficiency in the manual, but a recruit who has already sufficient knowledge of fire-arms to shoot a squirrel will get along very well on the field of battle.

Exemption from disease is not the least of the advantages gained by the recruit in joining an old regiment. Few new regiments pass a year in the service without losing many by disease while the recruits who have joined this army during the past eighteen months have suffered little from this cause. This is due partly to the fact that surgeons and officers have learned to take care of men, but mainly to the fact that the men have learned to take care of themselves. Experience teaches the soldier many little arts not given in books, which lighten his toil, lessen his hardships, and preserve his health, and thus the recruit acquires with ease what others have learned as the fruit of a long and costly experience. This is of more importance than is supposed. The young soldier fears only the dangers of the battle field, but disease is his greatest enemy. A good illustration of this is found in the report of the casualties during the Mexican war by the Adjutant General dated Dec. 3d, 1849. According to that report there were employed during the Mexican war an aggregate of 100,454 men. Of these 1549 were killed in battle and died of wounds while 10,986 died of ordinary disease. It may be thought that the losses in action during this war have been comparatively much greater and if we were to credit the dispatches of sensational newspapers correspondents of regiments "decimated, cut to pieces, that went into the field with six hundred men and came out with but fifty" &c., we might grant it, but old soldiers know how much such stories amount to and are thankful that they are not at the mercy of these blood thirsty knights of the quill, who think nothing of annihilating a regiment with a single stroke of the pen. But some one will ask, "Did not our army lose twenty eight hundred killed at Gettysburg?"[26] True, yet that was but three to one hundred of those engaged, and that and Chancellorsville where our loss was much less, are the only engagements of magnitude in which the army participated during the past year, while perhaps as many as a hundred and fifty thousand different men have belonged to it during the time. Besides, this army[27] has proportionately lost more than any other large army in the country.

I would not wish to depreciate the real dangers of the battle-field, but there has been so much exaggeration upon the subject that it seemed a few facts in reference to it might be useful.

A . A . C .

Living in Virginia proved interesting to these soldiers from Vermont. Terrain was flatter, soil often clay, and weather much hotter in the summers. The weather was a constant subject of discussion, and it was often compared with that of home. During the winter there was ample time in which to erect proper quarters. Vermonters had mastered the building techniques.

January 28, 1864
From the Vermont Brigade
Camp of the Vermont Brigade
Jan. 20, 1864.

An unusual number of citizens have recently visited this army. They express much surprise to find the men in so comfortable quarters, and many declare that our style of living is preferable to that at the Washington hotels.

Chaplain Webster,[28] of the Sixth Vermont Regiment, has recently procured of the Christian Commission a Chapel Tent, which, through his energetic efforts, seconded by members of the Regiment, has been raised upon stockades, and furnished with a desk, seats, a stove, &c, and forms a very comfortable and commodious place of worship. It is, I think, the first of the kind in the brigade since the winter of 1861-2.

Those who think this portion of the "Sunny South" has anything in common with those regions where flowers blossom and oranges ripen in January would have such ideas quickly dispelled by a brief visit here at this season. During most of the time since the first of the month the ground has been covered with snow, and the cold has been so intense that, on some days, a clear sun at mid-day would make no impression upon the snow, or the frozen earth where its surface was exposed. Just now, however, it is quite warm; heavy rains have fallen, and the depth of the mud does honor to the anniversary of the famous "Mud Fleet" expedition of one year ago.[29]

Detachments of recruits continue to arrive. Their unmilitary ways are a source of much amusement, but there is no disposition to vex the new arrivals, on the part of the old soldiers. They are too well pleased to have their assistance for this; and so they go to work with a will to help build their tents, and make them generally comfortable.

The construction of tents, or rather huts, for winter quarters, has become quite an art. Many of these structures display more skill, and are really more comfortable than the dwellings of the poorer citizens about here. The old soldier never waits for orders to build winter quarters, but whenever the army halts more than two days at a time, he proceeds to fell trees and "confiscate" unoccupied buildings, and soon the camp rings with the sound of the saw, axe and hatchet. He builds of logs or boards a box-like structure from six to ten feet square, according to the number who are to occupy it, for which the shelter tent makes an excellent roof, and fills also the place of windows. The interstices are "daubed with untempered mortar," that is, Virginia's "sacred soil," whose adhesive qualities render it invaluable as building material. A bedstead is made of poles, and covered with "Virginia feathers,"[30] while tables and chairs are improvised of hard bread boxes, &c. A fireplace in one corner, containing a blazing fire, makes all look bright and comfortable. As the tents of a company are always laid out in the form of a street, the camp of a regiment thus becomes a miniature village, and when built with taste is not without artistic effect. Thus snugly housed, the soldier laughs at the storm, and, so far as the substantial elements of comfort are concerned, is as well off as anybody in the world.

A.A.C.

Since the Army of the Potomac meant to stay in the vicinity of Brandy Station and Culpeper, the local citizenry found their Southern allegiance swaying if oaths of allegiance meant having their property left undamaged. A few even romanced or married Union soldiers.

February 19, 1864[31]

From the Vermont Brigade — More Re-Enlistments
Conjunction of Mars and Venus
Protection of Property, &c.

Camp near Brandy Station, Va.

[No date]

The usual quiet prevails here and it does not seem probable that it will be disturbed for some time. Veterans are returning daily in large numbers and receive a right hearty welcome. All seem as well pleased to return as they were to go home, and many came back several days before the expiration of their furloughs. Surely a soldier's life is not without its attractions, when those who had been absent from home for nearly three years, could not stay with their friends for the short period of thirty-five days.

The return of the veterans has given a new impetus to re-enlisting, as it is now expected that those who re-enlist will receive their furloughs immediately. Upwards of a hundred will probably leave the brigade for Vermont in a few days.

That remarkable conjunction of Mars and Venus recently noticed in some localities has also been visible in this region.[32] There have been several marriages of soldiers with Virginia's fair daughters, in this vicinity, and judging from appearances there is a prospect of several more. Ladies, who a year ago, were no doubt, affected with the most violent Yankee phobia, are now often seen escorted by Union officers and soldiers, and if they hate "those horrid Yankees" very badly, appearances are deceptive. The soldiers are getting to be on the best of terms with the citizens about here. The latter confess that our boys don't steal any more than the rebels, so there is no cause for quarreling on that score. Few families remain in the immediate vicinity of the camps, but at the houses nearer the picket line, groups of soldiers often gather in the evening before broad fire places and "fight their battles o'er again," while members of the family relate incidents told by their friends, just now on the other side of the Rapidan, with an occasional sarcastic remark which shows where their real sympathies are. A soldier, perhaps, tells how his regiment was surrounded at Fair Oaks; that there was a long line of rebels in front of us, we could see nothing but rebels and, "There," interrupts some pretty secesher, "that's exactly where I'd like to be!" All join in a hearty laugh which follows, and the hero of Fair Oaks grows suspicious that after all, his society is not so agreeable as that of some of those fellows of butternut hue,[33] who tent beyond the Rapidan would be.

However friendly these people may seem they never forget their secession sympathies, and though the men are more cautious, the women never hesitate to avow their enthusiasm for the "Southern cause," and their faith in its success.

The practice of granting safeguards to such citizens as may request it, where the army is in camp, has no doubt contributed much to the good feeling existing between the soldiers and those whom they are "subjugating." The term "safeguard" is applied both to the document given the owner of the property protected and to the non-commissioned officer or soldier stationed to enforce it. These guards are stationed not only at the houses in the vicinity of the camps, but often some distance beyond the picket line, where scouting parties from both sides render property especially insecure. When they are beyond the outposts they are also furnished with a safeguard, which reads something like this: "As the bearer is sta-tioned here solely to protect this property, if he is captured or injured in any way, this house and the adjoining buildings will be burned to the ground." Of course they are never harmed. Since the duties of a safeguard are much lighter than service in camp, the benefit is mutual, and while the guards are faithful in their trust, the families with which they are stationed treat them as one of their own members, and share with them the best they have. But enough for this time of secessionists and their property.

A.A.C.

Crane found himself caught up in the re-enlistment fervor and re-enlisted himself. The *Rutland Herald* made note of his appearance in the town as he was en route to Virginia after his furlough home. The paper stated Crane was "ready to do gallant service on the resumption of active military operations, and he will do it, when opportunity offers. Success to him."[34] Upon returning to Virginia, Crane immediately reopened his correspondence with the *Rutland Herald*. Camp life was improving and was less routine for both officer and enlisted man.

March 30, 1864
From the Vermont Brigade
Camp of the Vermont Brigade
March 25th, 1864.

On returning "to the front" after a few weeks absence, but little change is apparent. I could not, however, help noticing the improved appearance of the different camps. Though always kept scrupulously clean by a rigidly enforced system of inspection, they seem to have been policed with unusual care of late, a measure of no doubtful value at this season of the year.

The forests in the vicinity of the camps have been largely encroached upon this winter. Fire-wood for cooking purposes is drawn by government teams, but the men have to "forage" for their own tent-fires, and having exhausted the supply of stumps, boughs, &c., in the vicinity are now compelled to "back" wood a distance of from two to three miles. Let no one say the Army of the Potomac is doing nothing.

Much regret is felt here at the transfer of Gen. Howe[35] from the command of our division. Although not covetous of popular applause, we think few officers have won so deservedly the respect and esteem of all under their command.

Literary societies have been in successful operation for some weeks in the 3d, 4th, and 6th Vermont Regiments, and very generally, I believe, throughout the army. Weekly meetings are held in which the exercises consist of an oration, the reading of the "Vermont Volunteer,"[36] or some other journal yet unknown to fame, and a discussion of some popular question. The following are fair specimens of the subjects discussed, given in the interrogatory form: Is army life demoralizing? Ought the property of the rebels to be confiscated? Is there more to admire than condemn in the life and character of John Brown? These meetings are held in the Chapel tents, which though very large, are always crowded to overflowing.

A severe snow-storm prevailed here on the afternoon and evening of the 22d inst. It was accompanied by a violent north wind, and some whose duties compelled them to be out of doors, declared that they never before suffered so much from the cold. The thawing snow affords the boys much amusement at their favorite sport of snow-balling. Day before yesterday a regular engagement was fought by the 2d and 6th Vt. Regiments, in which there were charges and countercharges, a great waving of banners, and much noise of battle, of shouting and blowing of bugles; also there was much blood shed (principally from the noses of the combatants,) many were captured and re-captured, and innumerable deeds of mighty valor were performed on either side.

"Long time in even scale the battle hung."

But as an impartial chronicler I am compelled to admit that the brave veterans of the 6th, after contending long with vastly superior numbers, were at last forced to retire from the field, which they did in good order contesting the ground inch by inch.

I have nothing to indicate that the confidence of the army in Gen. Meade[37] has been weakened, though all are pleased that Lieut. Gen. Grant[38] is to establish his headquarters here. Gen. Grant came down from Washington yesterday and is expected to review the army as soon as the condition of the ground will admit.

A . A . C .

The arrival of General U.S. Grant announced that an advance would soon be under way. The Army of the Potomac discovered the new commander-in-chief would accompany their army, which indicated the soldiers would be in for serious work. Drill and target practice became more common, as did the harbingers of spring.

April 5, 1864
From the Vermont Brigade
Near Brandy Station, Va.
March 31, 1864.

An unusual amount of rain has fallen here during the past week and cold north winds have prevailed as might be conjectured since the ranges of the Blue Ridge are still covered with snow.

In spite of the cold weather, one sees many indications of Spring, in the vicinity of the outposts. Robins and other birds are numerous and lively, the reddish brown of the hillsides is rapidly changing to green, and beyond the lines the farmers are plowing as if intending to put in their crops as usual. In that large region occupied by the army, however, there is little left to mark the changes of the season, and in time a large portion of Virginia might well adopt those lines of the poet:

> "Seasons return, but not to me returns
> Spring, or the sweet approach of even or morn."

Target practice, by all three arms of the service, has recently taken the place, in part, of the ordinary drills, throughout the army. This most essential branch of military training has been, heretofore too much neglected, and a wonderful improvement has already resulted from the few hours thus far devoted to its practice. Owing to the long range of the rifled musket now in use, a small variation in the aim or a slight error in estimating distance, even if the aim is accurate, will render the fire of a regiment, directed against a line of battle quite within range, entirely harmless.

Six deaths have occurred in the Sixth Regiment during the past Winter. The measles, typhoid fever and pneumonia have been the prevailing diseases. It must interest all friends of the soldier to know that the hospital arrangements of the regiments here, have been this Winter, as nearly perfect as possible under the circumstances. The beds are supplied with everything necessary for comfort by the Sanitary Commission, an abundance of suitable food is furnished, reading matter is furnished by the Christian Commission and other sources, experienced surgeons are on duty at all hours of the night and day, and it is certain that only in very few cases could the sick receive better care at home than here.

A.A.C.

Recruiting for the five veteran Vermont regiments had been successful, and the men anticipated the start of the campaign. Weather, as usual, remained a constant topic of conversation.

April 11, 1864
From the Vermont Brigade
Camp of the Vermont Brigade
April 6th, 1864.

In this region March "went out like a lion" and April came in like the biggest of lions. We had rain, snow and sleet alternately, and for three days it has rained incessantly; those who have the good fortune to be in camp don't mind it, rather like it in fact, since at such times they have no fears of drills, reviews or marches before their eyes. But there is no help for the unlucky fellows who happen to be detailed for a three days tour of picket duty. There is much poetry in war, and the veteran soldier will find some mirth-provoking subject upon the most wearisome march, or even in the midst of danger, but I have yet to meet with one who could discover any amusement in walking his beat on the picket line, through the long night hours when the rain has made his blanket as porous as a sponge and his hands are so benumbed with cold as scarcely to be able to hold his musket.

No signs of a movement are yet apparent, and the statement published in the New York papers to the effect that all sutlers were ordered to leave this army by the 4th of April must have been premature. They are, on the contrary, remarkably lively just now, owing to the arrival of the paymaster.

Major Mason has just completed the payment of our brigade for the months of January and February, 1864.

This Brigade is now one of the largest in the army, drawing rations for upwards of 3,400 men. *And yet there is room.* The Fourth Vermont numbers less than the minimum, while the Fifth and Sixth are sadly deficient, and it is in consequence impossible to fill the vacancies occurring among the commissioned officers of those regiments, though there are numerous worthy non-commissioned officers who have nobly earned promotion.

It is reported here that those who have enlisted for the Seventeenth Vermont are to be assigned to this Brigade. If so, we can assure them of a right hearty welcome. It is certainly to be hoped that some arrangement might be made satisfactory to them. If they are anxious to tread the path of glory, they could hardly travel in better company than they could find here.

The army is in good condition in every respect, probably never better, except that some of the recruits are suffering from the diseases incidental to acclimation.

We doubt if the rebels ever faced so fine an army as that which Gen. Grant will lead in the ensuing campaign.

    A.A.C.

While drill and target practice were essential for a soldier's survival, reviews were not. In fact, they were not greeted enthusiastically by the troops. The closer it came to the opening of a campaign, the frequency of reviews increased.

The Vermont Brigade got their first glimpse of their new division commander, General George W. Getty. He was a West Point graduate, had been a division commander with the IX Corps, and most recently, the acting inspector general for the Army of the Potomac.

April 21, 1864
From the Vermont Brigade
Near Brandy Station, Va.
April 15, 1864.

Preparations for the ensuing campaign are going rapidly forward, though it must not be supposed they have just commenced. They began when the army went into winter quarters on the 3d of December, and since that time, though externally has been quiet, a vast deal of work has been performed. Unserviceable ordnance[39] has been repaired or replaced by new, all wagons, ambulances, caissons, gun-carriages, etc., have been repainted and repaired, and all unserviceable animals sent to Washington to recuperate while their places are filled with new ones. In fact everything pertaining to the army has been carefully inspected and put in marching and fighting order. When the weather would admit, the men have been subjected to long and fatiguing drills both for instruction and exercise. Thus treated, an army does not deteriorate in camp, but improves daily in health and discipline.

Recently, however, certain measures have been taken which point more directly to immediate movements. On the 13th inst. all surplus baggage was sent to Alexandria to be stored, and to-day the sutlers packed up all unsold goods and started for Washington. If found within the lines of the army after tomorrow their goods will be confiscated and themselves set to work on the fortifications. It is not probable that the Government will get many cheap laborers in this way. After all that has been said of sutlers we think them the least deserving the abuse they receive, of all that large class of persons who are making fortunes from the government and the army. Lately their prices have not been exorbitant, considering the personal and pecuniary risks they encounter, and many of them display courage and enterprise worthy of a better cause. I must confess we are a little sorry to see them leave this morning for the commissary's bill of fare is quite limited, and pork and hard tack are not very desirable for a steady diet in the summer months. But "hunger is the best sauce" and exercise is nearly as good, so we shall not be likely to want an appetite.

We have had a few days of comparatively pleasant weather, and drills and reviews are again in order. Our brigade was reviewed day before yesterday, by Gen. Getty, our new division commander. His review differed from some we have attended, in this that the object of the general seemed rather to see than to be seen. Of Gen. Getty we know but little save from his appearance, which however speaks strongly in his favor. The division now consists of four brigades.

You were correct in stating that the Vermont brigade is now the 2d Brigade, 2d Division, 6th Corps and might have added that it has retained that designation since June 1862. Few if any brigades in this army have remained intact and preserved their numerical designation so long. We had been thinking for some time that we wanted a Brigadier, and the appointment of Col. Grant[40] whose history is so closely identified with that of the brigade seems universally satisfactory. It is certainly gratifying in these days of political engineering, to know that it is still possible to win promotion by deserving it.

The transfer of the old Third corps to the Second[41] has been followed by "conduct prejudicial to good order and military discipline" on the part of some officers and men of the former who persist in treating with disrespect the badge of the Second corps. The old Third was justly proud of its reputation and not being accustomed to lower one's colors to the enemy, finds it difficult to yield up its organization and its distinction badge, borne on its brigade, division and corps colors on many well fought fields, to a rival in the contest for fame. Nothing serious is likely to result from it, but the ill feeling engendered is certainly to be regretted.

A.A.C.

Reviews and preparations for the coming campaign continued. A grand review was staged at Brandy Station for General U.S. Grant himself, and meant much work for every soldier in the army. Still, the soldiers kept themselves occupied with various forms of recreation.

April 28, 1864
From the Vermont Brigade
Camp near Brandy Station, Va.
April 23, 1864.

We are now having warm, dry weather, but still be quietly in camp and see no signs of an immediate change of programme. I suppose you of the North are anxiously waiting for the army to do something, but it is not a little remarkable that we who are more directly interested endure the delay with a great deal of patience. Soldiers, like many people who do not wear blue clothes, are gifted with a kind of mental inertia, usually denominated laxness. I think which is quite indispensable in the army. This may seem strange to those who think soldiers endowed with natures entirely different from those of other people, but the truth is that soldiers are not so much different from other people as other people are apt to think. Many seem to suppose while most persons have a decided aversion to sleeping on the ground, don't like stale bread and pork fat more than three times a day, object to carrying a load of fifty pounds forty miles per twenty-four hours, and have an especial horror of the noise, smoke, sulphurous smell, exploding shells, whizzing cannon shot, and other concomitants of the battle-field, that all these things have a peculiar charm to the soldier, who likes to march with blistered feet, never cares what he eats and drinks, cannot sleep in comfortable quarters, but revels in fiendish delight in the carnage of the battle-field. It is hardly necessary to add that this is a false impression. I would by no means imply that a regard for the wishes of the soldier ever delayed the movement of an army, for the way they are treated during an active campaign, shows conclusively that such minor items as the sleep, rest, food and safety of the soldier never enter into the calculations of those who are planning an engagement.

So much then in extenuation of the very complacent manner in which the army endures delays which caused so much apprehension in the minds of others. There is, however, still room for hope. Reviews usually precede the opening of a campaign, and the past week has been distinguished by an unusual number of them. On Monday, the 18th, the Sixth corps was reviewed by Lieut. Gen. Grant accompanied by Gen. Meade and the three corps commanders, Generals Sedgwick, Hancock and Warren.[42] The day was a fine one, and, at eleven o'clock there were assembling upon the field near the house of John M. Botts, many thousand men completely armed and equipped, each wearing his best uniform, white gloves included. Generals with their brilliant staffs were busily engaged forming their commands in line, aides were riding furiously in every direction as though the fate of a battle were at stake, the whole forming a rather bright picture in which prancing steeds, brilliant uniforms, glittering gun barrels, and star-spangled banners formed the most prominent features. At length the line was formed, the general with his staff appeared in front of the corps, in column by company and followed by the artillery of the corps, marched past the reviewing officer, officers saluting, colors dropping, as they passed, etc., etc.

Of course I have not attempted to describe the full ceremony of a review, which is a very ceremonious affair, since I fear the reading of such a description would be even more tiresome than the reality. Yet a review is by no means an idle parade, since it gives a general an opportunity to determine almost at a glance the condition of the clothing, arms, equipments and general efficiency of his entire command.

Horse racing has of late become almost a daily occurrence here. It is about the same as horse racing elsewhere. A large crowd of men, some on horseback and some on foot, assemble on "the course," two horses run as fast as they can, assisted by the whipping of their riders; one usually comes out ahead, an indefinite amount of money is supposed to change hands among the sporting fraternity, and then the performance is repeated so long as there are horses to run or men to bet. The horses occasionally run over a few soldiers, but it remarkable that very few casualties are known to have occurred in this way.

Furloughs not to exceed thirty days are now to be granted to six enlisted men in each regiment to enable them to attend the free military school at Philadelphia for the purpose of preparing for an examination before the board of managers of applicants for commissions in colored regiments. A preparatory examination is first required before a board now in session at Corps Head Quarters. It is evident that there will be no lack of applicants.

A.A.C.

St. Patrick's Day festivities

Off-duty soldiers of the Irish Brigade celebrated a St. Patrick's Day at their Falmouth, Va., encampment with this steeplechase, depicted in all its grandeur by Harper's Weekly, *which described the competition as being "indulged in with a realism that might have elicited the highest applause of the most famous race-grounds of the country."*

Letters to Vermont

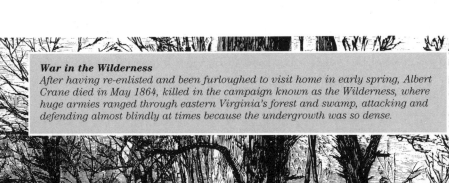

War in the Wilderness

After having re-enlisted and been furloughed to visit home in early spring, Albert Crane died in May 1864, killed in the campaign known as the Wilderness, where huge armies ranged through eastern Virginia's forest and swamp, attacking and defending almost blindly at times because the undergrowth was so dense.

On May 4, the Army of the Potomac finally broke camp. The time of inevitable waiting ended for Crane and the soldiers of the Vermont Brigade. Action was imminent, and it arrived much sooner than expected. The next day, May 5, Getty's Division was ordered to defend the vital intersection of the Orange Plank Road and Brock Road in the region termed the Wilderness, against the advance of General A.P. Hill's Third Corps. The fighting was horrific, and continued at the same intensity the following day.

The Vermont Brigade was in the forefront, augmenting its reputation as the "Bully Brigade." It suffered more than forty percent casualties. The *Rutland Herald* soon was printing the names of killed, wounded, and missing from the two-day conflict. The lists were long, and they shocked the whole state. In the edition of May 12, the following was printed:

> Capt A.A. Crane.— A special dispatch brings us the sad announcement that Capt. A.A. Crane of the 5th Vt. is among the killed in the recent Virginia battles. All who read the letters from the Vermont Brigade signed "A.A.C.," which have appeared in our columns from time to time need not be told that Capt. Crane was a young man of fine culture, of good talents and kindly disposition. He was also a brave and gallant officer.[43]

The *Herald* misstated Crane's correct rank and regiment, but the other facts were correct. On May 5, Lieutenant Albert Crane and his company commander, Captain Riley Bird, had died in the hard fighting for a road intersection in the Virginia Wilderness. The *Herald* printed further details two weeks later:

> "We learn that Lieut. Crane was not killed instantly, as at first reported, but died in an ambulance while being moved to a hospital about an hour after receiving his death wound."[44]

On Sunday, June 12, in the Congregational Church in Bridport, the Crane family held a funeral service in memory of their son. The sermon was delivered by Reverend Dr. Labaree, of Middlebury College, Crane's school for two years. After the service, a marble stone, carved with crossed flags and swords, was placed in Central Cemetery.

Like many others, Crane's body was not returned to Vermont. The stone in Bridport is to his memory, while in the Fredericksburg National Cemetery his remains lie with 15,000 other Union soldiers. The *Rutland Herald* summarized it best when it wrote of First Lieutenant Albert A. Crane upon receiving word of his death in the Wilderness:

He had seen much service and gave promise of much usefulness. He is now added to the long list of braves, who have died that their country might live.[45]

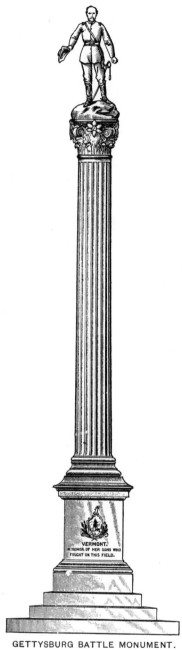

GETTYSBURG BATTLE MONUMENT.

In remembrance of soldiers

After the Civil War, many monuments were erected in Vermont and on the fields of battle, such as this one at Gettysburg commemorating the Second Vermont Brigade's action in the repulse of Pickett's charge; the fifty-foot high base is of Vermont granite, supporting a bronze statue of the brigade commander, General George J. Stannard.

Afterword

The letters of Albert A. Crane close out Volume I. Reading that he died in the tangled forests of the Wilderness in 1864 is a poignant reminder of the casualties of war: men, boys, struck down at a young age with their future unfilled. Crane, Lewis Dutton, and thousands of others, both Union and Confederate, made the ultimate sacrifice while fighting for what they believed in.

Vermont, with its population of 315,098 at the start of the war, put 34,238 men in the field, more than ten percent of the total population. Of that number, 5,224 died in battle, of wounds, in prison, or of disease. Unknown thousands carried to their postwar graves the physical or mental scars of this conflict to keep the United States one nation.

Vermont did its part.

A second volume of Letters to Vermont will follow, with six additional correspondents and their wartime experiences — along the Gulf of Mexico, as prisoners, as part of the garrison at Washington, and battling the cavalry of the Army of Northern Virginia.

General Notes

George Harper Houghton (ca.1824-1870)

Houghton learned daguerreotype photography in Brattleboro, Vermont, in the 1850s. For a few years he operated a studio in Kilbourn City, Wisconsin, to supplement his income as a carpenter. By 1859 he had returned to Brattleboro, where he opened a portrait studio. He was popular with newly enlisted soldiers who wanted carte-de-visites, small photographs of themselves in uniform, usually taken before they went off to war. In the spring of 1862, Houghton followed the First Vermont Brigade to the Virginia Peninsula, where he photographed scenes of army life in the field, including camps, troops drilling, artillery units, slave families, and battlefields. In early 1863 he photographed the Second Vermont Brigade at its encampment near Wolf Run Shoals in Virginia. Houghton died in Wisconsin in 1870.

James Hope (1818-1892)

Considered one of the most important landscape artists of the 19th century, Hope was born in Scotland, emigrated to Canada with his family at the age of three, then moved to Fair Haven, Vermont, in 1834. He was a working artist — with studios in Montreal, Castleton, Vermont, and New York City — by the time he enlisted in the 2nd Vermont, serving as a captain and a topographical engineer. He painted several Civil War scenes, including a view of the First Bull Run battle and four scenes of the Battle of Antietam. Hope died in 1892 in Watkins Glen, New York, where he had a studio and gallery.

Civil War Military Organization

Armies — Usually two or more corps; in the Union Army under the command of a major general; in the Confederate Army under either a full general or lieutenant general.

Corps — Two or more divisions under the command, in the Union Army, of a major general; in the Confederate Army, of a lieutenant general.

Division — Two or more brigades under the command of a major general. In the Union Army divisions were often commanded by brigadier generals.

Brigades — Units formed of two or more regiments early in the war; later four to five or more regiments became standard as regimental strength was reduced by casualties. A battery of artillery was sometimes included in the brigade, which was under the command of a brigadier general or a senior colonel.

Regiments — Commanded by a colonel, this unit consisted of ten companies of infantry or twelve troops of the cavalry. In the Union Army there existed, on paper, regiments of artillery which consisted of ten batteries, but in the field batteries were usually assigned to various formations on an individual basis. Confederate artillery was often organized in "battalions" of several batteries, attached to divisions or corps.

Companies — The smallest administrative unit in the army; the company was usually under the command of a captain. Termed "troops" in the cavalry, "batteries" in the artillery. Batteries in the Union Army were of six guns, in the Confederate Army, there were four. The company was a soldier's "home," the group of men with whom he was most closely associated throughout his military life.

Unit Designations

In the Union Army all units were designated by numbers: e.g. the Vermont Brigade consisted (for most of the war) of the 2nd, 3rd, 4th, 5th, and 6th Vermont regiments. It was officially designated the 2nd Brigade, 2nd Division, VI Army Corps, Army of the Potomac.

In the Confederate Army brigades, divisions and corps were often referred to by the commander's name. This could cause problems when the commander was killed or wounded and subsequently replaced by another officer. Artillery batteries were referred to either by the commanding officer's name or by their own special titles, e.g., Rockbridge Artillery, Washington Artillery.

Ranks in the Union Army

Lieutenant general — three gold stars.

Major general — two gold stars.

Brigadier general — one gold star.

Colonel — gold eagle.

Lieutenant colonel — silver oak leaf.

Major — gold oak leaf.

Captain — two gold bars.

1st lieutenant — one gold bar.

2nd lieutenant — as for 1st Lieutenant, but with no bar.

Sergeant major — three curved stripes over three chevrons.

1st sergeant — diamond above three chevrons.

Sergeant — three chevrons.

Corporal — two chevrons.

Private — no rank insignia.

Commissioned officers commonly wore shoulder-straps — rectangles of colored cloth — blue for infantry, yellow for cavalry, and red for artillery; straps displayed a metallic embroidered rank insignia. They were bordered in gold embroidery, and were sewn to each shoulder of the uniform coat.

Non-commissioned officers wore large cloth chevrons on both sleeves made of cloth lace or ribbon (silk or worsted) in the color of their branch of service, for example yellow chevrons in the cavalry.

Other Military Terms

Adjutant — Regimental officer who managed the administration of the unit, such as issuing daily orders and maintaining regimental books.

Artificer — Skilled tradesman who served in units that maintained wagons and equipment, and worked on special construction projects, such as fortifications, bridges, or railroads

Chaplain — At the regimental level, an enlisted clergyman who conducted religious services and ceremonies.

Picket guard — Small groups of soldiers stationed in a chain (or line) of posts beyond their unit's main line; serving defensively as guards, they watched for the approach of the enemy, and for infiltrators, scouts, and suspicious persons. Picket duty was a routine part of the soldier's military life.

Provost guard — Military police, headed by a provost marshal.

Quarter master — An commissioned or non-commissioned officer whose duty it is to assign living quarters or camps for the troops and to provide them with rations, ammunition, clothing, equipment, etc. Quarter Masters were found at all levels — from company to army, with a corresponding increase in rank.

Skirmishers — Soldiers sent out ahead of the main line of battle to act as "feelers" to determine enemy movements and positions, thus helping to prevent the main force being surprised or to prepare the way for an advance. At times, especially in densely wooded terrain, whole regiments or brigades would form massive skirmish lines during battle.

Sutlers — Independent civilian contractors permitted to accompany the army and sell wares — such as food items, beverages, and personal supplies — not normally supplied through the military.

1 Early in the war, gray was typically worn by state militia companies, and the first three Vermont infantry regiments were attired in this color. The 2nd and 3rd Vermont Regiments were later issued uniforms of blue. Of course, the Confederate use of gray led to confusion on the battlefield early in the war.

2 Benjamin Underwood was the first Vermont soldier to lose his life in the conflict. Before the war ended, 5,223 would join him; he died of an undetermined illness, not in battle.

3 U.S. Senator Benjamin Wade of Ohio.

4 J. Wolcott Phelps, colonel of the 1st Vermont Regiment.

5 Both vessels saw action in March 1862 against the Confederate ironclad *Virginia*. The *Cumberland* was sunk in the engagement.

6 Edmund A. Morse of Rutland, whom McManus would have known before the war.

7 Members of the 7th New York Regiment.

8 Major-General Benjamin Butler of Massachusetts, the local commanding officer.

9 William Howard Russell, special correspondent, considered one of the most authoritative writers of the war.

10 John Boardman Page, state treasurer of Vermont during the war years, and later governor, 1867-1868; Frederick Chaffee was a merchant who had served in the Rutland Light Guard and had designed their militia uniforms.

11 *Rutland Courier*, November 29, 1861.

12 *Rutland Herald*, January 7, 1864, and February 25, 1864.

Notes to Chapter 2 "*Sigma*"

1 Vermont Adjutant-General Henry Baxter.

2 Newton H. Ballou.

3 Richard Smith.

4 William T. Burnham.

5 James H. Walbridge.

6 Volney S. Fullam.

7 David L. Sharpley.

8 George J. Stannard, commander of the 9th Vermont.

9 Francis V. Randall.

10 Henry Whiting.

11 Elijah S. Brown.

12 The band was dissolved in 1862.

[13] The editor has found no detailed account of why the Winooski company was replaced by the company from Vergennes.

[14] Vermont Governor Erastus Fairbanks.

[15] Sabin is referring to firearms. The 2nd Vermont received not rifled muskets as expected, but an issue of obsolete Springfield muskets.

[16] Newton Stone.

[17] Erastus Fairbanks.

[18] Perley P. Pitkin.

[19] John Howe.

[20] William W. Henry.

[21] John S. Tyler.

[22] The Shenandoah River flows northward, so the lower end of the valley is near Maryland and West Virginia.

[23] Secession or Secessionist.

[24] Edward Hastings Ripley.

[25] First Lieutenant Samuel H. Kelley.

[26] John C. Stearns.

[27] Second Lieutenant Alfred C. Ballard, a *Herald* correspondent known as "A.C.B."

[28] Captain Charles Jarvis of Company D.

[29] Major General John Wool, the seventy-eight-year-old commander of the Department of Virginia and a veteran of both the War of 1812 and the Mexican War.

[30] Members of the 1st Rhode Island Cavalry Regiment. Four of this regiment's companies were from New Hampshire.

[31] Commanding heights north of town and the Potomac River.

[32] East of town and the Shenandoah River.

[33] The 3rd Maryland Potomac Home Brigade Infantry.

[34] Battery of light artillery from Indiana.

[35] Captain Silas F. Rigby.

[36] Colonel George J. Stannard

[37] Union intelligence in 1862 usually inflated the size of Robert E. Lee's Army of Northern Virginia. In reality, Lee had approximately 40,000 men.

[38] Linus E. Sherman.

[39] The other three officers were Captain David W. Lewis and Lieutenants Erastus W. Jewett and Justus Dartt.

[40] This camp was located a quarter mile from Camp Douglas; it became the 9th Vermont's home for one month before the regiment moved to Camp Douglas.

[41] Disloyal cowards.

[42] Lieutenant Colonel Dudley K. Andross.

[43] Colonel Dixon Miles.

[44] Aldace Walker, letter to his father, March 18, 1863; Vermont Historical Society, Montpelier, Vt.

Notes to Chapter 3 "L.T.D."

[1] The Goshen town clerk has no record of Dutton's birth. It was either in 1838 or 1839.

[2] Three years was the length of the enlistments; the Second Regiment was raised in June 1861

[3] In honor of Vermont's adjutant general, H. Horace Baxter.

[4] Breed N. Hyde, the regiment's first lieutenant colonel.

[5] Dutton changed his pseudonym from "D," to "L.D.," to "L.T.D." and "Ell Tee Dee."

[6] Unidentified.

[7] Lieutenant John T. Greble, 2nd United States Artillery, a Vermont native.

[8] Battle of Big Bethel.

[9] Baxter did not recover sufficiently, and Proctor replaced him as regimental quartermaster.

[10] Wheelock G. Veazey.

[11] David T. Corbin.

[12] Thomas Nelson. The rank of colonel was honorary.

[13] Captain Mooer never served in the regiment. The Calais company was mustered in under the command of Elon O. Hammond.

[14] Nelson D. Adams, who directed the brigade band until the end of the war.

[15] Known also by his nickname of "Baldy," earned from his thinning hair.

[16] Quartermaster general for the state of Vermont.

[17] Cloth covering for a cap with a flap to protect the back of the neck.

[18] Colonel John W. Phelps, 1st Vermont Regiment, still on duty at Fortress Monroe. Phelps was promoted to brigadier general before he could be offered the colonelcy of the 3rd Regiment.

[19] Edwin Stoughton subsequently was selected as colonel of the 4th Vermont Regiment.

[20] United States Army.

[21] The campsite is now covered by the headquarters building of the Central Intelligence Agency.

[22] The soldiers in camp.

²³ Senator James Henry Lane of Kansas, an ardent supporter of Lincoln, emancipation, and arming of slaves.

²⁴ A bold nickname, considering the 5th Vermont had not seen any action.

²⁵ December 20 engagement between forces out foraging the Virginia countryside. Dranesville is halfway between Alexandria and Leesburg.

²⁶ A division, composed of three brigades made up of regiments referred to as Pennsylvania Reserves and commanded by Brigadier General George McCall.

²⁷ The colonel of the 5th Vermont was Henry Smalley, who had been recruited for the command from the Regular Artillery.

²⁸ Lewis A. Grant, eventually commander of the Vermont Brigade from the Fredericksburg Campaign of December 1862 until the conclusion of the war.

²⁹ "Z" was a frequent civilian contributor of letters to the editor.

³⁰ General George B. McClellan. Dutton is describing a form of punishment.

³¹ Regimental campsite before Camp Griffin.

³² 5th Pennsylvania Cavalry Regiment, nicknamed after Lincoln's first secretary of war, Simon Cameron of Pennsylvania.

³³ Commander of the detachment, 5th Pennsylvania Cavalry. He cannot be identified.

³⁴ Brigadier General William F. "Baldy" Smith, who commanded the division of which the Vermont Brigade was a part. Smith's Division was a component of Erastus Keyes's IV Corps.

³⁵ Members of the 5th Pennsylvania Cavalry.

³⁶ Battle of Mill Springs, January 9, 1862; Confederate Brigadier General Felix Zollicoffer was killed in the engagement.

³⁷ La Mountain was another early American balloonist.

³⁸ Thaddeus Lowe, who implemented the new technology of aerial reconnaissance by balloon and a rival of La Mountain.

³⁹ La Mountain was a common surname in this Vermont town west of Brandon.

⁴⁰ This was a way of acquiring a medical disability discharge.

⁴¹ See the letters of "E.R.R." for more details of this expedition.

⁴² General Ambrose Burnside's expedition to Roanoke Island.

⁴³ This is quite a colorful metaphor.

⁴⁴ Due to a shortage of manpower, the Confederacy implemented a conscription act a year before the Union.

⁴⁵ Dutton had no liking for Confederate soldiers, and certainly wanted them to pay a hard price for their role in the war.

⁴⁶ Very early American style football.

⁴⁷ Captain of Company H, Charles W. Seagar of Brandon.

⁴⁸ This peninsula is the land between the James and York rivers.

[49] Site of the first line of Confederate defenses.

[50] Private Peter Brady was the first 5th Vermont soldier injured in combat.

[51] This is a description of the engagement at Lee's Mills.

[52] Dutton's term for Southerners.

[53] Magruder's surrender was pure rumor.

[54] The Pamunkey River drains into the York River at West Point, Virginia.

[55] Dutton is referring to Wilson Ager's "coffee-mill gun," a hopper-fed weapon that proved to be rather ineffective. The Gatling gun, introduced in limited quantities in 1864, proved more effective as the first true machine gun.

Notes to Chapter 4 "E.R.R."

[1] Major General Benjamin Butler.

[2] Some of these troops were destined to be on the expedition to capture Port Royal, South Carolina.

[3] Battery E, 3rd United States Artillery. It bore the name of its battery commander in the Mexican War. It had just participated in the first battle of Bull Run.

[4] One of the original proprietors of the Maryland colony.

[5] Railroad cars.

[6] Colonel of the 21st Massachusetts Regiment.

[7] Brigadier General Thomas W. Sherman.

[8] John A. Andrew, wartime governor of Massachusetts.

[9] Sergeant William H. Button of Sheldon, Company A, 5th Vermont Regiment.

[10] Brigadier General Ambrose Burnside of Rhode Island.

[11] Commodore David Porter.

[12] Maryland legislature came into session.

[13] Confederate fortifications opposite Fortress Monroe.

[14] This was a 3.67-inch bore, rifled field piece with a long range.

[15] A large seacoast artillery piece.

[16] Brigadier General Jesse Reno, killed at South Mountain, Maryland, on September 14, 1862.

[17] Lieutenant Colonel Alberto C. Maggi.

[18] The name of regiment's colonel is incorrect; it should be Augustus Moore.

[19] The body of water south of Roanoke Island.

[20] Though this ship was smashed to pieces, the crew did not suffer any loss.

[21] Navy Captain Louis M. Goldsborough, commander of the Union's North Atlantic Blockading Squadron.

[22] Elizabeth City was the southern terminus of the Dismal Swamp Canal, which connected Norfolk, Virginia, with Albemarle Sound.

[23] In the Confederate Army.

[24] Better known today as tuberculosis.

[25] *Rutland Weekly Herald*, June 19, 1862.

[26] Correct spelling is New Bern.

[27] Reed is describing the battlefield of March 14, 1862, outside New Bern.

[28] Fought on April 19, 1862.

[29] Charles T. Campbell.

[30] Colonel William S. Clark.

[31] Better known as the *Virginia*.

[32] Also sunk by the *Virginia*.

[33] The Army of the Potomac.

[34] Named after the brigade commander, Colonel Edward Ferrero.

[35] A landing approximately ten miles northeast of Fredericksburg.

[36] Brigadier General King led a division in General Irwin McDowell's III Corps, which was under the overall command of John Pope.

[37] Confederate General Thomas "Stonewall" Jackson.

[38] Henry A. Wise, governor of Virginia from 1856-1860.

[39] Salt pork.

[40] Reed is referring to the Orange and Alexandria Railroad; the troops probably mounted the cars at Rappahannock Station.

[41] Another name for the engagement at Cedar Mountain.

[42] Confederate cavalry commander Major General James Ewell Brown "JEB" Stuart.

[43] Cavalry under the direction of Stuart.

[44] Now the site of Walter Reed Army Hospital in Washington, D.C.

[45] Paroled prisoners.

[46] Lieutenant Colonel Joseph P. Rice was killed at Chantilly on September 1, 1862. The 21st Massachusetts suffered its greatest number of casualties in this engagement, nearly 150 of fewer than 400 engaged.

[47] Edwin R. Reed Pension Record, National Archives, Washington, D.C.

Notes to Chapter 5 "*B*"

[1] Blunt, a native of St. Johnsbury, had served in both the 3rd and 6th Vermont Regiments.

[2] "First Families of Virginia."

3 James Kemper, later a major general in the Confederate Army.

4 A hard biscuit made of flour, salt, and water.

5 Stoughton, of Bellows Falls, had been colonel of the 4th Vermont Regiment.

6 Henry H. Baxter of Rutland, who in 1861 had served as Vermont's adjutant general.

7 Fought on September 1, 1862.

8 Until 1988 the site lay relatively undisturbed, but since has been covered with townhouses.

9 Town southeast of Fairfax.

10 This is inaccurate; Stuart's force numbered about 1,800.

11 Roswell Farnham.

12 Confederate General Thomas "Stonewall" Jackson.

13 Battle of Fredericksburg, December 13, 1862.

14 Landon was on furlough.

Notes to Chapter 6 "J.C.W."

1 The wording of this sentence is unclear and two words are illegible, but the reference is to April 19, 1861, when the 6th Massachusetts Regiment (militia) was attacked by a pro-secession mob while the troops were changing train stations in Baltimore on their way to protect Washington. Four soldiers and twelve civilians were killed.

2 From the start of the war, a majority of the citizens of Baltimore were pro-Southern and many Union troops chose to avoid the city in transit.

3 Brush huts.

4 Adoniram J. Blakeley.

5 Private Elias S. Baker.

6 Private Francis Nash.

7 Major General Ambrose Burnside who, as the new commander of the Army of the Potomac, was advancing on Fredericksburg.

8 No packs.

9 Colonel William T. Nichols, commander of the 14th Vermont.

10 Colonel Asa Blunt, commander of the 12th Vermont.

11 Better known as "hardtack," a quarter-inch-thick hard cracker of unleavened flour. The crackers were not known for their taste and were quite unpopular.

12 Williams could be describing the First Bull Run of July 21, 1861, or the Second Bull Run, August 29-30, 1862.

13 Split rail fences.

14 Full packs.

[15] Lieutenant Colonel Charles W. Rose.

[16] Major General Franz Sigel.

[17] Major General Nathaniel P. Banks.

[18] *Rutland Herald*, 25 December 1862.

[19] Confederate cavalry commander Major General J.E.B. Stuart.

[20] This raid is also described by "B" in a letter dated January 2, 1863.

[21] Major Nathaniel B. Hall.

[22] Captain Ransom O. Gore.

[23] Captain John C. Thompson.

[24] Sergeant Harley G. Sheldon.

[25] The word "vice," in military terms, means "to replace."

[26] Lieutenant Lewis P. Fuller.

[27] Battle of Chancellorsville, considered to be Robert E. Lee's greatest victory.

[28] Major General Joseph Hooker, commander of the Army of the Potomac, who replaced Ambrose Burnside after his failures as army commander.

[29] Many Union regiments which had enlisted for two-year terms were scheduled to leave the Army of the Potomac in May and June.

[30] Similar to a modern pup tent.

[31] Tents made from government-issued shelter halves. Soldiers would put several together to make a shelter.

[32] Brigadier General George J. Stannard, commander of the 2nd Vermont Brigade.

[33] Confederate General Robert E. Lee.

[34] This was the sound of a cavalry engagement at the town of Aldie, Virginia, between Confederates under Colonel Thomas Munford and Union horsemen led by Brigadier General Judson Kilpatrick.

[35] Many of these nine-month regiments were greeted with ill-regard by three-year veterans for the shortness of their enlistments and because substantial enlistment bounties had been paid.

Notes to Chapter 7 "A.A.C."

[1] Brigadier General Thomas H. Neill, commander of the 3rd Brigade.

[2] Brigadier William Brooks, one-time commander of the Vermont Brigade, now commander of a division in the VI Corps.

[3] Confederate Major General Richard Anderson's division, part of Longstreet's Corps.

[4] This engagement was fought around Bank's Ford.

[5] Battery A, 1st Maryland.

6 On spherical case shot, a hollow cannonball filled with bullets, there was a fuse which could be set for a certain number of seconds so it would explode the shot in front of the advancing enemy's lines, scattering the bullets.

7 Battery commander was Captain J.H. Rigby.

8 Colonel Elisha Barney, commander of the 6th Vermont.

9 Crane is sarcastically referring to the rapid retreat of the Confederates.

10 Two of the captured field officers were Colonel Leroy Stafford, 9th Louisiana, and Colonel Trevanion Lewis, 8th Louisiana.

11 Frank Butterfield.

12 Though the army had been defeated, public sentiment apparently rebounded quickly.

13 Union paper currency.

14 *Rutland Herald*, August 26, 1863; Crane Service Record.

15 The Vermont Brigade again would be in this region in May 1864.

16 Pioneers were soldiers who assisted in road-clearing, bridge-building, while waiters were often soldiers on detached duty to members of the general and field officer staff.

17 Regiments always had large numbers of men on some form of detached duty which reduced their combat-effective ranks.

18 Tague was a private in Company A, 5th Vermont; Blowers a private in Company A, 2nd Vermont.

19 Newton Stone was with the 2nd Vermont.

20 The byword when McClellan commanded the Army of the Potomac while it lay inactive outside Washington during the winter of 1861-1862.

21 Those re-enlisted men on furlough.

22 Liberal rationing of alcohol.

23 It can be gathered from this sentiment of Crane's that the *New York Herald* favored the Democratic Party policy of achieving peace over victory.

24 French-Canadian.

25 This comment was directed at the Germans, who were ridiculed for their poor fighting ability.

26 Actual Federal deaths were 3,155.

27 Army of the Potomac.

28 Alonzo Webster.

29 This is a reference to General Burnside's failed flanking maneuver in January 1863, when the weather turned wet and bitter. That expedition became known as the "Mud March."

30 This could refer to either "acquired" feathers from geese or ducks, or pine boughs; Crane does not clarify.

31 This letter was not dated in the paper.

Chapter Notes

[32] Crane is humorously speaking of the God of War meeting the Goddess of Love.

[33] Often the Confederate soldiers did not wear uniforms of gray, but those that had been dyed with butternuts.

[34] *Rutland Weekly Herald*, March 17, 1864.

[35] Brigadier General Albion Howe, who was transferred to command of the Artillery Depot in Washington and also directed the Office of the Inspector of Artillery.

[36] Probably the poem composed by Julia Ripley Dorr of Rutland.

[37] Major General George G. Meade, commander of the Army of the Potomac. There was some belief that since Grant was planning to accompany the Army of the Potomac, he had little confidence in Meade's capabilities.

[38] Ulysses S. Grant, commander-in-chief of the Union armies.

[39] Artillery pieces.

[40] Brigadier General Lewis A. Grant. He had entered the service as a major in the 5th Vermont and had led the brigade since February 1863.

[41] The consolidation of several of the corps of the Army of the Potomac into larger units was met with great uproar. Men had strong loyalty to their old corps and hated to see the units broken up. To ease the transition, men were able to retain the old corps badges, which they were proud to display.

[42] Major General John Sedgwick, VI Corps; Winfield S. Hancock, II Corps; and Gouverneur Warren, V Corps.

[43] *Rutland Herald*, May 12, 1864.

[44] *Rutland Herald*, May 31, 1864.

[45] *Rutland Herald*, May 12, 1864.

Acknowledgments

No book can be completed by an individual. One person takes the role of coming up with the idea and then following through, but must be supported by a cast.

This book would not be complete without noting the assistance of Springfield, Vt., Town Librarian Russ Moore; and also the assistance of the Rutland Free Library and the Rutland Historical Society, who permitted me to pore over the Civil War volumes of the *Rutland Herald*. The town clerks of Rutland City, Castleton, Clarendon, Bridport, Goshen, and Poultney — all in Vermont — were most helpful in allowing me to search vital records, and they assisted in the search. The National Archives and Veterans Administration answered my requests for service and pension records, and the Chicago Historical Society tracked down the obituary of Albert Sabin.

Other archivists and librarians were also of great assistance, especially Paul Carnahan and Barney Bloom of the Vermont Historical Society and Jeff Marshall of Special Collections of the University of Vermont.

I always appreciated the words of support from my friend, Nick Picerno of Springfield, Vermont, encouraging me to see this project to completion and giving helpful hints to trace down leads on the writers.

Ron Toelke and Barbara Kempler-Toelke did excellent work in layout, design, and production, and Stuart Murray oversaw the editing of the book and the assembling of those final details. Much appreciation goes to Tordis Ilg Isselhardt, publisher of Images from the Past, who saw my work's potential as a book.

Great words of thanks go to my wife Betsy, who supported my work on this project and exhibited a world of patience as I deliberately transcribed the letters from photocopied newsprint to computer. Without her urging, the project might not have been published and would have remained in a file cabinet.

Sources of Illustrations

Front cover, 6-7, 26 (top), 62-63, 170 (bottom): Courtesy Vermont Historical Society

Back cover, 25, 31, 40: The Bennington Museum, Bennington, Vermont

ii, 3, 18-19, 58 (top), 72-73, 88, 126 (bottom), 130-131, 135, 140-141, 143, 146 (bottom), 150, 155, 158, 178-179: Special Collections, Bailey/Howe Library, University of Vermont, Burlington

viii, xiv, 10-11, 12, 16, 46, 86, 90, 96, 100 (middle), 118, 166, 168-169, 181, 204: Various sources including *The American Conflict : A History of the Great Rebellion* Vols. I and II, Horace Greeley, O.D. Case & Co., Hartford, 1864 and 1866

xii-xiii, 14: Rutland Historical Society, Rutland, Vermont

22-23, 26 (middle and bottom), 52-53, 83, 92-93, 96 (bottom), 112-113, 146 (middle), 162-163, 170 (top and middle), 199: *Official Portfolio of War and Nation: The Civil War in the United States*, Marcus J. Wright (ed.), G. J. Stanley, Washington, 1907

24, 79, 95, 96 (top), 104-105, 106, 108, 126 (top), 132, 161, 173, 202-203: *Harper's Pictorial History of the Civil War* Parts First and Second, Alfred H. Guersey and Henry M. Alden, McDonnell Bros., Chicago, 1866 and 1868

146 (top): S.L. Griffith Memorial Library, Danby, Vermont

Bibliography

Benedict, George G. *Army Life in Virginia*. Burlington, Vt: Free Press Association, 1895.

—. *Vermont in the Civil War*. 2 vols. Burlington, Vt: Free Press Association, 1886–88.

Boatner, Mark. *The Civil War Dictionary*. New York: David McKay Co., 1959.

Catton, Bruce. *Glory Road*. Garden City, N.Y.: Doubleday and Co., 1952.

—. *Mr. Lincoln's Army*. Garden City, N.Y.: Doubleday and Co., 1951.

—. *A Stillness at Appomattox*. Garden City, N.Y.: Doubleday and Co., 1952.

Davis, William C., ed. *The End of an Era*. Vol. 6 of *The Images of War*. Garden City, N.Y.: Doubleday & Co., 1984.

Editors of Time–Life Books. *The Civil War*. 30 vols. Alexandria, Va.: Time–Life Books, 1983–1987.

Faust, Patricia L. *Historical Times Illustrated Encyclopedia of the Civil War*. New York: Harper & Row, 1986.

Fisk, Wilbur. *Hard Marching Every Day*. Eds. Emil and Ruth Rosenblatt. Lawrence, Kan.: University Press of Kansas, 1992.

Frye, Dennis E. "The Siege of Harpers Ferry." *Blue & Gray Magazine 5* (August–September 1987).

Furguson, Ernest B. *Chancellorsville 1863 — The Souls of the Brave*. New York: Alfred A. Knopf, 1992.

Hayes, Lyman Simpson. *History of the Town of Rockingham, Vermont*. Bellows Falls, Vt.: n.p., 1907.

Hearn, Chester G. *Six Years of Hell*. Baton Rouge, La.: Louisiana State University Press, 1996.

Hennessy, John J. *Return to Bull Run*. New York: Simon & Schuster, 1993.

Hyde, Arthur L. and Frances P. *Burial Grounds of Vermont*. Bradford, Vt.: Vermont Old Cemetery Association, 1991.

Johnston, Robert U. and Clarence C. Buel, eds. *Battles and Leaders of the Civil* War. 4 vols. New York: Century, 1887–1888.

McPherson, James M. *Battle Cry of Freedom*. New York: Ballantine Books, 1988.

Military Service Records and Pension Records, National Archives, Washington, D.C.

Murfin, James V. *The Gleam of Bayonets*. New York: Bonanza Books, 1965.

Peck, Theodore. *Revised Roster of Vermont Volunteers*. Montpelier, Vt.: Press of the Watchman, 1892.

Pension Record, Veteran Administration, White River Junction, Vt.

Rhea, Gordon. *The Battle of the Wilderness May 5–6, 1864*. Baton Rouge, La.: Louisiana State University Press, 1994

Ripley, Edward Hastings. *Vermont General*. Ed. Otto Eisenschiml. New York: Devin–Adair Company, 1960.

Rutland Herald. Rutland, Vt.

Rutland Weekly Herald, Rutland, Vt.

Sauers, Richard. "Burnside in North Carolina." *Blue & Gray Magazine* 5 (August 1988).

Sears, Stephen W. *Chancellorsville*. Boston: Houghton Mifflin Co., 1996.

—. *To the Gates of Richmond*. New York: Ticknor & Fields, 1992.

Stackpole, Edward J. *Chancellorsville*. Harrisburg, Pa.: Stackpole Books, 1958.

Sturtevant, Ralph Orson. *Pictorial History of the Thirteenth Regiment Vermont Volunteers War of 1861–1865*. n.p., 1910.

Teetor, Paul R. *A Matter of Hours*. Rutherford, N.J.: Fairleigh Dickinson University Press, 1982.

United States Census, 1850.

United States Census, 1860.

United States War Department. *The War of the Rebellion: A Compilation of the Official Records of the Union and Confederate Armies*. 128 parts in 70 vols. and atlas. Washington, D.C.: Government Printing Office, 1880–1901.

Warner, Ezra J. *Generals in Blue*. Baton Rouge, La.: Louisiana State University Press, 1964.

Warner, Ezra. *Generals in Gray*. Baton Rouge, La.: Louisiana State University Press, 1959.

Williams, John C. *History and Map of Danby, Vermont*. Rutland, Vt.: McLean and Robbins, Independent Office, 1869.

—. *Life In Camp*. Claremont, N.H.: Claremont Manufacturing Co., 1864.

Index

Note: Illustrations and maps are indicated by ***bold italics***

1st Maryland Battery, 174
1st Massachusetts Regiment, 151-52
1st Rhode Island Cavalry Regiment, 47
1st Vermont Artillery, 4
1st Vermont Brigade, ***6-7***, ***70***, 91, 172, 177, 195, 197 fighting ability, 164, 170-71, 200
1st Vermont Cavalry, 154
1st Vermont Regiment, 128
    at camp in Brattleboro, Vt., ***18-19***
    at Camp Butler, 17-24
    disbanding of, 24
    at Fortress Monroe, 14-17
    recruitment and mustering, 13-14
    Rutland Company (Rutland Light Guard, K), 13-14, 17, 24
    Woodstock Company, 17
    See also McManus, M.J.
2nd Massachusetts Battery, 137
2nd U.S. Sharpshooters, Company E, 3
2nd Vermont Brigade, 137, 145, ***146***, 147, 153, 155, 159, 160, 161, 164, 165, 177, 204
2nd Vermont Regiment, 28, ***170, 178-79***
    Bennington Company, (A), 28, 30, 32, 35
    Brattleboro Company, 42
    departure for south, 38, 43
    with 1st Vermont Brigade, 70, 171, 174
    Fletcher Company (H), 28, 29, 34, 35, 38
    hospital of, 28
    Ludlow Company (J), 30
    Montpelier Company (F), 28, 33, 42
    mustering ceremony, 40
    training and provisioning, 28-43, 65, 68
    Tunbridge Company, 28, 40
    Vergenne Company, 66
    Waterbury Company (D), 28, 42
    Winooski Co. (Green Mountain Guard), 34, 36-37

See also Sabin, Albert E.
3rd Maryland Regiment, 50
3rd Vermont Regiment, ***62-63***, 171
    in Lee's Mills battle, 88
    mustering and deployment of, 69-70
    raising and recruitment, 59-60
    Springfield Company, 66
    training and provisioning of, 60-68
    Wells River Company, 66
    See also Dutton, Lewis T.
4th Vermont Regiment, 70, 153, 171, 192, 195
5th New Hampshire Regiment, 5
5th Pennsylvania Cavalry Regiment ("Cameron's Dragoons"), 79-81
5th Vermont Regiment
    at battle at Savage's Station, 95
    at battle of Williamsburg, 89-91
    at Camp Griffin, ***3***, 24, 70-84
    camp near Brandy Station, 193
    casualties and illness, 71, 77, 78, 80, 89, 91-95, 101
    Brandon Company (H), 70, 95
    march to Alexandria, 84
    Mine Run campaign, 182
    recruitment and training, 70-74
    re-enlistment, 185-86, 195
    at Yorktown and Lee's Mills battles, 87-89
    See also Dutton, Lewis T..
VI Army Corps, 174, 177, 198
6th Vermont Regiment, 70, ***170***
    in Banks Ford battle, 174-75
    casualties among, ***178-79***, 194
    enlistment and mustering, 171
    in Funkstown, Md. battle, 177
    I Company, ***170***
    in Lee's Mills battle, 88-89
    Middlebury Company (A), 171-72
    in Mine Run campaign, 180-82
    in the Peninsular Campaign, 172
    in the Wilderness campaign, 200
    winter quarters (Brandy Station, Va.), 180-99
    See also Crane, Albert A.
7th Louisiana Regiment, 175

7th Massachusetts Battery, 116
7th Vermont Regiment, 4
IX Corps, 119, 121, 195
9th Louisiana Regiment, 175
9th New Jersey Regiment, 111
9th Vermont Regiment, 31, **40**, 159
  battle and capture at Harper's Ferry, 27, 48-51
  at Camp Sigal (Winchester, Va.), 44-48
  at parole camp, 49, 51-56
  training and mustering, 44-45
  See also Sabin, Albert R.
10th Vermont Regiment, 127
11th Vermont Regiment, 127
12th Vermont Regiment, ***xii-xiii, 126, 135***
  with 2nd Vermont Brigade, 128, 149, 153, 154-55, 156, 157, 160
  at Camp Vermont, 128-34, 149
  Company B, 137
  Company G, 137
  disbanding of, 145
  at Fairfax Court House, 134-39
  at Gettysburg, 145
  recruitment of, 128
  Rutland Light Guards (Company K), 128
  at Warrenton, Va., 160
  at Wolf Run Shoals, ***130-31, 140-41***, 145
  See also "B"
13th Vermont Regiment, 137, 149, 151-56, 165
14th Vermont Regiment, 142
  Camp Vermont (Alexandria, Va.), 148-53
  Company A, 158
  Company B, 149, 158-59
  Company G, 149, 159
  Company H, 150, 159
  Company K, 149, 157, 159
  Fairfax Court House, Va., 154-57
  Gettysburg, 165
  recruitment and mustering of, 147-48
  return to Vermont, 165
  Wolf Run Shoals, 157-65
  See also Williams, John C.

15th Vermont Regiment, 142, 145
  at Camp Vermont, 149
  duty near Occoquan Creek, 151-52
  duty near Fairfax Station, 154-56
16th Vermont Regiment, 142, 149, 153, 155-56, 165
17th Vermont Regiment, 195
21st Massachusetts Regiment
  with the Burnside Expedition, 102-16
  casualties among, 98, 102, 107, 111, 115, 124-25
  with McClellan's march to Richmond, 116-19
  with IX Corps, 119-25
  Worcester Company (A), 97, 99
  recruitment and training, 97-102
  See also Reed, Edwin R.
26th Pennsylvania Regiment, 152
32nd, 33rd Ohio Regiments, 50
51st New York Regiment, 103, 111
57th Pennsylvania Regiment, 116
125th New York Regiment, 153

A

A tents. *See* camps; shelter
Acquia Creek Landing, 120
Adams, Nelson D., 66
adjutants, 208
Albemarle Sound, N. C., 103, 111
  maps of, ***106, 108***
alcohol, 66, 102, 107, 176, 186
Alexandria, Va., 85
  Camp Vermont at, 128-33
allotment law, 76
ambulances, 68, 184, 196. *See also* wagons
amputations, 110-11. *See also* casualties
Anderson, Richard, 174
Andrews, John A., 101
Annapolis and Elk Bridge Railroad, 98
Annapolis, Md., 97-102, 103
Arlington Heights, Va., 148
arms. See weapons
Army of Northern Virginia, 2, 119, 160,

172, 175. *See also* Lee, Robert E.

Army of the Potomac, 2, 48, 139, 155, 195
  under Burnside, 154-55
  under Grant, 193-200
  under Hooker (pursuit of Lee), 2, 145, 160-65, ***162-63, 170***, 172-77
  under McClellan (Peninsular Campaign/March on Richmond), 47, 84-94, 139
  winter quarters (Brandy Station), 183-93
  See also battle descriptions; troop movement and individual regiments

Army of Virginia (Union), 119

artificers, 208

artillery. *See* weapons

B

"B"
  letters from Camp Vermont, 128-33
  letters from Fairfax Court House, 134-38
  letters from Wolf Run Shoals, 139-44
  See also 12th Vermont Regiment

Baker, Elias S., 149-50

Ballard, Alfred C. ("A.C.B."), 45, 51

balloon surveillance, 80, ***90***. *See also* intelligence

Ballou, Newton H., 28

Baltimore, Lord, 98

Baltimore, reception of troops in, ***26***, 45, 148

bands, regimental, 35, 66, 74, 99. *See also* recreation

Banks Ford (Fredericksburg, Va.), battle at, 174-75

Banks, Nathaniel P., 121, 154

Barney, Elisha, 175

Barrett, James, 4

battle descriptions
  Banks Ford, 174-75
  Bull Run, second battle of, 122-25
  Fairfax Court House defense, 137-39, 156-57
  Harper's Ferry, 49-50

Harriet Lane engagement, 17
  Lee's Mills, 87-89
  Marye's Heights, Fredericksburg, 174
  Mine Run campaign, 180-83
  Monticello engagement, 15
  Roanoke Island, 110-14
  Williamsburg, 89-91

battles, preparation for, 36-39, 41, 115, 137-38, 149, 152, 156, 174, 196. *See also* battle descriptions; camp life; troop movement

Baxter, Henry H., 28, 69, 135

bayonets. *See* weapons

Beaufort, N. C., 114

Bellows Falls *Argus*, 20

Bellows Falls, Vt., 69

Bennington Regimental Band, 35

Benson, Vt., 125

Big Bethel, battle at, 21, ***22-23***, 66

Bird, Riley, 200

blacks, 20. *See also* slaves

Blakeley, Adoniram J., 149

Blowers, George E., 183-84

Blue Ridge-Fredericksburg area, ***118***

Blunt, Asa P., ***126***, 127, 151, 157

Boston Rifle Company, 20

Botts, John M., house of, 198

Bowie knife. See weapons

Brady, Peter, 88

Brandon, Vt., 24, 27, 59, 70, 101

Brandy Station
  battle at, 161
  winter quarters at, 183-99

Brattleboro, encampment at, ***18-19***, 44, 148

breastworks. *See* battle descriptions; weapons

Bridport, Vt., 171, 201

Bristol, Vt., 172

Brooks, William, 174

Brown, Elijah S., 34

Brown, John, 76, 192

Buel, D. H., 42

Bull Run, 152
  first battle of, 70, 98

second battle of, 48, 118, 122-25

burials, 15-17, 24, 57, **58**, 91, 95, 107, 136-37, **178-79**, 201. *See also* casualties

Burlington Regimental Band, 66

Burlington *Times*, 54-56

Burlington, Vt., 27
    Camp Underwood, 28-43
    farewell to 2nd Regiment, 43
    1st Methodist Church, 36
    Fire Companies, 33
    support from women of, 34-35, 36

Burnham, William T., 28, 29, 35, 38

Burnside, Ambrose (Burnside Expedition), 81, 101-116, 119, 150, 154, 172

bushwhackers, 45

Butler, Benjamin, 21, 98

Butterfield, Frank, 175

Button, William H., 101

C

Cain, William J., 28

Caledonia County, Vt., 60, 68

Camden, NJ, 148

Cameron's Dragoons, 78, 81

camp life
    disciplinary actions, 28, 33, 36-37, 42, 77-78, 183-84
    drills and training, 32, 37, 65-66, 67, 70-71, 81, 102, 120, 152, 155-56, 158, 160, **170**, 187, 193-96
    false alarms, rumors, 70-71, 126, 149, 151-52, 155, 159, 186
    illness, 44, 47, 49, 58, 66, 69, 78, 102, 107
    monotony, 30, 37, 70-71, 77, 158, 171
    morale, 4, 32, 38, 44, 56, 65, 66, 69, 129, 142-44, 176, 186, 197
    parades, reviews, 3, 29, 40, 44, 71, **72-73**, 83, 101, 115, 122, **140-41**, 196, 197, 198
    during parole, 51-53, 122-23, 124-125
    picket/guard duty, 20, 45, 71, 74, 76-79, 99, 123-24, 126, 130-32, 134, 142, 145, 149-52, 154-56, 159-60,

185, 191, 195, 208
    recreation and leisure, 33, 35, 40, 83-84, 100-101, **135**, 143-44, 156, **170**, 186-87, 191-93, 198-99
    religious observances, 21, 36, 42, 189, 192, 208
    rigors of, 74, 99, 102, 120-21, 133, 195
    sanitation, 3, 67, 192
    scouting expeditions, 17, 21, 151
    weather's effects on, 33, 77-78, 81, 85, 89, 120, 126, 160, 165, 193-95
    See also battles; camps; civilians; clothing and equipment; food and rations; shelter; troop movement *and individual regiments*

camps
    Advance, 78
    Andrew (New Bern, N.C.), 115
    Baxter (St. Johnsbury, Vt.), 59, 61, **62-63**
    at Brandy Station, Va., 183-99
    at Brattleboro, Vt., **18-19**
    Butler (Newport News, Va.), 17-24
    at Cedar Mountain, Va., 121
    Chase, 148
    Douglas (Chicago), 51, **52-53**
    Ferraro (Fredericksburg, Va.), 120-21
    at Falmouth, Va., 172, 174
    field, 87, 134, 137, 139, 142, 148, 151, 157, 158
    Fortress Monroe (Va.), **12**, 15-16
    Griffin, **3**, 25, **58**, **72-73**, 171
    Seward, 148
    Simeon (Newport News, Va.), 117
    Tyler (Chicago), 51, 54-56
    Underwood (Burlington, Vt.), 28-43
    Vermont (Alexandria, Va.), 128-32, 149-50, 152
    at Wolf Run Shoals, 139, 145, **155**, 157, **158**
    winter quarters, 3, 6-7, 62-63, 74, 148, 154-57, 172, 183-99
    See also battle descriptions; food & rations; marches; shelter; troop movement *and individual regiments*

Cantine, George, 4

casualties
    from accidents, 20, 81, 89, 98, 107, 149, 158

from battle, 74, 79, 82, 88, 91, 109-114, 124, 138, 156, 175, 177, 188, 200
from disease, 15, 67, 71, 77, 80, 102, 107, 110, 117, 150, 187-88, 194
See also battle descriptions; burials; horses; hospitals

Cavendish (Vt.), 66

Cedar (Slaughter's) Mountain, Va., battle at, 96, 121, 123

censorship, 1-2. *See also* newspapers

Centreville, Va., 80, 82, 122, 124, 134

Chancellorsville campaign, 2, 175

Chantilly battleground, 137-38

chapel tents, 189, 192. *See also* shelter

Chase, J. B., 34

Chase, Z. G., 29

Chickahominy River, 94

Christmas holidays, 135, 136, 185-86

citizen-soldiers. See recruitment; volunteer army

City of New York (steamer), **104-105**, 107

civilians, Union
criticisms of soldiers by, 54-56, 160
reluctance to enlist, 28, 47-48, 128
morale of, 176
support and relief for troops, **26**, 33-36, 41, 45, 68, 74, 94, 124, 146, 148
sutlers, 74, **83** 195, 196, 208
visits to Union camps, 21-24, 33-35, 39, 41, 42-43, 189
See also Confederates: civilians; newspapers; noncombatants

clothing and equipment
in battle, 175
Confederate, 82, 177
disposal of on capture, 54-55
of 1st Vermont Regiment, 13
on marches and drills, 17, 74, 85, 102, 115, 120, 137, 153, 198
of 2nd Vermont Regiment, 28, 30-32, 36-37
shoes, 34
tack, 68
of 3rd Vermont Regiment, 65-68

winter, 17
See also Quarter Masters

Colvin, Nora (Mrs. J.C. Williams), 167

communications. See telegraph

Concord, NH, 68

Confederate
civilians, 45, 90-91, 120, 190-91
property, 85, 91, 120, 132-33, 189, 191
soldiers, 80, 82, 109, 111, 176-77
See also prisoners *and individual battles*

confiscation, 65

Congress (warship), 117

Connecticut Valley, 60

conscription. *See* recruitment

Corbin, David T., 66

court martial, 42

Crane, Albert A. ("A.A.C.")
background and enlistment, 171
burial and memorials to, 201
illness, 172
letters from Brandy Station, Va., 180-99
letters from northern Virginia, 174-77
in New York City, 177
promotions, 172
re-enlistment and furlough, 192
wounding and death, 200
See also 1st Vermont Brigade; 6th Vermont Regiment

Cross, Edward, 5

Culpeper, Va.
battle of, 47, 121
relations with locals at, 190-91
Court House, 121
See also Brandy Station

Cumberland (war ship), 17, 117

Custis, Martha Dandridge, 91

D

Danby, Vt., 3, 167

Dartmouth College, 47

Davis (Quarter Master General), 30, 68

defenses. *See* battle descriptions; camp life; weapons

Denver, CO, 167

deserters
    among new recruits, 42, 187
    execution of, 183-84
    See also disciplinary actions

disciplinary actions
    for absence without leave, 42
    for disobedience, insubordination, 28, 36-37
    for minor infractions, 33
    "Virginia overcoats," 77-78
    for desertion, 183-84

discipline. See drills and training

disease and illness, 47, 51, 58, 69, 78, 91,102, 107, 142, 165-66, 187-88, 195
    post-war, 125, 165-66

Dorr, Julia Ripley, x

draft riots, 177

draft. *See* recruitment

Dranesville, battles at, 74, 79, 157

drills and training
    Camp Griffin, 70-74, **72-73**
    clothing for, 120
    of new recruits, 187
    in use of arms, 37, 66
    in Vermont, 30-33, 37, 61, 65-66
    while waiting for action, 70-74, 81, 102, 152, 155-56, 158, 160, 193-96
    during winter, 77, 196
    See also camp life

Duncklee, J.J., 33

Dutton, Lewis T. ("L.T.D.")
    birth and background, 59
    enlistment, 70
    letters from Camp Baxter, 59-70
    letters from Camp Griffin, 70-84
    letters during the Peninsular Campaign, 85-95
    memorial to, 95
    physical description, 70
    wounding, death and burial, 95
    See also 3rd Vermont Regiment; 5th Vermont Regiment

dysentery. *See* disease

E

Early, Jubal, 172, 175

Elizabeth City, N.C., 110, 111

executions, 183-84

F

Fair Oaks, Va., battle at, 94, 176

Fairbanks & Company, 68

Fairbanks Scale Company, 65

Fairbanks, Erastus, 13, 38, 40, 65, 68-70

Fairfax Court House, Va., 134, 137, 151, 153

Fairfax Station, 139, 151, 156, 164

Falls Church (Va.), 75, 85

Falmouth, Va., 172, 199

false alarms. *See* camp life

Farnham, Roswell, 139

flags, **25**, 33-34, **40**

Floyd gun. *See* weapons

fly tents. *See* shelter

food and rations
    cooking, 67, 192
    costs, 17, 20-21
    in Confederate camps, 88, 177
    for prisoners and parolees, 56, 124
    foraging (pilfering) for, 121, 150, 152
    hard tack, 99, 117, 121, 123, 133, 180, 196
    in hospitals, 91-94, 194
    on holidays, 100, 101, 133, 180
    on marches, 115, 123, 134, 136-38, 142, 151-52, 154, 180, 182
    salted meat, 117, 121, 180, 196
    in Union camps, 109, 117, 133, 143, 196
    in Vermont training camps, 32-33, 36, 61
    See also Quarter Masters; supply depots; sutlers

Fort Hatteras, 107

Fort Macon, N. C., 114

fortifications. See battle descriptions; weapons

Fortress Monroe, **12,** 15-16, 20, 87, 103, 117, 119

Frayser's Farm, battle at, 86
Fredericksburg, Va., **6-7**, 119, 123, 150, 152, 154, 164, 172, 176
  battles at, 5, 139, 155, 159, 174-75
  National Cemetery, 201
Fredonia, N. Y., 57
French-Canadian soldiers, 187
Fullam, Volney S., 30
Fuller, Lewis P., 159
furloughs, 184-185, 199

G

gambling, 170
German soldiers, 21, 187
Germanna Ford, 182
Getty, George W., 195, 200
Gettysburg, 5, 145, **161**, 165, **166-69**, 172, 177, **204**
Goldsborough, Louis M., 107
Gordonsville Rd., 174
Gore, Ransom O., 158
Goshen, Vt., 59, 95
Grant, Lewis A., 75, 197
Grant, Ulysses S., 175, 193, 198
Grebble, John T., 66
Groveton, Va., battle at, 122
Guinon, William, 28

H

Hall, Henry M., 3
Hall, Nathaniel B., 159
Hancock, Winfield S., 198
hard tack. See food and rations
Harper's Ferry, W. Va., **26**, **46**, 48-51, 154
Harriet Lane (steamer), 17-20
Harrison's Landing, Va., 117
Hatch, Assistant Quarter Master, 20
Hatch, W. B., 69
Henry, Lieut. William W., 42
Hill, A. P., 200
Hilton Head, SC, hospital at, **96**
homesickness, 4, 44, 101. *See also* camp life: morale

Hooker, Joseph, 2, 160, 172, 174-75
Hope, James, 6, 82, 206
horseracing, **170**, 198-99, **199**
horses, 55, 68, 74, 82, 90, 94, 138, 156, 196. *See also* wagons
hospitals, 3, 28, 68
  in Baltimore, 95
  at Camp Ferrero, 120
  conditions in, 3, 110-114, 117, **143**, 194
  floating, 91, 116
  at Harper's Ferry, 51
  at Hilton Head, SC, **96**
  at Naval Academy, 98
  at New Bern, 115
  at Roanoke Island, 111-14
  at Savage's Station, 95
  at White House, Va., 91-94
  See also casualties; disease
Houghton, George Harper, 126, 155, 206
housing. See shelter
Howe, Albion, 192
Howe, John, 40
Hyde, Breed N., 61, 66

I

intelligence, military, 45, 76, 80, 82, 87. *See also* newspapers
Irish soldiers, 187

J

Jackson, Thomas "Stonewall," 44, 45, 48, 96, 120-21, 139
James River, 87, 116-17
Jarvis, Charles, 47
Johnston, Joseph E., 84, 89, 94

K

Kelley, Samuel H., 45
King, Rufus, 120
Kingsley, Levi G., 128, 139
Knox, Bertha (Mrs. J.C. Williams), 167

L

La Mountain, John, 80
Ladd, Adjutant, 38
Landon, Walter C., 128, 133, 142
Lane, James Henry, 71
Larabee, Rev. Dr., 201
Lee, Robert E., 2, 48, 91, 94, 118, 121-22, 164-65, 172, *173*, 175, 177. *See also* Army of Northern Virginia
Lee, William H.F., 91
Lee's Mills, battle at, 87-89
leisure activities. *See* camp life: recreation
Lewinsville, Va., 75, 78
Life in Camp (Williams), 167
Lincoln, Abraham, 116, 127, 171
living quarters. *See* shelter
London *Times*, 21
Lonergan (Green Mountain Guard), 34, 36
Longstreet, James, 122, 124
Lord, W. H., 34
Lowe, Thaddeus, 80

M

Mackey, Helen (Mrs. Albert Sabin), 57
Maggi, Alberto C., 103
Magruder, John, 87, 89, 91
mail, 61, 107
    importance of, 2, 4, 47, 129
    regularity and speed of, 2, 5, 17, 44, 187
Malvern Hill, battle of, 13, 86, 176
Manassas, Va., 80, 82, 84
Manley, Sylvia (Mrs. Edwin Reed)
maps
    Blue Ridge-Fredericksburg area, *118*
    Cedar Mountain area, *96*
    Fortress Monroe area, *12*
    Gettysburg area, *161*
    Gettysburg battle (Pickett's charge), *166*
    Harper's Ferry-Fredericksburg

area, *46*
    Lee's 1863 invasion route, *173*
    Mine Run area, *181*
    North Carolina coast, *108*
    Peninsula below Williamsburg, *79*
    Richmond, battlefields east of, *86*
    Richmond, eastern approach, *16*
    Roanoke Island, *106*
    United States, 1861-1865, *10-11*
    Vermont in the 1860's, *viii*
marches
    into battle, 87-88, 110, 120, 137-39, 174, 180-82
    equipment on, 115, 198
    fitness for, 115
    making camp during, 87, 134, 139, 142, 144, 151-52, 153, 155, 180-182
    preparations for, 134, 137
    rigors of, 85, 120-24, 134, 137-42, 151-154, 180-82
    training, 33, 74, 102-103, 155
    troop movement via, 48-49, 51, 85, 87-88, 94, 115, 121-24, 139-40, 148, 151-54, 158-59, 160-65, *162-63*, *170*
    See also battle descriptions; troop movement
Marye's Heights, battle for. *See* Fredericksburg
Maryland, raids into, 160,164
McCall, George, 74
McClellan, George, 47, 50, 78, 80, 84, 87-89, 94, 116, 117. *See also* Army of the Potomac
McManus, Martin J. ("M.J.M.")
    background and enlistment in 1st Vermont, 13
    death and burial, 24
    enlistment in 5th Vermont, 24
    letters from Camp Butler, 17-24
    letters from Fort Monroe, 15-16
    post-military career, 24
    promotions, 14, 24
    See also 1st Vermont Regiment
Mead, Alexis, 28
Meade, George, 170, 172, 177, 180, 198
measles. *See* disease
memorials and monuments, 95, 204

Merrill, G. A., 61, 66
Merrimack (iron clad war ship), 117
Middlebury College, 27, 171, 201
Miles, Dixon, 48-49, 51, 56
military
    organization, 206-208
    terms, 208
Mill Springs, battle of, 80
Mine Run, battle, 180-83, *181*
Minneapolis, MN, 167
Minnesota (war ship), 17
money. *See* pay
Monticello (war ship), 15
Montpelier *Patriot*, 34
Montpelier, Vt., 28, 30, 33, 35, 171
Moore, Augustus, 99, 103
morale
    of Army of the Potomac, 3, 47, 84
    on Burnside expedition, 109
    public, 176
    See also camp life: morale
Morse, Edmund A., 20
Mosby, John S., *146*, 157, 160
Mt. Vernon, 132
"Mud March." See Burnside, Ambrose
muskets. *See* weapons

N

Nash, Francis, 150
Naval Academy. See U.S. Naval
    Academy
Negroes. *See* blacks, slaves
Neil, Thomas H., 174
Nelson, Thomas, 66
Neuse River, 111
New Bern, N. C., battle at, 96, 109,
    111-14, *112-13*, 155
    camp and hospital at, 115
New York City
    reception of troops, 38, 148
    draft riots, 177
New York *Herald*, 1, 186-87
New York *Times*, 1, 45
New York Zouaves, 66
Newport News, 116

newspapers
    correspondents and reporters for,
    1-4, 28, 30, 42
    criticisms of army and soldiers in,
    20-21, 34, 54-56
    criticisms of civilians in, 60
    inaccuracy of information in, 2, 5,
    47, 60, 95, 99, 195
    as source of information for civil-
    ians, 5, 8, 129
    as source of information and sup-
    port for soldiers, 4, 47, 64, 81, 98,
    119, 186
    strategic importance of, 1-2, 45, 76
    See also camp life: recreation; cen-
    sorship and *individual soldier-
    correspondents*
Nichols, William T., 151, 153, 158,
    160
non-combatants, 180
Norfolk, Va., 86
North Clarendon, Vt., 97
Northerner (steamer), 102-109
nurses. *See* hospitals

oath of allegiance, 82. *See also* trea-
    son
Occoquan River, 131, 139, 152, 155,
    157
officers
    dislike or resentment towards, 51,
    102
    popularity and respect for, 15, 28,
    38, 45, 66, 85, 116, 153
    privateering by, 54-55
    quartering of, 78, 101
    training responsibilities, 29
    See also battles; camp life
onward movement. See Richmond,
    Va., advance on
Orange County, Vt., 60
Orange, Mass., 97
Orleans County, Vt., 68
Orwell, Vt., 80
outfitting. *See* clothing and
    equipment

P

Page, John Boardman, 21, 24
Pamlico Sound, N. C., 107, *108*
Pamunkey River, 91, *92-93*
parades. *See* camp life: parades
Parker, George, 171
parole, 51-53, 122-23, 124-25. *See also* camp life: during parole
Passumpsic Valley, 60
pay
    Union soldiers', 24, 40, 42, 76, 124, 165, 195
    Confederate soldiers', 82
Peck, E. W., 33
Peninsular Campaign. *See* Army of the Potomac; McClellan
Pennsylvania, invasion of, 172
Phelps, John W., 14, 15, 69
Philadelphia, reception of troops in, *146*, 148, 199
photographers, 126, 155, 206
picket guards, picket duty. *See* camp life: picket duty
Pickett's Division, 165, *166*, *168-69*
pilfering/pillaging
    by Union soldiers, 88, 107, 121-22, 133, 152, 189
    by Confederate soldiers, 176-77
    See also souvenirs
pilot bread. See food and rations
pioneers, 180
Pitkin, Perley P., 40
Poland, Chief Justice, 61
politics, politicians, soldiers' views on, 76, 81, 142-45, 186, 197
Pope, John, 119, 121-22
Port Monmouth, N. J., 148
Port Royal, SC, 99
Porter, David, 101
Potomac River, 46, 99, 129-30
prisoners
    Confederate civilians, 98, 110
    Confederate soldiers, 20, 79-80, 81-82, 98, 107, 109, 111, 138, 152, 156, 175, 177
    treatment of, 50-51, 54-56, 82, 124-25, 177
    Union soldiers, 47, 50, 124-25
    See also parole; spies
privates, treatment of, 102
Proctor, Redfield (Quarter Master), 68
provisioning. *See* food and rations; clothing and equipment; weapons
Provost Marshal guards, 101-102, 124, 183, 208. *See also* camp life: disciplinary actions

Q

Quarter Masters, 4, *12*, 20-21, 30-32, 34, 40, 88, 208. *See also* food and rations; pay; shelter

R

railroads, 91
    baggage trains, 153, 155
    guarding of, 98-99, 120, *150*
    importance of, 26, 47, 120, 139
    mail trains, 47
    troop transport via, 43, 56, 120, 121, 153
Randall, Francis V., 33-34, 42
Rapidan River, 121, 180, *181*, 191
Rappahannock River, 119, 164, 175
rations. See food and rations
recreation and leisure, *135*, 156
    athletic contests, 83-84
    band concerts, 35, 40
    dances, 101
    dinners, 33
    discussions, 143-44, 192
    holiday observances, 83-84, 100-101, 133, 135-36, 152, 180, 185-86
    horse races, *170*, 198-99
    reading, 186-87
    snow ball fights, 193
    visits and tours, 132, 137-38, 190-91
recruitment, 13, 14, 35-37, 39, 43-44, 60, 171, 177
    avoiding, 28, 48, 60, 127
    draft, 44, 48, 60, 82, 127, 177
    fitness for service, 29-30, 48, 120-21
    reenlistment, 24, 184-86, 190

See also volunteer army *and individual regiments*

Reed, Edwin R. ("E.R.R., America")
  birth and background, 97
  capture and parole, 122, 124-25
  discharge, post-war life and death, 125
  hospital detail, 110-19
  illnesses and injuries, 97, 111, 114, 125
  letters from Camp Andrew (New Bern N. C.), 115
  letters from Camp Ferrero (Fredericksburg, Va.), 120-21
  letters from Camp Simeon (Newport News, Va.), 117-19
  letters from Cedar Mountain, Va., 121-22
  letters from Newport News, Va., 116-19
  letters from Roanoke Island, N. C., 110-14
  letters from the *Northerner*, 102-109
  letters from U.S. Naval Academy (Annapolis), 98-100
  See also 12th Massachusetts Regiment

Reno, Jesse, 103, 116, 124

Rhode Island cavalry, 47

Rice, Joseph P., 124

Richmond, Va., advance on, *16*, 84-95, *88*, 116, 119, 139, 150, 176

rifle pits. *See* battle descriptions; weapons

rifles. *See* weapons

Rigby, J.H., 174

Rigby, Silas F., 50

Ripley, Edward Hastings, 45

Ripley, William Y. W., 13, *14*

roads
  as military sites, 109, 137-38, 152, 157, 165, 174, 200
  conditions, 75, 90, 139, 142, 144
  cutting, 142
  See also battles; troop movements

Roanoke Island, N. C., 103, *106*, 107
  battle for, 81, 109-110

Roanoke, Va., 109

Rockingham, Vt., 27

Rose, Charles W., 154, 158

Russell, William Howard, 21

Rutland and Burlington Railroad, 43

Rutland *Herald*, **xiv**, 1, 2-4, 59, 63, 98, 101, 114-15, 129, 145, 147, 172, 200-01

Rutland Juvenile Company, 35

Rutland Light Guard, xii-xiii, 13, 24, 128-29. *See also* 1st Vermont Regiment; 12th Vermont Regiment

Rutland *Weekly Herald. See* Rutland *Herald*

Rutland, Vt., 5, 13, 24

S

Sabin, Albert R. ("Sigma"), **26**
  birth, background, 27
  enlistment, 27, 43-44
  marriages, 44, 57
  letters from Camp Underwood (Vt.), 27-43
  letters from Camp Sigal (Va.), 43-48
  letters from Harper's Ferry, 48-51
  letter from Camp Tyler (Chicago), 54-56
  at Middlebury College, 27, 43, 56
  post-war academic career, 56-57
  death and memorials, 57

safeguards, 191

salt horse, (salt beef). *See* food and rations

Sanitary Commission, 194. *See also* hospitals

sanitation. See camp life

Savage's Station, 86, 95

Sawyer's gun. *See* weapons: artillery

scouting. *See* camp life: scouting

sea journeys, hazards of, 102-107

Sedgwick, John, 172, 198

Seven Days' Battles, 86, 88, 93, 94

Seven Pines, Va., battle at, 94

Sharpley, David L., 30

Sheldon, Harley G., 159

shelter, 60, 78, 101, *130-31*, 132, 134, *135*, 148, 150, 153, 160, 189-90
in the field, 120, 131, *132*, 149, 151, 153, 160
winter quarters, 74, *126*, 148, 150, 154-57, 188-90
See also camps; hospitals
Shenandoah River, 46, 55, 164
Sherman, Linus E., 51
"Sherman's Battery," 98
Ship Island, 4
shipwrecks, *104-105*, 106-107
shoes. *See* clothing and equipment
short rations. *See* food and rations: on marches
Sickle's brigade, 152
Sigel, Franz, 154
skirmishers, skirmishes, 20-21 47, *58*, 79-82, 88, 126, 137-38, 159-60, 180-82, 208
slaves, 79, 82
small pox. *See* disease
Smalley, Henry, 75, 81, 85
Smith, Richard, 28, 40
Smith, William F., 67, 80
Soldier's Home (Washington, DC), 124
soldiers, nature of, 197-98
Somerville, Mass., 125
South Mills, N. C., 114
souvenirs, 117, 136. *See also* pilfering
Spaulding, Wesley, 28
spies, 101, 110, 152. *See also* intelligence
St. Johnsbury, 60-61
St. Patrick's Day celebrations, 199
Stannard, George J., *31*, 32, 38, 51, 159, 160, *204*
state militia. *See* recruitment
Stearns, Eli L., 28
Stearns, John C., 45
Stone, Louriston D., 28, 38
Stone, Newton, 183
stores and equipment, destruction of, 49, 54-55, *92-93*, 122

Stoughton, Charles, *146*
Stoughton, Edwin, 69, 138, *146*, 153, 155, 156-57
Stoughton, H.E., 69
Strite, Capt., 29, 38
Stuart, James Ewell Brown ("Jeb"), 123, 156-57
raid at Fairfax Court House, 137-39
supply depots
Fortress Monroe, 20
White House Landing, *88*, 91, *92-93*
See also Quarter Masters
sutlers. *See* civilians
Swanton, Vt., 101

T

Tague, John, 183-84
telegraphs, 21, 90, 107
tents. *See* camps; shelter
Thanksgiving, 100-101, 133, 152, 180
Thompson, John C., 158
Thoroughfare Gap, 164
train stations. *See* railways
treason, legal definition of, 61-64. *See also* war: support for
troop movement
by boat, *96*, 101, 102-109, 119, 148
by foot, 48-49, 51, 85, 87-88, 94, 115, 121-24, 134, 137-42, 139-40, 148, 151-54, 158-59, 160-65, *162-63*, *170*
by train, 43, 49, 121, 146, 148, 153
See also battle descriptions; marches
troop strength
Confederate, 49, 50-51, 87, 107, 116, 138, 172, 183
Union, 15, 45, 49, 98-99, 101, 116, 120, 134, 154, 156, 160, 172
See also battle descriptions; newspapers
Tyler, John S., 42
typhoid fever. *See* disease.

U

U.S. Naval Academy, 97, **100**, 103
Underwood, Benjamin, 15-17
Underwood, Levi, 27
uniforms. *See* camp life; clothing and equipment; Quarter Masters
Union army, standing orders, 111, 122
Union I Corps, 145
Union Mills, Va., **150**, 161
United States 1861-1865, map of, **10-11**

V

Veazey, Wheelock G., 66
Vermont brigades. *See* 1st Vermont Brigade; 2nd Vermont Brigade
Vermont Cavalry, 103
Vermont soldiers
    criticisms of, 160, 164
    marriages in Virginia, 190-91
    patriotism of, 144, 185-86
    re-enlistment by, 185-86
    skill and bravery of, 89, 157, 160, 164, 170, 175, 187, 200
    See also newspapers *and individual soldier-correspondents*
"Vermont Volunteer, The," (Dorr), x, 192
Vermont, *viii*
    avoiding conscription in, 28, 47-48, 128
    passion for news in, 64
    patriotism of, 60, 65, 69
    pride in, 44, 60, 68-69, 144
"Veteran" regiments, 186
"Virginia overcoat," 77-78
Virginia, 90
    countryside, 45, 75, 116, 129-32, 188
    marriages with Union soldiers, 190-91
    soil, 75, 78
    weather in, 17, 120, **126**, 189, 193-94

See also battles; maps; troop movement
volunteer army, 71, 102, 127. *See also* recruitment

W

Wade, Benjamin, 15
wagons, ammunition and baggage, 68, 145, 182, 196. *See also* ambulances
waiters, 180
Walbridge, James H., 30, 32, 35
Walker, Aldace, 4
Wallingford, Vt., 4
war
    changing attitudes towards, 5, 43, 55, 127, 142-44
    desire for end to, 110, 119, 120, 142-43
    profit-making from, 51, 82, 143
    support for, 32, 39, 43, 60, 64-65, 69, 73, 75-77, 82, 88-89, 91, 144, 185-86
Warren, Gouverneur, 198
Washburn, Peter, 21
Washington *Morning Chronicle*, 187
Washington, D.C., 129
    arrival of troops at, 148
    defense of, 24, 150, 164, 170
    See also 2nd Vermont Regiment, 5th Vermont Regiment
Washington, George, 98, 132
    birthday celebrations, 83-84
weapons
    artillery, 50, 103, 119, 159
    bayonets, 68, 175
    Bowie knife, 114
    complaints about, 3, 37-38, 39-40
    Confederate, 17, 37, 80, 90, 107, 115, 123, 174
    costs of, 68
    destruction of, 55
    mines (percussion shells), 89
    muskets, rifled, 37-38, 66-68, 103, 194
    muskets, smooth-bore, 37, 38
    repeating rifles, 94
    satisfaction with, 67-68
    spiking, 90

See also battle descriptions; troop movement

weather
  as factor in battles and campaigns, 17, 85, 139-42, 142-44, 156, 182, 185, 189
  and sea wrecks, 103-107
  in Virginia, 17, 120 **126**, 129, 189, 193-94
  See also camp life: weather's effects on

Wells River, Vt., 60

West Point, 14, 61, 69, 195

Westminster, MD, 145

White House Landing, Va., **88**, 91-94
  burning of, **92-93**, 94

White Sulphur Springs, Va., 123

Whiting, Henry, 34, 38, 40

Wilderness Campaign, 180, 202, **200-201**

Williams, John C. ("J.C.W."), **146**
  background and enlistment, 146-147
  letters from Camp Vermont, 148-53
  letters from Fairfax Court House, 154-56
  Life in Camp, 167
  illnesses, 157, 165-66
  physical description, 147
  pension, 167
  voluntary reduction in rank, 157
  letters from Wolf Run Shoals, 158-65
  post-war life and death, 166-67
  See also 14th Vermont Regiment

Williams, Martin, 147

Williamsburg, Va., engagement at, 89-91

winter quarters
  Army of the Potomac, 183-99
  Vermont Brigades, 18, 62-63, 154-57, 172

Wise, Henry A., 120

Wolf Run Shoals, camp at, 139, 145, **155**, 157, **158**
  ford at, 142, 160

women
  in camp, 77, 101
  as nurses, 117
  rights of, 76
  support and relief activities of, **27**, 33-34, 36, 68

wood, 75, 85
  foraging for, 192

Wool, John, 47

Worthen, Harry, **146**

Y

Yorktown, Va., 87, 119

Z

Zollicoffer, Felix, 80

The Editor

Donald Wickman is a Vermont historian with an intense interest in the American Civil War. Wickman also has earned a reputation as an authority on Mount Independence, the Revolutionary War site in Orwell, Vermont. His work has been published in several journals including *New Jersey History*, *Vermont History*, *Rutland Historical Society Quarterly*, and *Bulletin of the Fort Ticonderoga Museum*.

Born and raised in New Jersey, Wickman received a B.S. in Plant Science from the University of Maine at Orono, an M.Ed. in Agricultural Education from Rutgers University, New Brunswick, N.J., and an M.A. in History from the University of Vermont in Burlington.

Recipient of the 1996 Weston Cate, Jr. Research Fellowship from the Vermont Historical Society, and until recently Educator/Research Assistant at the Lake Champlain Maritime Museum in Vergennes, Vermont, Wickman is a full-time horticulturist and adjunct faculty member at Community College of Vermont.

IMAGES FROM THE PAST

publishing history in ways that help people see it for themselves

Other books from our press that you might enjoy

THE HONOR OF COMMAND: GENERAL BURGOYNE'S SARATOGA CAMPAIGN, JUNE-OCTOBER 1777

by Stuart Murray

Leaving Quebec in June, the northern British army's commanding officer, Major General John Burgoyne was confident in his ability to strike a decisive blow against the rebellion in the colonies. Instead, the stubborn rebels fought back, slowed his advance and inflicted irreplaceable losses, leading to his defeat and surrender at Saratoga on October 17, 1777 — an important turning point in the American Revolution.

Burgoyne's point of view as the campaign progresses is expressed from dispatches to Lord George Germain, British Colonial Secretary, addresses to his army, and exchanges with friends and fellow officers. Maps, sketches, engravings, and contemporary portraits depict the Lake Champlain-Hudson River Valley corridor from St.-Jean's to Saratoga; General Burgoyne, individual uniformed soldiers, the Baron and Baroness von Riedesel, and the death and burial of Simon Fraser. Index.

7" x 10"; 128 pages; 39 prints and engravings, 3 paintings, and 8 maps; index; listing of area historic sites, and selected bibliography

ISBN 1-884592-03-1 Paperback: $14.95

BENNINGTON'S BATTLE MONUMENT: MASSIVE AND LOFTY

by Tyler Resch

The design and construction of the 306' dolomite tower dedicated in 1891 to commemorate a significant Revolutionary War victory. Includes contemporary newspaper articles and photographs; portraits of Presidents Hayes and Harrison; sketches of rejected designs; a birdseye view of the town in 1887; and a narrative and vertigo-inducing photos that show how they change the light bulb on the top.

7" x11"; 64 pages; 42 modern and historical photographs; 16 sketches, prints and ephemera.

ISBN 1-884592-00-7 Paperback: $9.95

RUDYARD KIPLING IN VERMONT:
BIRTHPLACE OF THE JUNGLE BOOKS

by Stuart Murray

This book fills a gap in the biographical coverage of the important British author who is generally described as having lived only in India and England. It provides the missing links in the bitter-sweet story that haunts the portals of Naulakha, the distinctive shingle style home built by Kipling and his American wife near Brattleboro, Vermont, where the Kiplings lived for four years and the first two of their three children were born.

All but one of Kipling's major works stem from these years of rising success, happiness and productivity; but because of a feud with his American brother-in-law, Beatty, which was seized on by newspaper reporters eager to put a British celebrity in his place, the author and his family left their home in America forever in 1896.

6" x 9"; 198 pages; Excerpts from Kipling poems, 21 historical photos; 6 book illustrations; and 7 sketches convey the mood of the times, character of the people, and style of Kipling's work. Extensive index.

ISBN 1-884592-04-X Hardcover: $29.00

ISBN 1-884592-05-8 Paperback: $18.95

NORMAN ROCKWELL AT HOME IN VERMONT:
THE ARLINGTON YEARS, 1939-1953

by Stuart Murray

The story of Norman Rockwell's dynamic years in the Vermont village where he painted some of his greatest works, including "The Four Freedoms" and "Saying Grace." Inspired by the "everyday life of my neighbors," the artist created storytelling pictures that have touched the hearts of millions around the world.

7" x 10"; 96 pages; 13 Rockwell paintings and sketches and 32 historical photographs in black and white; index; regional map, list of area museums, selected bibliography

ISBN 1-884592-02-3   Paperback $14.95

REMEMBERING GRANDMA MOSES

by Beth Moses Hickok

The story of Christmastime 1934 when the author at 23 was considering marriage to Frank Moses, a widower with two young daughters, and the 74 year old Anna Robertson Moses, grandmother to Frances and Zoan, had not yet become the world's much loved and admired artist, Grandma Moses. Told in affectionate detail including word for word conversations with Grandma Moses gathered from the author's journals and letters to her mother. Hickok, a first-time published author at 83, provides a direct link to the famous artist.

6" x 9"; 64 pages; portraits of Grandma Moses from 1947 and 1949, 9 historical and 9 contemporary photographs in black and white; yarn painting by the artist in color.

ISBN 1-884592-01-5 Paperback: $12.95

REMEMBERING GRANDMA MOSES (tape)

by Beth Moses Hickok

The complete book read by the author in 1996 with additional stories about Grandma Moses's childhood and life with her husband Thomas Moses, and her artistry in the kitchen.

Yarn painting by the artist in color and black and white photograph of the author at the artist's gravesite as cover art; chronology and map enclosed.

ISBN 1-884592-06-6 60 minute audio cassette: $12.00

ALLIGATORS ALWAYS DRESS FOR DINNER: AN ALPHABET BOOK OF VINTAGE PHOTOGRAPHS

by Linda Donigan and Michael Horwitz

A book of late 19th and early 20th century photographs full of glimpses into lives distant from our own by place and time; a book of letters and phrases that adults and children can savor both alone and together; an activity book of discoveries and excursions; and more.

Each two-page spread offers a surprising visual treat: Beholding Beauty — a beautifully dressed and adorned Kikuyu couple; Fluted Fingers — a wandering Japanese Zen monk playing a bamboo recorder; Man and Machine — a proud drill press operator at his station; and Working the Bandwagon — the Cole Brothers Circus Band on an elaborate 1879 Lion and Mirror wagon.

9 1/4" x 9 3/4"; 64 pages; 28 duotone photographs; A-Z information appendix.

ISBN 1-884592-08-2 Hardcover: $25.00

Available at your local bookstore or from Images from the Past, Inc., 888-442-3204 for credit card orders; P.O. Box 137, Bennington, Vermont 05201 with check or money order. When ordering, please add $3.50 shipping and handling for the first book and $1 for each additional. Add 5% sales tax for shipments to Vermont.